THE

POEMS

OF

THOMAS PARNELL

AND

THOMAS TICKELL.

Tho Parnell

THE

POETICAL WORKS

OF

THOMAS PARNELL.

WITH A LIFE,

BY OLIVER GOLDSMITH.

BOSTON:
LITTLE, BROWN AND COMPANY.
NEW YORK: EVANS AND DICKERSON.
PHILADELPHIA: LIPPINCOTT, GRAMBO AND CO.
M.DCCC.LIV.

RIVERSIDE, CAMBRIDGE:
PRINTED BY H. O. HOUGHTON AND COMPANY.

STEREOTYPED BY STONE AND SMART.

CONTENTS.

THE

LIFE OF THOMAS PARNELL.*

BY OLIVER GOLDSMITH.

THE life of a scholar seldom abounds with adventure. His fame is acquired in solitude; and the historian, who only views him at a distance, must be content with a dry detail of actions by which he is scarcely distinguished from the rest of mankind. But we are fond of talking of those who have given us pleasure; not that we have any thing important to say, but because the subject is pleasing.

Thomas Parnell, D. D., was descended from an ancient family, that had for some centuries been settled at Congleton, in Cheshire. His father, Thomas Parnell, who had been attached to the Commonwealth party, upon the Restoration went over to Ireland; thither he carried a large personal fortune, which he laid out in lands in that kingdom. The estates he purchased there, as

* The Miscellaneous Works of Oliver Goldsmith, including a variety of pieces now first collected. By James Prior.

also that of which he was possessed in Cheshire, descended to our poet, who was his eldest son, and still remain in the family. Thus want, which has compelled many of our greatest men into the service of the muses, had no influence upon Parnell; he was a poet by inclination.

He was born in Dublin, in the year 1679, and received the first rudiments of his education at the school of Dr. Jones, in that city. Surprising things are told us of the greatness of his memory at that early period; as of his being able to repeat by heart forty lines of any book at the first reading; of his getting the third book of the Iliad in one night's time, which was given in order to confine him for some days. These stories, which are told of almost every celebrated wit, may perhaps be true; but for my own part, I never found any of those prodigies of parts, although I have known enow that were desirous, among the ignorant, of being thought so.

There is one presumption, however, of the early maturity of his understanding. He was admitted a member of the College of Dublin at the age of thirteen, which is much sooner than usual, as at that university they are a great deal stricter in their examination for entrance, than either at Oxford or Cambridge. His progress through the college course of study was probably marked with but little splendor; his imagination might have been too warm to relish the cold logic of Burgersdicius, or the dreary subtleties of Smiglesius; but it is certain, that as a classical scholar, few could equal him. His own compositions show this; and the deference which the most eminent men of his time paid him upon that head, put it beyond a doubt. He took the degree of master of arts the 9th of July, 1700; and in the same year he was ordained a deacon by William, bishop of Derry, having a dispensation from the primate, as being under twenty-three years of age. He was admitted into priest's orders about three years after, by William, archbishop of Dublin; and on the 9th of February, 1705, he was collated by Sir George Ashe, bishop of Clogher, to the archdeaconry of Clogher.

About that time also he married Miss Anne Minchin, a young lady of great merit and beauty, by whom he had two sons, who died young, and one daughter. His wife died some time before him; and her death is said to have made so great an impression on his spirits, that it served to hasten his own. On the 31st of May, 1716, he was presented by his friend and patron, archbishop King, to the vicarage of Finglass, a benefice worth about four hundred pounds a year, in the diocese of Dublin; but he lived to enjoy his preferment a very short time. He died at Chester, in July, 1717, on his way to Ireland, and was buried in Trinity Church in that town, without any monument to mark the place of his interment.* As he died without male issue, his estate devolved to his only nephew, Sir John Parnell, baronet, whose father was younger brother to the archdeacon, and one of the justices of the King's Bench in Ireland.

Such is the very unpoetical detail of the life of a poet. Some dates, and some few facts scarcely more interesting than those that make the ornaments of a country tomb-stone, are all that remain of one whose labors now begin to excite universal curiosity. A poet, while living, is seldom an object sufficiently great to attract much attention; his real merits are known but to a few, and these

* Since the above passage was printed off, the editor has been favored with the following communication from Mr. Donovan, of Anson-street, Liverpool:

"In the summer of 1834, I happened to be for a short time in Chester, and, among other little pursuits to which I devoted my leisure hours while there, I endeavored to discover whether Parnell was really interred without any monument in Trinity Church in that city, as Goldsmith writes, or not. I made the search among the monuments which I proposed, and made also minute inquiries, but in vain; and I think I may say, that no monument does exist. My next inquiry was, whether they had even any record of his interment; and to ascertain this, I obtained permission to search the Registry. I examined, without effect, the year 1717, but, pursuing the list, I found, to my no small surprise, the following entry, in its proper order of date, in the register of interments of 1718:—

'THOMAS PARNELL, D. D.
'18 *October*, 1718,'

being one year and three months after the time which Goldsmith mentions as the period of his decease."

are generally sparing in their praises. When his fame is increased by time, it is then too late to investigate the peculiarities of his disposition; the dews of the morning are past, and we vainly try to continue the chase by the meridian splendor.

There is scarcely any man but might be made the subject of a very interesting and amusing history, if the writer, besides a thorough acquaintance with the character he draws, were able to make those nice distinctions which separate it from all others. The strongest minds have usually the most striking peculiarities, and would consequently afford the richest materials: but in the present instance, from not knowing Dr. Parnell, his peculiarities are gone to the grave with him; and we are obliged to take his character from such as knew but little of him, or who, perhaps, could have given very little information if they had known more.

Parnell, by what I have been able to collect from my father and uncle, who knew him, was the most capable man in the world to make the happiness of those he conversed with, and the least able to secure his own. He wanted that evenness of disposition which bears disappointment with phlegm, and joy with indifference. He was ever very much elated or depressed, and his whole life was spent in agony or rapture. But the turbulence of these passions only affected himself, and never those about him; he knew the ridicule of his own character, and very effectually raised the mirth of his companions, as well at his vexations as at his triumphs.

How much his company was desired, appears from the extensiveness of his connections, and the number of his friends. Even before he made any figure in the literary world, his friendship was sought by persons of every rank and party. The wits at that time differed a good deal from those who are most eminent for their understanding at present. It would now be thought a very indifferent sign of a writer's good sense, to disclaim his private friends for happening to be of a different party in politics; but it was then otherwise; the Whig wits held the Tory wits in great contempt, and these retaliated in their turn. At the head of one party were Addison, Steele, and Congreve; at that of the other, Pope, Swift, and Arbuthnot. Parnell was a friend to both sides, and with a liberality becoming a scholar, scorned all those trifling distinctions, that are noisy for the time, and ridiculous to posterity. Nor did he emancipate himself from these without some opposition from home. Having been the son of a Commonwealth's man, his Tory connections on this side of the water gave his friends in Ireland great offence. They were much enraged to see him keep company with Pope, and Swift, and Gay; they blamed his undistinguishing taste, and wondered what pleasure he could find in the conversation of men who approved the treaty of Utrecht, and disliked the Duke of Marlborough. His conversation is said to have been extremely pleasing; but in what its peculiar excellence consisted is now unknown. The letters which were written to him by his friends, are full of compliments upon his talents as a companion, and his good-nature as a man. I have several of them now before me. Pope was particularly fond of his company, and seems to regret his absence more than any of the rest. A letter from him follows thus:

"London, July 29.

"Dear Sir:—I wish it were not as ungenerous as vain to complain too much of a man that forgets me, but I could expostulate with you a whole day upon your inhuman silence: I call it inhuman; nor would you think it less, if you were truly sensible of the uneasiness it gives me. Did I know you so ill as to think you proud, I would be much less concerned than I am able to be, when I know one of the best-natured men alive neglects me; and if you know me so ill as to think amiss of me, with regard to my friendship for you, you really do not deserve half the trouble you occasion me.

"I need not tell you, that both Mr. Gay and myself have written several letters in vain; and that we were constantly inquiring, of all who have seen Ireland, if they saw you, and that (forgotten as we are) we are every day remembering you in our most agreeable hours. All this is true: as that we are sincerely lovers of you, and deplorers of your absence, and that we form no wish more ardently than that which brings you over to us, and places you in your old seat between us. We have lately had some distant hopes of the Dean's design to revisit England: will not you accompany him? or is England to lose every thing that has any charms for us, and must we pray for banishment as a benediction? I have once been witness of some, I hope all of your splenetic hours: come, and be a comforter in your turn to me, in mine.

"I am in such an unsettled state, that I can't tell if I shall ever see you, unless it be this year: whether I do or not, be ever assured, you have as large a share of my thoughts and good wishes as any man, and as great a portion of gratitude in my heart as would enrich a monarch, could he know where to find it. I shall not die without testifying something of this nature, and leaving to the world a memorial of the friendship that has been so great a pleasure and pride to me. It would be like writing my own epitaph, to acquaint you with what I have lost since I saw you, what I have done, what I have thought, where I have lived, and where I now repose in obscurity. My friend Jervas, the bearer of this, will inform you of all particulars concerning me; and Mr. Ford is charged with a thousand loves, and a thousand complaints, and a thousand commissions to you on my part. They will both tax you with the neglect of some promises which were too agreeable to us all to be forgot: if you care for any of us, tell them so, and write so to me. I can say no more, but that I love you, and am, in spite of the longest neglect of happiness, dear sir, your most faithful, affectionate friend and servant,

"A. POPE.

"Gay is in Devonshire, and from thence he goes to Bath. My father and mother never fail to commemorate you."

Among the number of his most intimate friends was Lord Oxford, whom Pope has so finely complimented upon the delicacy of his choice.

> "For him thou oft hast bid the world attend,
> Fond to forget the statesman in the friend;
> For Swift and him despis'd the farce of state,
> The sober follies of the wise and great;
> Dexterous the craving, fawning crowd to quit,
> And pleas'd to 'scape from flattery to wit."

Pope himself was not only excessively fond of his company, but under several literary obligations to him for his assistance in the translation of Homer. Gay was obliged to him upon another account; for, being always poor, he was not above receiving from Parnell the copy-money which the latter got for his writings. Several of their letters, now before me, are proofs of this; and as they have never appeared before, it is probable the reader will be much better pleased with their idle effusions, than with any thing I can hammer out for his amusement.

"Binfield, near Oakingham, Tuesday.

"DEAR SIR:—I believe the hurry you were in hindered your giving me a word by the last post, so that I am yet to learn whether you got well to town, or continue so there. I very much fear both for your health and your quiet; and no man living can be more truly concerned in any thing that touches either than myself. I would comfort myself, however, with hoping, that your business may not be unsuccessful, for your sake; and that at least it may soon be put into other proper hands. For my own, I beg earnestly of you to return to us as soon as possible. You know how very much I want you; and that, however your business may depend on any other, my business depends entirely upon you; and yet still I hope you will find your man, even though I lose you the mean while. At this time, the more I love you, the more I can spare you; which alone will, I dare say, be a reason to you to let me have you back the sooner.

"The minute I lost you, Eustathius, with nine hundred pages and nine thousand contradictions of the Greek characters, arose to view! Spondanus, with all his auxiliaries, in number a thousand pages (value three shillings), and Dacier's three volumes, Barnes's two, Valterie's three, Cuperus, half in Greek, Leo Allatus, three parts in Greek, Scaliger, Macrobius, and (worse than all) Aulus Gellius! All these rushed upon my soul at once, and whelmed me under a fit of the headache. I cursed them all religiously, damned my best friends among the rest, and even blasphemed Homer himself.

"Dear sir, not only as you are a friend, and a good-natured man, but as you are a Christian and a divine, come back speedily, and prevent the increase of my sins; for, at the rate I have begun to rave, I shall not only damn all the poets and commentators who have gone before me, but be damned myself by all who come after me. To be serious; you have not only left me to the last degree impatient for your return, who at all times should have been so (though never so much as since I knew you in the best health here), but you have wrought several miracles upon our family; you have made old people fond of a young and gay person, and inveterate papists of a clergyman of the church of England; even nurse herself is in danger of being in love in her old age, and (for all I know) would even marry Dennis for your sake, because he is your man, and loves his master. In short, come down forthwith, or give me good reasons for delaying, though but a day or two, by the next post. If I find them just, I will come up to you, though you know how precious my time is at present: my hours were never worth so much money before; but perhaps you are not sensible of this, who give away your own works. You are a generous author; I a hackney scribbler: you a Grecian, and bred at a university; I a poor Englishman, of my own educating: you a reverend parson, I a wag; in short, you are Dr. Parnelle (with an *e* at the end of your name,) and I, your most obliged and affectionate friend and faithful servant,

A. POPE.

"My hearty service to the Dean, Dr. Arbuthnot, Mr. Ford, and the true genuine shepherd, J. Gay of Devon. I expect him down with you."

We may easily perceive by this, that Parnell was not a little necessary to Pope in conducting his translation; however, he has worded it so ambiguously, that it is impossible to bring the charge directly against him. But he is much more explicit when he mentions his friend Gay's obligations in another letter, which he takes no pains to conceal.

"DEAR SIR:—I write to you with the same warmth, the same zeal of good-will and friendship, with which I used to converse with you two years ago, and can't think myself absent, when I feel you so much at my heart. The picture of you which Jervas brought me over, is infinitely less lively a representation than that I carry about with me, and which rises to my mind whenever I think of you. I have many an agreeable reverie through those woods and downs where we once rambled together; my head is sometimes at the Bath, and sometimes at Letcomb, where the Dean makes a great part of my imaginary entertainment, this being the cheapest way of treating me; I hope he will not be displeased at this manner of paying my respects to him, instead of following my friend Jervas's example, which, to say the truth, I have as much inclination to do as I want ability.

"I have been ever since December last in greater variety of business than any such men as you (that is, divines and philosophers) can possibly imagine a reasonable creature capable of. Gay's play, among the rest, has cost much time and long-suffering, to stem a tide of malice and party, that certain authors have raised against it; the best revenge on such fellows is now in my hands, I mean your Zoilus, which really transcends the expectations I had conceived of it. I have put it into the press, beginning with the poem Batrachom; for you seem, by the first paragraph of the dedication of it, to design to prefix the name of some particular person. I beg, therefore, to know for whom you intend it, that the publication may not be delayed on this account, and this as soon as is possible. Inform me, also, upon what terms I am to deal with the bookseller, and whether you design the copy-money for Gay, as you formerly talked; what number of books you would have yourself, &c. I scarcely see any thing to be altered in this whole piece; in the poems you sent I will take the liberty you allow me: the story of Pandora, and the Eclogue upon Health, are two of the most beautiful things I ever read. I do not say this to the prejudice of the rest, but as I have read these oftener. Let me know how far my commission is to extend, and be confident of my punctual performance of whatever you enjoin. I must add a paragraph on this occasion in regard to Mr. Ward, whose verses have been a great pleasure to me; I will contrive they shall be so to the world, whenever I can find a proper opportunity of publishing them.

"I shall very soon print an entire collection of my own madrigals, which I look upon as making my last will and testament, since in it I shall give all I ever intend to give (which I'll beg yours and the Dean's acceptance of). You must look on me no more a poet, but a plain commoner, who lives upon his own, and fears and flatters no man. I hope before I die to discharge the debt I owe to Homer, and get upon the whole just fame enough to serve for an annuity for my own time, though I leave nothing to posterity.

"I beg our correspondence may be more frequent than it has been of late. I am sure my esteem and love for you never more deserved it from you, or more prompted it from you. I desired our friend Jervas (in the greatest hurry of my business) to say a great deal in my name, both to yourself and the Dean, and must once more repeat the assurances to you both, of an unchanging friendship and unalterable esteem. I am, dear sir, most entirely, your affectionate, faithful, obliged friend and servant,

"A. Pope."

From these letters to Parnell, we may conclude, as far as their testimony can go, that he was an agreeable, a generous, and a sincere man. Indeed, he took care that his friends should always see him to the best advantage; for, when he found his fits of spleen and uneasiness, which sometimes lasted for weeks together, returning, he returned with all expedition to the remote parts of Ireland, and there made out a gloomy kind of satisfaction, in giving hideous descriptions of the solitude to which he retired. It is said of a famous painter, that, being confined in prison for debt, his whole delight consisted in drawing the faces of his creditors in caricature. It was just so with Parnell. From many of his unpublished pieces which I have seen, and from others that have appeared, it would seem that scarcely a bog in his neighbourhood was left without reproach, and scarcely a mountain reared its head unsung. "I can easily," says Pope, in one of his letters, in answer to a dreary description of Parnell's, "I can easily image to my thoughts the solitary hours of your eremitical life in the mountains, for some parallel to it in my own retirement at Binfield:" and in another place, "We are both miserably enough situated, God knows; but of the two evils, I think the solitudes of the South are to be preferred to the deserts of the West." In this manner Pope answered him in the tone of his own complaints; and these descriptions of the imagined distress of his situation served to give him a temporary relief: they threw off the blame from himself, and laid upon fortune and accident a wretchedness of his own creating.

But though this method of quarrelling in his poems with his situation, served to relieve himself, yet it was not easily endured by the gentlemen of the neighborhood, who did not care to confess themselves his fellow-sufferers. He received many mortifications upon that account among them; for, being naturally fond of company, he could not endure to be without even theirs, which, however, among his English friends he pretended to despise. In fact, his conduct, in this particular, was rather splenetic than wise; he had either lost the art to engage, or did not employ his skill in securing those more permanent, though more humble connections, and sacrificed for a month or two in England, a whole year's happiness by his country fireside at home.

However, what he permitted the world to see of his life was elegant and splendid; his fortune (for a poet) was very considerable, and it may easily be supposed he lived to the very extent of it. The fact is, his expenses were greater than his income, and his successor found the estate somewhat impaired at his decease. As soon as ever he had collected in his annual revenues, he immediately set out for England, to enjoy the company of his dearest friends, and laugh at the more prudent world that were minding business and gaining money. The friends to whom, during the latter part of his life, he was chiefly attached, were Pope, Swift, Arbuthnot, Jervas, and Gay. Among these he was particularly happy; his mind was entirely at ease, and gave a-loose to every harmless folly that came uppermost. Indeed, it was a society in which, of all others, a wise man might be most foolish, without incurring any danger or contempt. Perhaps the reader will be pleased to see a letter to him from a part of this junto, as there is something striking even in the levities of genius. It comes from Gay,

Jervas, Arbuthnot, and Pope, assembled at a chop-house near the Exchange, and is as follows:

"My dear Sir:—I was last summer in Devonshire, and am this winter at Mrs. Bonyer's. In the summer I wrote a poem, and in the winter I have published it, which I have sent to you by Dr. Ellwood. In the summer I ate two dishes of toad-stools, of my own gathering, instead of mushrooms; and in the winter I have been sick with wine, as I am at this time, blessed be God for it! as I must bless God for all things. In the summer I spoke truth to damsels; in the winter I told lies to ladies. Now you know where I have been, and what I have done, I shall tell you what I intend to do the ensuing summer; I propose to do the same thing I did last, which was to meet you in any part of England you would appoint; don't let me have two disappointments. I have longed to hear from you, and to that intent I teased you with three or four letters; but, having no answer, I feared both yours and my letters might have miscarried. I hope my performance will please the Dean, whom I often wished for, and to whom I would have often wrote, but for the same reasons I neglected writing to you. I hope I need not tell you how I love you, and how glad I shall be to hear from you; which, next to the seeing you, would be the greatest satisfaction to your most affectionate friend and humble servant, J. G."

"Dear Mr. Archdeacon:—Though my proportion of this epistle should be but a sketch in miniature, yet I take up this half page, having paid my club with the good company both for our dinner of chops and for this paper. The poets will give you lively descriptions in their way; I shall only acquaint you with that which is directly my province. I have just set the last hand to a couplet; for so I may call two nymphs in one piece. They are Pope's favourites, and though few, you will guess must have cost me more pains than any nymphs can be worth. He has been so unreasonable as to expect that I should have made them as beautiful upon canvas as he has done upon paper. If this same Mr. P. should omit to write for the dear frogs, and the Pervigilium, I must entreat you not to let me languish for them, as I have done ever since they have crossed the seas: remember by what neglects, &c., we missed them when we lost you, and therefore I have not yet forgiven any of those triflers that let them escape and run those hazards. I am going on at the old rate, and want you and the Dean prodigiously, and am in hopes of making you a visit this summer, and of hearing from you both, now you are together. Fortescue, I am sure, will be concerned that he is not in Cornhill, to set his hand to these presents, not only as a witness, but as a *serviteur très-humble,*

"C. JERVAS."

"It is so great an honour to a poor Scotchman to be remembered at this time of day, especially by an inhabitant of the Glacialis Ierne, that I take it very thankfully, and have, with my good friends, remembered you at our table in the chop-house in Exchange-alley. There wanted nothing to complete our happiness but your company, and our dear friend the Dean's. I am sure the whole entertainment would have been to his relish. Gay has got so much money by his 'Art of Walking the Streets,' that he is ready to set up his equipage; he is just going to the Bank to negotiate some exchange-bills. Mr. Pope delays his second volume of his Homer till the martial spirit of the rebels is quite quelled; it being judged that the first part did some harm that way. Our love again and again to the dear Dean. *Fuimus torys,* I can say no more. ARBUTHNOT."

"When a man is conscious that he does no good himself, the next thing is to cause others to do some. I may claim some merit this way, in hastening this testimonial from your friends above-writing: their love to you indeed wants no spur, their ink wants no pen, their pen wants no hand, their hand wants no heart, and so forth, (after the manner of Rabelais, which is betwixt some meaning and no meaning); and yet it may be said, when present thought and opportunity is wanting, their pens want ink, their hands want pens, their hearts want hands, &c., till time, place, and conveniency concur to set them writing, as at present, a sociable meeting, a good dinner, warm fire, and an easy situation do, to the joint labour and pleasure of this epistle.

"Wherein if I should say nothing I should say much, (much being included in my love,) though my love be such, that if I should say much, I should yet say nothing, it being (as Cowley says) equally impossible either to conceal or to express it.

"If I were to tell you the thing I wish above all things, it is to see you again; the next is to see here your treatise of Zoilus, with the Batrachomuomachia, and the Pervigilium Veneris, both of which poems are master-pieces in several kinds; and I question not the prose is as excellent in its sort as the Essay on Homer. Nothing can be more glorious to that great author, than that the same hand that raised his best statue, and decked it with its old laurels, should also hang up the scarecrow of his miserable critic, and gibbet up the carcass of Zoilus, to the terror of the witlings of posterity. More, and much more, upon this and a thousand other subjects, will be the matter of my next letter, wherein I must open all the friend to you. At this time I must be content with telling you, I am faithfully your most affectionate and humble servant, A. POPE."

If we regard this letter with a critical eye, we must find it indifferent enough; if we consider it as a mere effusion of friendship, in which every writer contended in affection, it will appear much to the honour of those who wrote it. To be mindful of an absent friend in the hours of mirth and feasting, when his company is least wanted, shows no slight degree of sincerity. Yet probably there was still another motive for writing thus to him in conjunction. The above named, together with Swift and Parnell, had some time before formed themselves into a society, called the Scribblerus Club, and I should suppose they commemorated him thus, as being an absent member.

It is past a doubt that they wrote many things in conjunction, and Gay usually held the pen; and yet I do not remember any productions which were the joint effort of this society, as doing it honour.

There is something feeble and quaint in all their attempts, as if company repressed thought, and genius wanted solitude for its boldest and happiest exertions. Of those productions in which Parnell had a principal share, that of the Origin of the Sciences from the Monkeys in Ethiopia, is particularly mentioned by Pope himself, in some manuscript anecdotes which he left behind him.* The Life of Homer, also, prefixed to the translation of the Iliad, is written by Parnell and corrected by Pope; and, as that great poet assures us in the same place, this correction was not effected without great labour. "It is still stiff," says he, "and was written still stiffer; as it is, I verily think it cost me more pains in the correcting than the writing it would have done."† All this may be easily credited; for every thing of Parnell's that has appeared in prose, is written in a very awkward, inelegant manner. It is true, his productions teem with imagination, and show great learning; but they want that ease and sweetness for which his poetry is so much admired, and the language is also shamefully incorrect. Yet, though all this must be allowed, Pope should have taken care not to leave his errors upon record against him, or put it in the power of envy to tax his friend with faults that do not appear in what he has left to the world. A poet has a right to expect the same secrecy in his friend as in his confessor; the sins he discovers are not divulged for punishment but pardon. Indeed, Pope is almost inexcusable in this

* ["The Origin of the Sciences from the Monkeys in Ethiopia, was written by me, Dean Parnell, and Dr. Arbuthnot." POPE: Spence's Anecdotes, p. 201. Singer's edit. 1820.]

† [Spence's Anecdotes, p. 138.]

instance, as what he seems to condemn in one place he very much applauds in another. In one of the letters from him to Parnell, above-mentioned, he treats the Life of Homer with much greater respect, and seems to say, that the prose is excellent in its kind. It must be confessed, however, that he is by no means inconsistent: what he says in both places may very easily be reconciled to truth; but who can defend his candour and sincerity?

It would be hard, however, to suppose that there was no real friendship between these great men. The benevolence of Parnell's disposition remains unimpeached; and Pope, though subject to starts of passion and envy, yet never missed an opportunity of being truly serviceable to him. The commerce between them was carried on to the common interest of both. When Pope had a Miscellany to publish, he applied to Parnell for poetical assistance, and the latter as implicitly submitted to him for correction. Thus they mutually advanced each other's interest or fame, and grew stronger by conjunction. Nor was Pope the only person to whom Parnell had recourse for assistance. We learn from Swift's letters to Stella, that he submitted his pieces to all his friends, and readily adopted their alterations. Swift, among the number, was very useful to him in that particular; and care has been taken that the world should not remain ignorant of the obligation.

But in the connection of wits, interest has generally very little share; they have only pleasure in view, and can seldom find it but among each other. The Scribblerus Club, when the members were in town, were seldom asunder; and they often made excursions together into the country, and generally on foot. Swift was usually the butt of the company; and if a trick was played he was always the sufferer. The whole party once agreed to walk down to the house of Lord B——,* who is still living, and whose seat is about twelve miles from town. As every one agreed to make the best of his way, Swift, who was remarkable for walking, soon left the rest behind him, fully resolved, upon his arrival, to choose the very best bed for himself; for that was his custom. In the mean time, Parnell was determined to prevent his intentions, and taking horse, arrived at Lord B——'s by another way long before him. Having apprised his lordship of Swift's design, it was resolved, at any rate, to keep him out of the house; but how to effect this was the question. Swift never had the smallpox, and was very much afraid of catching it; as soon, therefore, as he appeared, striding along at a distance from the house, one of his lordship's

* [Lord Bathurst. He lived to extreme old age; and is alluded to by Burke, in one of his speeches on American affairs, as having witnessed almost the infancy and maturity of the colonies.]

servants was despatched to inform him that the smallpox was then making great ravages in the family, but that there was a summer-house with a field-bed at his service, at the end of the garden. There the disappointed Dean was obliged to retire, and take a cold supper that was sent out to him, while the rest were feasting within. However, at last they took compassion on him; and, upon his promising never to choose the best bed again, they permitted him to make one of the company.

There is something satisfactory in these accounts of the follies of the wise; they give a natural air to the picture, and reconcile us to our own. There have been few poetical societies more talked of, or productive of a greater variety of whimsical conceits, than this of the Scribblerus Club; but how long it lasted I cannot exactly determine. The whole of Parnell's poetical existence was not of more than eight or ten years' continuance. His first excursions to England began about the year 1706, and he died in the year 1717:* so that it is probable the club began with him, and his death ended the connection. Indeed, the festivity of his conversation, the benevolence of his heart, and the generosity of his temper, were qualities that might serve to cement any society, and that could hardly be replaced when he was taken away. During the two or three last years

* [He died in July 1717, in his thirty-eighth year.]

of his life, he was more fond of company than ever, and could scarcely bear to be alone. The death of his wife, it is said, was a loss to him that he was unable to support or recover.* From that time he could never venture to court the muse in solitude, where he was sure to find the image of her who inspired his attempts. He began therefore to throw himself into every company, and to seek from wine, if not relief, at least insensibility.† Those helps that sorrow first called for assistance, habit soon rendered necessary, and he died before his fortieth year, in some measure a martyr to conjugal fidelity.

Thus in the space of a very few years, Parnell attained a share of fame, equal to what most of his contemporaries were a long life in acquiring. He is only to be considered as a poet; and the

* ["I am heartily sorry for poor Mrs. Parnell's death. She seemed to be an excellent, good-natured young woman, and I believe the poor lad is much afflicted."—Swift's Journal to Stella, Aug. 24, 1711.]

† [Ruffhead, on the authority of Warburton, has given a different account of the cause which led to Parnell's intemperance:—"When he had been introduced by Swift to Lord Treasurer Oxford, and had been established in his favor by the assistance of Pope, he soon began to entertain ambitious views. The walk he chose to shine in was *popular preaching:* he had talents for it, and began to be distinguished in the mob places of Southwark and London, when the Queen's sudden death destroyed all his prospects. This fatal stroke broke his spirits; he took to drinking, became a sot, and soon finished his course."—See Spence's Anecdotes.]

universal esteem in which his poems are held, and the reiterated pleasure they give in the perusal, are a sufficient test of their merit. He appears to me to be the last of that great school that had modelled itself upon the ancients, and taught English poetry to resemble what the generality of mankind have allowed to excel. A studious and correct observer of antiquity, he set himself to consider nature with the lights it lent him; and he found that the more aid he borrowed from the one, the more delightfully he resembled the other. To copy nature is a task the most bungling workman is able to execute; to select such parts as contribute to delight, is reserved only for those whom accident has blest with uncommon talents, or such as have read the ancients with indefatigable industry. Parnell is ever happy in the selection of his images, and scrupulously careful in the choice of his subjects. His productions bear no resemblance to those tawdry things which it has for some time been the fashion to admire; in writing which the poet sits down without any plan, and heaps up splendid images without any selection; where the reader grows dizzy with praise and admiration, and yet soon grows weary, he can scarcely tell why. Our poet, on the contrary, gives out his beauties with a more sparing hand; he is still carrying his reader forward, and just gives him refreshment sufficient to support him to his journey's end. At the end of his course, the reader regrets that his way has been so short; he wonders that it gave him so little trouble, and so resolves to go the journey over again.

His poetical language is not less correct than his subjects are pleasing. He found it at that period in which it was brought to its highest pitch of refinement; and ever since his time it has been gradually debasing. It is indeed amazing, after what has been done by Dryden, Addison, and Pope, to improve and harmonize our native tongue, that their successors should have taken so much pains to involve it into pristine barbarity. These misguided innovators have not been content with restoring antiquated words and phrases, but have indulged themselves in the most licentious transpositions and the harshest constructions, vainly imagining, that the more their writings are unlike prose, the more they resemble poetry: they have adopted a language of their own, and call upon mankind for admiration. All those who do not understand them are silent, and those who make out their meaning are willing to praise, to show they understand. From these follies and affectations the poems of Parnell are entirely free. He has considered the language of poetry as the language of life, and conveys the warmest thoughts in the simplest expression.

Parnell has written several poems beside those published by Pope; and some of them have been made public with very little credit to his reputation. There are still many more that have not yet seen the light, in the possession of Sir John Parnell, his nephew; who, from that laudable zeal which he has for his uncle's reputation, will probably be slow in publishing what he may even suspect will do it injury.* Of those which are

* In the year 1788, a large addition was made to our poet's works, in a volume called, "The Posthumous Works of Dr. T. Parnell, containing Poems Moral and Divine, and on various other subjects."[1] They are described by the editor, as having been given by the author to the late Benjamin Everard, and since his death, found by his son among other manuscripts. The receipt annexed in Swift's handwriting, shows that they are certainly genuine.

Dec. 5, 1723.

I have received from Benjamin Everard, Esq., the above writings of the late Doctor Parnell, in four stitched volumes of manuscript, which I promise to restore to him on demand.

JONATHAN SWIFT.

Although these volumes were communicated to him by Swift, Pope, with admirable taste and judgment, contented himself with revising and polishing the few pieces which Parnell had selected for publication. Spence says,[2] "In the list of papers ordered to be burnt, were the pieces for carrying on the Memoirs of Scribblerus, and *several copies of verses by Dean Parnell.* I interceded in vain for both. As to the *latter, he said, that they would not add any thing to the Dean's character.*" These might have been duplicates, or perhaps transcripts made by Pope from the manuscripts mentioned

[1] Mr. Nicholls collected some additional poems, which now appear in Anderson's and Chalmers's *Collections.*

[2] Spence's *Anecdotes*, p. 290.

usually inserted in his works, some are indifferent, and some moderately good, but the greater part are excellent. A slight stricture on the most striking shall conclude this account, which I have already drawn out to a disproportionate length.

"Hesiod, or the Rise of Woman," is a very fine illustration of a hint from Hesiod. It was one of his earliest productions, and first appeared in a miscellany published by Tonson. Of the three songs that follow, two of them were written upon the lady he afterwards married. They were the genuine dictates of his passion, but are not excellent in their kind.

The Anacreontic, beginning with, "When Spring came on with fresh delight," is taken from a French poet whose name I forget, and, as far as I am able to judge of the French language, is better than the

above. Johnson says, "of the large appendages which I find in the last edition, I can only say, that I know not whence they came, nor have ever inquired whither they are going. They stood upon the faith of the compilers." Of their authenticity, after what I have observed, no reasonable doubt can be entertained; but of the prudence of publishing what Pope, and indeed previously Parnell himself, had rejected from their acknowledged inferiority, an estimate can easily be formed, when we consider that probably no one has ever heard a passage or line quoted from the volume; or has deposited a single image or sentiment from it in his memory; while the former poems of Parnell are familiar to old and young, the delight of the general reader, and approved by the most refined judges of poetical merit. Rev. J. Mitford's *Life of Parnell*, 63, 64.

original. The Anacreontic that follows, "Gay Bacchus," &c., is also a translation of a Latin poem, by Aurelius Augurellus, an Italian poet, beginning with,

> "Invitat olim Bacchus ad cœnam suos
> Comum, Jocum, Cupidinem."

Parnell, when he translated it, applied the characters to some of his friends; and as it was written for their entertainment, it probably gave them more pleasure than it has given the public in the perusal. It seems to have more spirit than the original; but it is extraordinary that it was published as an original and not as a translation. Pope should have acknowledged it, as he knew. The "Fairy Tale" is incontestably one of the finest pieces in any language. The old dialect is not perfectly well preserved; but this is a very slight defect, where all the rest is so excellent.

The "Pervigilium Veneris" (which, by the by, does not belong to Catullus) is very well versified; and in general all Parnell's translations are excellent. The "Battle of the Frogs and Mice," which follows, is done as well as the subject would admit; but there is a defect in the translation, which sinks it below the original, and which it was impossible to remedy,—I mean the names of the combatants, which in the Greek bear a ridiculous allusion to their natures, have no force to the English reader.* A bacon-eater was a good name for a mouse, and Pternotractas in Greek was a very good sounding word, that conveyed that meaning. Puff-cheek would sound odiously as a name for a frog, and yet Physignathos does admirably well in the original.

The "Letter to Mr. Pope" is one of the finest compliments that ever was paid to any poet; the description of his situation at the end of it is very fine, but far from being true. That part of it where he deplores his being far from wit and learning, as being far from Pope, gave particular offence to his friends at home. Mr. Coote, a gentleman in his neighbourhood, who thought that he himself had wit, was very much displeased with Parnell for casting his eyes so far off for a learned friend, when he could so conveniently be supplied at home.†

* ["Goldsmith has very properly remarked, that in this poem, the Greek names have not in English their original effect."—JOHNSON.]

† My learned and excellent friend, Mr. Barker, of Thetford, has kindly pointed out to me the following passage relating to Parnell's Hymn to Contentment:

"On the pursuit and attainment of this heavenly tranquillity, the classical and pious reader will perhaps not be displeased to meet a beautiful Ode from the "Divina Psalmodia of Cardinal Bona," on which Parnell manifestly formed his exquisite Hymn to *Contentment.* The insertion will be more readily pardoned, as this imitation has escaped the notice of Dr. Johnson, and, it is believed, of all other critics and commentators."

The translation of a part of the Rape of the Lock into monkish verse, serves to show what a master Parnell was of the Latin; a copy of verses made in this manner, is one of the most difficult trifles that can possibly be imagined. I am assured that it was written upon the following

"O Sincera parens beatitatis,
Cœli delicium, Deique proles,
Pax, terræ columen, decusque morum,
Pax cunctis potior ducum triumphis,
Quos mundi colis abditos recessus?
Hic te sollicito requirit æstro
Urbanos fugiens procul tumultus.
Hic inter scopulos, vagosque fluctus
Spumantis pelagi latere credit.
Hic deserta petit loca, et per antra
Te quærens, varias peragrat oras
Qua lucens oritur, caditque Titan.
Hic, ut te celer adsequatur, aurum
Congestum colit, atque dignitatum
Regalem sibi præparat decorem.
Hic demens juga scandit, et remotos
Perscrutatur agros; tamen supernæ
Hi pacis nequeant bonis potiri.
Cur sic ergo tuum, benigna, numen
Celans, implacidum relinquis orbem?
Pacem sic ego sciscitabar. Illa
Respondet.—Proprio imperare cordi
Si nosti, tibi cognitumque numen
Possessumque meum est; sinu receptam
Sic me perpetuo coles amore."

See Sermons on subjects chiefly practical, by J. Jebb, D. D. F. R. S. Bishop of Limerick, Ardfert, and Aghadoe, third ed. London, 1824, p. 94. *Appendix II. to Rev. John Mitford's Life of Parnell.*

occasion. Before the Rape of the Lock was yet completed, Pope was reading it to his friend Swift, who sat very attentively, while Parnell, who happened to be in the house, went in and out without seeming to take any notice. However, he was very diligently employed in listening, and was able, from the strength of his memory, to bring away the whole description of the Toilet pretty exactly. This he versified in the manner now published in his works; and the next day, when Pope was reading his poem to some friends, Parnell insisted that he had stolen that part of the description from an old monkish manuscript. An old paper with the Latin verses was soon brought forth, and it was not till after some time that Pope was delivered from the confusion which it at first produced.*

The "Book-worm" is another unacknowledged translation, from a Latin poem by Beza. It was the fashion with the wits of the last age to conceal the places whence they took their hints or their subjects. A trifling acknowledgment would have made that lawful prize, which may now be considered as plunder.

The "Night Piece on Death" deserves every

* ["Mr. Harte told me that Dryden had been imposed on by a similar little stratagem. One of his friends translated into Latin verse, printed, and pasted on the bottom of an old hat-box, that celebrated passage, 'To die is landing on some silent shore, &c.,' and that Dryden, on opening the box, was alarmed and amazed."—WARTON.]

praise, and I should suppose, with very little amendment, might be made to surpass all those night pieces and churchyard scenes* that have since appeared. But the poem of Parnell's best known, and on which his best reputation is grounded, is the "Hermit." Pope, speaking of this in those manuscript anecdotes already quoted, says that "the poem is very good. The story," continues he, "was written originally in Spanish, whence probably Howel had translated it into prose, and inserted it in one of his letters. Addison liked the scheme, and was not disinclined to come into it." However this may be, Dr. Henry More, in his Dialogues, has the very same story;† and I have been informed by some, that it is originally of Arabian invention.

* [The Night Piece is indirectly preferred by Goldsmith to Gray's Churchyard; but, in my opinion, Gray has the advantage of dignity, variety, and originality of sentiment. JOHNSON.]

† I have added, in a note, the works of different authors, where, in my own very contracted line of reading, I have accidentally met with this fiction, and which shows it to have been more generally known, than Goldsmith, or probably Parnell, was aware.

1. Herolt Sermones de Tempore et Sanctis, fol. Nuremb. 1496, (Serm. liii.) 2. Gesta Romanorum, c. lxxx. 3. Sir Percy Herbert's Conceptions to his Son, 4to. 1652. 4. H. More's Divine Dialogues, p. 256, ed. 1743. 5. Howell's Letters, iv. 4. 6. Lutherana (Eng. Trans.) vol. ii. p. 127. 7. Voltaire's Zadig. vol. i. chap. xx. p. 125; and see Beloe's Anecdotes, vol. vi. p. 324; and Warton's Eng. Poetry, vol. i. p. cciv. cclxvi.;

With respect to the prose works of Parnell, I have mentioned them already; his fame is too well grounded for any defects in them to shake it. I will only add, that the Life of Zoilus was written at the request of his friends, and designed as a satire upon Dennis and Theobald, with whom his Club had long been at variance. I shall end this account with a letter to him from Pope and Gay, in which they endeavour to hasten him to finish that production.

"London, March 18.

"DEAR SIR:—I must own I have long owed you a letter, but you must own you have owed me one a good deal longer. Besides, I have but two people in the whole kingdom of Ireland to take care of, the Dean and you; but you have several, who complain of your neglect in England. Mr. Gay complains, Mr. Harcourt complains, Mr. Jervas complains, Dr. Arbuthnot complains, my Lord complains, I complain. (Take notice of this figure of iteration, when you make your next sermon.) Some say you are in deep discontent at the new turn of affairs; others, that

vol. iii. p. 41. See also Br. Mus. MS. Harl. 463. fol. 8. Epitres de Madam Antoinette Bourignon, Part: sec: Ep. xvii.

Antonia, who the *Hermit's* story fram'd,
A tale to prose-men known, by verse-men fam'd.
W. Harte's Courtier and Prince.

you are so much in the archbishop's good graces, that you will not correspond with any that have seen the last ministry. Some affirm that you have quarrelled with Pope (whose friends they observe daily fall from him, on account of his satirical and comical disposition); others, that you are insinuating yourself into the opinion of the ingenious 'Mr. What-do-ye-call-him.' Some think you are preparing your Sermons for the press, and others, that you will transform them into essays and moral discourses. But the only excuse that I will allow, is your attention to the Life of Zoilus. The Frogs already seem to croak for their transportation to England, and are sensible how much that doctor is cursed and hated, who introduced their species into your nation; therefore, as you dread the wrath of St. Patrick, send them hither, and rid the kingdom of those pernicious and loquacious animals.

"I have at length received your poem out of Mr. Addison's hands, which shall be sent as soon as you order it, and in what manner you shall appoint. I shall, in the mean time, give Mr. Tooke a packet for you, consisting of divers merry pieces. Mr. Gay's new farce, Mr. Burnet's Letter to Mr. Pope, Mr. Pope's Temple of Fame, Mr. Thomas Burnet's Grumbler on Mr. Gay, and the Bishop of Ailsbury's Elegy, written either by Mr. Cary or some other hand.

"Mr. Pope is reading a letter; and in the

mean time, I make use of the pen to testify my uneasiness in not hearing from you. I find success, even in the most trivial things, raises the indignation of Scribblers: for I, for my 'What-d'-ye-call-it,' could neither escape the fury of Mr. Burnet, or the German Doctor; then where will rage end, when Homer is to be translated? Let Zoilus hasten to your friend's assistance, and envious criticism shall be no more. I am in hopes that we may order our affairs so as to meet this summer at the Bath: for Mr. Pope and myself have thoughts of taking a trip thither. You shall preach, and we will write lampoons; for it is esteemed as great an honour to leave the Bath for fear of a broken head, as for a Terræ Filius of Oxford to be expelled. I have no place at court; therefore, that I may not entirely be without one everywhere, show that I have a place in your remembrance.

Yours, &c.

"A. Pope, and J. Gay.

"Homer will be published in three weeks."

I cannot finish this trifle without returning my sincerest acknowledgments to Sir John Parnell, for the generous assistance he was pleased to give me, in furnishing me with many materials, when he heard I was about writing the life of his uncle; as also to Mr. and Mrs. Hayes, relations of our poet; and to my very good friend M. Stevens, who, being an ornament to letters himself, is very ready to assist all the attempts of others.

TO THE

RIGHT HONOURABLE ROBERT, EARL OF OXFORD, AND EARL MORTIMER.

SUCH were the notes, thy once-lov'd poet sung,
'Till death untimely stopp'd his tuneful tongue.
O just beheld, and lost! admir'd, and mourn'd!
With softest manners, gentlest arts, adorn'd!
Blest in each science, blest in every strain!
Dear to the Muse, to Harley dear—in vain!

For him, thou oft hast bid the world attend,
Fond to forget the statesman in the friend;
For Swift and him, despis'd the farce of state,
The sober follies of the wise and great;
Dexterous, the craving, fawning crowd to quit,
And pleas'd to 'scape from flattery to wit.

Absent or dead, still let a friend be dear,
(A sigh the absent claims, the dead a tear)
Recall those nights that clos'd thy toilsome days,
Still hear thy Parnell in his living lays:
Who careless, now, of interest, fame, or fate,
Perhaps forgets that Oxford e'er was great;
Or deeming meanest what we greatest call,
Beholds thee glorious only in thy fall.

And sure if ought below the seats divine
Can touch immortals, 'tis a soul like thine:
A soul supreme, in each hard instance tried,
Above all pain, all anger, and all pride,
The rage of power, the blast of public breath,
The lust of lucre, and the dread of death.

In vain to deserts thy retreat is made;
The Muse attends thee to the silent shade:
'Tis hers, the brave man's latest steps to trace,
Re-judge his acts, and dignify disgrace.
When Interest calls off all her sneaking train,
When all the oblig'd desert, and all the vain;
She waits, or to the scaffold, or the cell,
When the last lingering friend has bid farewell.
Ev'n now she shades thy evening walk with bays,
(No hireling she, no prostitute to praise)
Ev'n now, observant of the parting ray,
Eyes the calm sun-set of thy various day,
Through fortune's cloud one truly great can see,
Nor fears to tell, that Mortimer is he.

A. Pope.

Sept. 25, 1721.

HESIOD;

OR, THE RISE OF WOMAN.

HESIOD; OR, THE RISE OF WOMAN.

What ancient times, those times we fancy wise,
Have left on long record of woman's rise,
What mortals teach it, and what fables hide,
What author wrote it, how that author died,
All these I sing. In Greece they fram'd the tale;
In Greece 'twas thought a woman might be frail,
Ye modern beauties! where the poet drew
His softest pencil, think he dreamt of you;
And warn'd by him, ye wanton pens, beware
How heaven 's concern'd to vindicate the fair.
The case was Hesiod's; he the fable writ:
Some think with meaning, some with idle wit;
Perhaps 'tis either, as the ladies please;
I wave the contest, and commence the lays.

In days of yore, no matter where or when,
'Twas ere the low creation swarm'd with men,
That one Prometheus, sprung of heavenly birth
Our author's song can witness, liv'd on earth.
He carv'd the turf to mould a manly frame,
And stole from Jove his animating flame.
The sly contrivance o'er Olympus ran,
When thus the monarch of the stars began.

O vers'd in arts! whose daring thoughts aspire
To kindle clay with never-dying fire!
Enjoy thy glory past, that gift was thine;
The next thy creature meets, be fairly mine:
And such a gift, a vengeance so design'd,
As suits the counsel of a God to find;
A pleasing bosom-cheat, a specious ill,
Which felt they curse, yet covet still to feel.

He said, and Vulcan straight the sire commands,
To temper mortar with ethereal hands;
In such a shape to mould a rising fair,
As virgin-goddesses are proud to wear;
To make her eyes with diamond-water shine,
And form her organs for a voice divine.
'Twas thus the sire ordain'd; the power obeyed;
And work'd, and wonder'd at the work he made;
The fairest, softest, sweetest frame beneath,
Now made to seem, now more than seem, to breathe.

As Vulcan ends, the cheerful queen of charms
Clasp'd the new-panting creature in her arms;
From that embrace a fine complexion spread,
Where mingled whiteness glow'd with softer red.
Then in a kiss she breath'd her various arts,
Of trifling prettily with wounded hearts;
A mind for love, but still a changing mind;
The lisp affected, and the glance design'd;
The sweet confusing blush, the secret wink,

The gentle-swimming walk, the courteous sink,
The stare for strangeness fit, for scorn the frown,
For decent yielding looks declining down,
The practis'd languish, where well-feign'd desire
Would own its melting in a mutual fire;
Gay smiles to comfort; April showers to move;
And all the nature, all the art, of love.

Gold-sceptred Juno next exalts the fair;
Her touch endows her with imperious air,
Self-valuing fancy, highly-crested pride,
Strong sovereign will, and some desire to chide:
For which, an eloquence, that aims to vex,
With native tropes of anger, arms the sex.

Minerva, skilful goddess, train'd the maid
To twirl the spindle by the twisting thread,
To fix the loom, instruct the reeds to part,
Cross the long weft, and close the web with art,
A useful gift; but what profuse expense,
What world of fashions, took its rise from hence!

Young Hermes next, a close contriving god,
Her brows encircled with his serpent rod;
Then plots and fair excuses fill'd her brain,
The views of breaking amorous vows for gain,
The price of favours, the designing arts
That aim at riches in contempt of hearts;
And for a comfort in a marriage life,
The little, pilfering temper of a wife.

Full on the fair his beams Apollo flung,
And fond persuasion tipp'd her easy tongue:
He gave her words, where oily flattery lays
The pleasing colours of the art of praise;
And wit, to scandal exquisitely prone,
Which frets another's spleen to cure its own.

Those sacred Virgins whom the bards revere,
Tun'd all her voice, and shed a sweetness there,
To make her sense with double charms abound,
Or make her lively nonsense please by sound.

To dress the maid, the decent Graces brought
A robe in all the dyes of beauty wrought,
And plac'd their boxes o'er a rich brocade
Where pictur'd loves on every cover play'd;
Then spread those implements that Vulcan's art
Had fram'd to merit Cytherea's heart;
The wire to curl, the close-indented comb
To call the locks, that lightly wander, home;
And chief, the mirror, where the ravish'd maid
Beholds and loves her own reflected shade.

Fair Flora lent her stores, the purpled Hours
Confin'd her tresses with a wreath of flowers;
Within the wreath arose a radiant crown;
A veil pellucid hung depending down;
Back roll'd her azure veil with serpent fold,
The purfled border deck'd the floor with gold.

Her robe (which closely by the girdle brac't
Reveal'd the beauties of a slender waist)
Flow'd to the feet; to copy Venus' air,
When Venus' statues have a robe to wear.

The new-sprung creature finish'd thus for harms,
Adjusts her habit, practises her charms,
With blushes glows, or shines with lively smiles,
Confirms her will, or recollects her wiles:
Then conscious of her worth, with easy pace
Glides by the glass, and turning views her face.

A finer flax than what they wrought before,
Through time's deep cave the sister Fates explore,
Then fix the loom, their fingers nimbly weave,
And thus their toil prophetic songs deceive.

Flow from the rock, my flax! and swiftly flow,
Pursue thy thread; the spindle runs below.
A creature fond and changing, fair and vain,
The creature woman, rises now to reign.
New beauty blooms, a beauty form'd to fly;
New love begins, a love produc'd to die;
New parts distress the troubled scenes of life,
The fondling mistress, and the ruling wife.

Men, born to labour, all with pains provide;
Women have time, to sacrifice to pride:
They want the care of man, their want they know,
And dress to please with heart-alluring show,

The show prevailing, for the sway contend,
And make a servant where they meet a friend.

Thus in a thousand wax-erected forts
A loitering race the painful bee supports;
From sun to sun, from bank to bank he flies
With honey loads his bag, with wax his thighs;
Fly where he will, at home the race remain,
Prune the silk dress, and murmuring eat the gain.

Yet here and there we grant a gentle bride,
Whose temper betters by the father's side;
Unlike the rest that double human care,
Fond to relieve, or resolute to share:
Happy the man whom thus his stars advance!
The curse is general, but the blessing chance.

Thus sung the Sisters, while the gods admire
Their beauteous creature, made for man in ire;
The young Pandora she, whom all contend
To make too perfect not to gain her end:
Then bid the winds that fly to breathe the spring,
Return to bear her on a gentle wing;
With wafting airs the winds obsequious blow,
And land the shining vengeance safe below.
A golden coffer in her hand she bore,
(The present treacherous, but the bearer more)
'Twas fraught with pangs; for Jove ordain'd above,
That gold should aid, and pangs attend on love.

Her gay descent the man perceiv'd afar,
Wondering he run to catch the falling star;
But so surpris'd, as none but he can tell,
Who lov'd so quickly, and who lov'd so well.
O'er all his veins the wandering passion burns,
He calls her nymph, and every nymph by turns.
Her form to lovely Venus he prefers,
Or swears that Venus' must be such as hers.
She, proud to rule, yet strangely fram'd to tease,
Neglects his offers while her airs she plays,
Shoots scornful glances from the bended frown,
In brisk disorder trips it up and down,
Then hums a careless tune to lay the storm,
And sits, and blushes, smiles, and yields, in form.

"Now take what Jove design'd," she softly cried,
"This box thy portion, and myself thy bride:"
Fir'd with the prospect of the double charms,
He snatch'd the box, and bride, with eager arms.

Unhappy man! to whom so bright she shone:
The fatal gift, her tempting self, unknown!
The winds were silent, all the waves asleep,
And heaven was trac'd upon the flattering deep;
But whilst he looks unmindful of a storm,
And thinks the water wears a stable form,
What dreadful din around his ears shall rise!
What frowns confuse his picture of the skies!

At first the creature man was fram'd alone,

Lord of himself, and all the world his own.
For him the Nymphs in green forsook the woods,
For him the Nymphs in blue forsook the floods;
In vain the Satyrs rage, the Tritons rave;
They bore him heroes in the secret cave.
No care destroy'd, no sick disorder prey'd,
No bending age his sprightly form decay'd,
No wars were known, no females heard to rage,
And poets tell us, 'twas a golden age.

When woman came, those ills the box confin'd
Burst furious out, and poison'd all the wind,
From point to point, from pole to pole they flew,
Spread as they went, and in the progress grew:
The Nymphs regretting left the mortal race,
And altering nature wore a sickly face;
New terms of folly rose, new states of care;
New plagues to suffer, and to please, the fair!
The days of whining, and of wild intrigues,
Commenc'd, or finish'd, with the breach of leagues;
The mean designs of well-dissembled love;
The sordid matches never join'd above;
Abroad, the labour, and at home the noise,
(Man's double sufferings for domestic joys);
The curse of jealousy; expense, and strife;
Divorce, the public brand of shameful life;
The rival's sword; the qualm that takes the fair;
Disdain for passion, passion in despair—
These, and a thousand, yet unnam'd, we find;
Ah fear the thousand, yet unnam'd, behind!

Thus on Parnassus tuneful Hesiod sung:
The mountain echoed, and the valley rung;
The sacred groves a fix'd attention show;
The crystal Helicon forbore to flow;
The sky grew bright; and (if his verse be true)
The Muses came to give the laurel too.
But what avail'd the verdant prize of wit,
If love swore vengeance for the tales he writ?
Ye fair offended, hear your friend relate
What heavy judgment prov'd the writer's fate,
Though when it happen'd, no relation clears,
'Tis thought in five, or five and twenty years.

Where, dark and silent, with a twisted shade
The neighb'ring woods a native arbour made,
There oft a tender pair for amorous play
Retiring, toy'd the ravish'd hours away;
A Locrian youth, the gentle Troilus he,
A fair Milesian, kind Evanthe she:
But swelling nature in a fatal hour
Betray'd the secrets of the conscious bower;
The dire disgrace her brothers count their own,
And track her steps, to make its author known.

It chanc'd one evening, ('twas the lover's day)
Conceal'd in brakes the jealous kindred lay;
When Hesiod wandering, mus'd along the plain,
And fix'd his seat where love had fix'd the scene:
A strong suspicion straight possess'd their mind,
(For poets ever were a gentle kind.)

But when Evanthe near the passage stood,
Flung back a doubtful look, and shot the wood,
"Now take," at once they cry, "thy due reward,"
And urg'd with erring rage, assault the bard.
His corpse the sea received. The dolphins bore
('Twas all the gods would do) the corpse to shore.

Methinks, I view the dead with pitying eyes,
And see the dreams of ancient wisdom rise:
I see the Muses round the body cry,
But hear a Cupid loudly laughing by;
He wheels his arrow with insulting hand,
And thus inscribes the moral on the sand.
"Here Hesiod lies: ye future bards, beware
How far your moral tales incense the fair:
Unlov'd, unloving, 'twas his fate to bleed;
Without his quiver Cupid caus'd the deed:
He judg'd this turn of malice justly due,
And Hesiod died for joys he never knew."

SONG.

When thy beauty appears,
In its graces and airs,
All bright as an angel new dropt from the sky;
At distance I gaze, and am aw'd by my fears,
So strangely you dazzle my eye!

But when without art,
Your kind thoughts you impart,
When your love runs in blushes through every vein;
When it darts from your eyes, when it pants
in your heart,
Then I know you're a woman again.

There 's a passion and pride
In our sex, she replied,
And thus (might I gratify both) I would do;
Still an angel appear to each lover beside,
But still be a woman to you.

A SONG.

Thirsis, a young and amorous swain,
Saw two, the beauties of the plain,
Who both his heart subdue:
Gay Cælia's eyes were dazzling fair,

Sabina's easy shape and air
With softer magic drew.

He haunts the stream, he haunts the grove,
Lives in a fond romance of love,
And seems for each to die;
Till each a little spiteful grown,
Sabina Cælia's shape ran down,
And she Sabina's eye.

Their envy made the shepherd find
Those eyes, which love could only blind;
So set the lover free:
No more he haunts the grove or stream,
Or with a true-love knot and name
Engraves a wounded tree

Ah Cælia! sly Sabina cried,
Though neither love, we're both denied;
Now to support the sex's pride,
Let either fix the dart.
Poor girl! says Cælia, say no more;
For should the swain but one adore,
That spite which broke his chains before,
Would break the other's heart.

SONG.

My days have been so wondrous free,
The little birds that fly
With careless ease from tree to tree,
Were but as bless'd as I.

Ask gliding waters, if a tear
Of mine increas'd their stream?
Or ask the flying gales, if e'er
I lent one sigh to them?

But now my former days retire
And I 'm by beauty caught,
The tender chains of sweet desire
Are fix'd upon my thought.

Ye nightingales, ye twisting pines!
Ye swains that haunt the grove!
Ye gentle echoes, breezy winds!
Ye close retreats of love!

With all of nature, all of art,
Assist the dear design;
O teach a young, unpractis'd heart,
To make my Nancy mine!

The very thought of change I hate,
  As much as of despair;
Nor ever covet to be great,
  Unless it be for her.

'Tis true, the passion in my mind
  Is mix'd with soft distress;
Yet while the fair I love is kind,
  I cannot wish it less.

ANACREONTIC.

WHEN spring came on with fresh delight,
To cheer the soul, and charm the sight,
While easy breezes, softer rain,
And warmer suns salute the plain;
'Twas then, in yonder piny grove,
That Nature went to meet with Love.

Green was her robe, and green her wreath,
Where'er she trod, 'twas green beneath;
Where'er she turn'd, the pulses beat
With new recruits of genial heat;
And in her train the birds appear,
To match for all the coming year.

Rais'd on a bank where daisies grew,
And violets intermix'd a blue,
She finds the boy she went to find;
A thousand pleasures wait behind,
Aside, a thousand arrows lie,
But all unfeather'd wait to fly.

When they met, the dame and boy,
Dancing Graces, idle Joy,
Wanton Smiles, and airy Play,
Conspir'd to make the scene be gay;

Love pair'd the birds through all the grove,
And Nature bid them sing to Love,
Sitting, hopping, fluttering, sing,
And pay their tribute from the wing,
To fledge the shafts that idly lie,
And yet unfeather'd wait to fly.

'Tis thus, when spring renews the blood,
They meet in every trembling wood,
And thrice they make the plumes agree,
And every dart they mount with three,
And every dart can boast a kind,
Which suits each proper turn of mind.

From the towering eagle's plume
The generous hearts accept their doom:
Shot by the peacock's painted eye,
The vain and airy lovers die:
For careful dames and frugal men,
The shafts are speckled by the hen:
The pies and parrots deck the darts,
When prattling wins the panting hearts:
When from the voice the passions spring,
The warbling finch affords a wing:
Together, by the sparrow stung,
Down fall the wanton and the young:
And fledg'd by geese the weapons fly,
When others love they know not why.

All this, as late I chanced to rove,

I learn'd in yonder waving grove.
And see, says Love, who called me near,
How much I deal with Nature here,
How both support a proper part,
She gives the feather, I the dart,
Then cease for souls averse to sigh
If Nature cross ye, so do I;
My weapon there unfeather'd flies,
And shakes and shuffles through the skies;
But if the mutual charms I find
By which she links you, mind to mind,
They wing my shafts, I poise the darts,
And strike from both, through both your hearts.

ANACREONTIC.

GAY Bacchus liking Estcourt's wine,
  A noble meal bespoke us ;
And for the guests that were to dine,
  Brought Comus, Love, and Jocus.

The god near Cupid drew his chair,
  Near Comus, Jocus plac'd :
For wine makes Love forget its care,
  And Mirth exalts a feast.

The more to please the sprightly god,
  Each sweet engaging Grace
Put on some clothes to come abroad,
  And took a waiter's place.

Then Cupid nam'd at every glass
  A lady of the sky ;
While Bacchus swore he'd drink the lass,
  And had it bumper-high.

Fat Comus toss'd his brimmers o'er,
  And always got the most ;
Jocus took care to fill him more,
  Whene'er he miss'd the toast.

They call'd, and drank at every touch;
  He fill'd and drank again;
And if the gods can take too much,
  'Tis said, they did so then.

Gay Bacchus little Cupid stung,
  By reckoning his deceits;
And Cupid mock'd his stammering tongue,
  With all his staggering gaits:

And Jocus droll'd on Comus' ways,
  And tales without a jest;
While Comus call'd his witty plays
  But waggeries at best.

Such talk soon set them all at odds;
  And, had I Homer's pen,
I'd sing ye, how they drank like gods,
  And how they fought like men.

To part the fray, the Graces fly,
  Who make 'em soon agree;
Nay, had the Furies selves been nigh,
  They still were three to three.

Bacchus appeas'd, rais'd Cupid up,
  And gave him back his bow;
But kept some darts to stir the cup
  Where sack and sugar flow.

Jocus took Comus' rosy crown,
 And gaily wore the prize,
And thrice in mirth he push'd him down,
 As thrice he strove to rise.

Then Cupid sought the myrtle grove,
 Where Venus did recline;
And Venus close embracing Love,
 They join'd to rail at wine.

And Comus loudly cursing wit,
 Roll'd off to some retreat,
Where boon companions gravely sit
 In fat unwieldy state.

Bacchus and Jocus, still behind,
 For one fresh glass prepare;
They kiss, and are exceeding kind,
 And vow to be sincere.

But part in time, whoever hear
 This our instructive song;
For though such friendships may be dear,
 They can't continue long.

A FAIRY TALE,

IN THE ANCIENT ENGLISH STYLE.

In Britain's isle and Arthur's days,
When midnight faeries daunc'd the maze,
Liv'd Edwin of the green;
Edwin, I wis, a gentle youth,
Endow'd with courage, sense, and truth,
Though badly shap'd he been.

His mountain back mote well be said
To measure heighth against his head,
And lift itself above:
Yet spite of all that nature did
To make his uncouth form forbid,
This creature dar'd to love.

He felt the charms of Edith's eyes,
Nor wanted hope to gain the prize,
Could ladies look within;
But one Sir Topaz dress'd with art,
And, if a shape could win a heart,
He had a shape to win.

Edwin, if right I read my song,
With slighted passion pac'd along
All in the moony light:

'Twas near an old enchaunted court,
Where sportive faeries made resort
To revel out the night.

His heart was drear, his hope was cross'd,
'Twas late, 'twas farr, the path was lost
That reach'd the neighbour-town;
With weary steps he quits the shades,
Resolv'd the darkling dome he treads,
And drops his limbs adown.

But scant he lays him on the floor,
When hollow winds remove the door,
A trembling rocks the ground:
And, well I ween to count aright,
At once an hundred tapers light
On all the walls around.

Now sounding tongues assail his ear,
Now sounding feet approachen near,
And now the sounds encrease;
And from the corner where he lay
He sees a train profusely gay
Come pranckling o'er the place.

But, trust me, gentles, never yet
Was dight a masquing half so neat,
Or half so rich before;
The country lent the sweet perfumes,
The sea the pearl, the sky the plumes,
The town its silken store.

Now whilst he gaz'd, a gallant drest
In flaunting robes above the rest,
With awfull accent cried,
What mortal of a wretched mind,
Whose sighs infect the balmy wind,
Has here presumed to hide?

At this the swain, whose venturous soul
No fears of magic art controul,
Advanc'd in open sight;
'Nor have I cause of dreed,' he said,
'Who view, by no presumption led,
Your revels of the night.

''Twas grief for scorn of faithful love,
Which made my steps unweeting rove
Amid the nightly dew.'
'Tis well, the gallant cries again,
We faeries never injure men
Who dare to tell us true.

Exalt thy love-dejected heart,
Be mine the task, or ere we part,
To make thee grief resign;
Now take the pleasure of thy chaunce;
Whilst I with Mab my partner daunce,
Be little Mable thine.

He spoke, and all a sudden there
Light musick floats in wanton air;
The monarch leads the queen;

The rest their faerie partners found,
And Mable trimly tript the ground
With Edwin of the green.

The dauncing past, the board was laid,
And siker such a feast was made
As heart and lip desire;
Withouten hands the dishes fly,
The glasses with a wish come nigh,
And with a wish retire.

But now to please the faerie king,
Full every deal they laugh and sing,
And antick feats devise;
Some wind and tumble like an ape,
And other-some transmute their shape
In Edwin's wondering eyes.

Till one at last that Robin hight,
Renown'd for pinching maids by night,
Has hent him up aloof;
And full against the beam he flung,
Where by the back the youth he hung
To spraul unneath the roof.

From thence, 'Reverse my charm,' he cries,
'And let it fairly now suffice
The gambol has been shown.'
But Oberon answers with a smile,
Content thee, Edwin, for a while,
The vantage is thine own.

Here ended all the phantome play;
They smelt the fresh approach of day,
    And heard a cock to crow;
The whirling wind that bore the crowd
Has clapp'd the door, and whistled loud,
    To warn them all to go.

Then screaming all at once they fly,
And all at once the tapers die;
    Poor Edwin falls to floor;
Forlorn his state, and dark the place,
Was never wight in sike a case
    Through all the land before.

But soon as Dan Apollo rose,
Full jolly creature home he goes,
    He feels his back the less;
His honest tongue and steady mind
Han rid him of the lump behind
    Which made him want success.

With lusty livelyhed he talks
He seems a dauncing as he walks;
    His story soon took wind;
And beauteous Edith sees the youth,
Endow'd with courage, sense and truth,
    Without a bunch behind.

The story told, Sir Topaz mov'd,
The youth of Edith erst approv'd,
    To see the revel scene:

At close of eve he leaves his home,
And wends to find the ruin'd dome
All on the gloomy plain.

As there he bides, it so befell,
The wind came rustling down a dell,
A shaking seiz'd the wall:
Up spring the tapers as before,
The faeries bragly foot the floor,
And musick fills the hall.

But certes sorely sunk with woe
Sir Topaz sees the elfin show,
His spirits in him die:
When Oberon cries, 'A man is near,
A mortall passion, cleeped fear,
Hangs flagging in the sky.'

With that Sir Topaz, hapless youth!
In accents faultering ay for ruth
Intreats them pity graunt;
For als he been a mister wight
Betray'd by wandering in the night
To tread the circled haunt.

'Ah losell vile!' at once they roar,
'And little skill'd of faerie lore,
Thy cause to come we know:
Now has thy kestrell courage fell;
And faeries, since a lie you tell,
Are free to work thee woe.'

Then Will, who bears the wispy fire
To trail the swains among the mire,
    The caitive upward flung;
There like a tortoise in a shop
He dangled from the chamber-top,
    Where whilome Edwin hung.

The revel now proceeds apace,
Deffly they frisk it o'er the place,
    They sit, they drink, and eat;
The time with frolick mirth beguile,
And poor Sir Topaz hangs the while
    Till all the rout retreat.

By this the starrs began to wink,
They shriek, they fly, the tapers sink,
    And down ydrops the knight:
For never spell by faerie laid
With strong enchantment bound a glade
    Beyond the length of night.

Chill, dark, alone, adreed, he lay,
Till up the welkin rose the day,
    Then deem'd the dole was o'er:
But wot ye well his harder lot?
His seely back the bunch has got
    Which Edwin lost afore.

This tale a Sybil-nurse ared;
She softly strok'd my youngling head,
    And when the tale was done,

'Thus some are born, my son,' she cries,
'With base impediments to rise,
And some are born with none.

'But virtue can itself advance
To what the favourite fools of chance
By fortune seem'd design'd;
Virtue can gain the odds of fate,
And from itself shake off the weight
Upon th' unworthy mind.'

THE VIGIL OF VENUS.

WRITTEN IN THE TIME OF JULIUS CÆSAR, AND BY SOME ASCRIBED TO CATULLUS.

Let those love now, who never lov'd before ;
Let those who always lov'd, now love the more.
The spring, the new, the warbling spring appears,
The youthful season of reviving years ;
In spring the loves enkindle mutual heats,
The feather'd nation choose their tuneful mates,
The trees grow fruitful with descending rain
And drest in differing greens adorn the plain.
She comes ; to-morrow Beauty's empress roves
Through walks that winding run within the groves ;
She twines the shooting myrtle into bowers,
And ties their meeting tops with wreaths of flowers,

PERVIGILIUM VENERIS.

Cras amet, qui numquam amavit ; quique amavit, cras amet.
Ver novum, ver jam canorum : vere natus orbis est,
Vere concordant amores, vere nubent alites,
Et nemus comam resolvit de maritis imbribus.
Cras amorum copulatrix inter umbras arborum
Implicat gazas virentes de flagello myrteo.

Then rais'd sublimely on her easy throne,
From Nature's powerful dictates draws her own.
Let those love now, who never lov'd before;
Let those who always lov'd, now love the more.

'Twas on that day which saw the teeming flood
Swell round, impregnate with celestial blood;
Wandering in circles stood the finny crew,
The midst was left a void expanse of blue;
There parent Ocean work'd with heaving throes,
And dropping wet the fair Dione rose.
Let those love now, who never lov'd before;
Let those who always lov'd, now love the more.

She paints the purple year with varied show,
Tips the green gem, and makes the blossom glow,

Cras Dione dicit, jura fulta sublimi throno.
Cras amet, qui numquam amavit; quique amavit, cras amet.

Tunc liquore de superno, spumeo ponti e globe,
Cærulas inter catervas, inter et bipedes equos,
Fecit undantem Dionen de maritis imbribus.
Cras amet, qui numquam amavit; quique amavit, cras amet.

Ipsa gemmis purpurantem pingit annum floribus,
Ipsa surgentes papillas de Favoni spiritu

She makes the turgid buds receive the breeze,
Expand to leaves, and shade the naked trees:
When gathering damps the misty nights diffuse,
She sprinkles all the morn with balmy dews;
Bright trembling pearls depend at every spray,
And kept from falling, seem to fall away.
A glossy freshness hence the rose receives,
And blushes sweet through all her silken leaves;
(The drops descending through the silent night,
While stars serenely roll their golden light,)
Close till the morn, her humid veil she holds;
Then deck'd with virgin pomp the flower unfolds.
Soon will the morning blush: ye maids! prepare,
In rosy garlands bind your flowing hair:
'Tis Venus' plant: the blood fair Venus shed,
O'er the gay beauty pour'd immortal red;
From Love's soft kiss a sweet ambrosial smell
Was taught for ever on the leaves to dwell;

Urguet in toros tepentes, ipsa roris lucidi,
Noctis aura quem relinquit, spargit humentes aquas
Et micant lacrymæ termentes decidivo pondere:
Gutta præceps orbe parvo sustinet casus suos;
In pudorem florulentæ prodiderunt purpuræ.
Humor ille, quem serenis astra rorant noctibus,
Mane virgines papillas solvit humenti peplo.
Ipsa jussit mane ut udæ virgines nubant rosæ,
Fusæ prius de cruore deque Amoris osculis,
Deque gemmis, deque flammis, deque solis pupuris.

From gems, from flames, from orient rays of light,
The richest lustre makes her purple bright;
And she to-morrow weds; the sporting gale
Unties her zone, she bursts the verdant veil:
Through all her sweets the rifling lover flies,
And as he breathes, her glowing fires arise.
Let those love now, who never lov'd before;
Let those who always lov'd, now love the more.

Now fair Dione to the myrtle grove
Sends the gay Nymphs, and sends her tender Love,
And shall they venture? Is it safe to go, [bow?
While Nymphs have hearts, and Cupid wears a
Yes, safely venture, 'tis his mother's will:
He walks unarm'd and undesigning ill,
His torch extinct, his quiver useless hung,
His arrows idle, and his bow unstrung.

Cras ruborem qui latebat veste tectus ignea,
Unico marita nodo non pudebit solvere.
Cras amet, qui numquam amavit; quique amavit, cras amet.

Ipsa nimfas diva luco jussit ire myrteo:
Et puer comes puellis. Nec tamen credi potest
Esse Amorem feriatum, si sagittas vexerit
Ite Nimfæ: posuit arma, feriatus est amor:
Jussus est inermis ire, nudus ire jussus est:
Neu quid arcu, neu sagitta, neu quid igne læderet.

And yet, ye Nymphs, beware, his eyes have charms,
And Love that's naked, still is Love in arms.
Let those love now, who never lov'd before;
Let those who always lov'd, now love the more.

From Venus' bower to Delia's lodge repairs
A virgin train complete with modest airs:
"Chaste Delia, grant our suit! or shun the wood,
Nor stain this sacred lawn with savage blood.
Venus, O Delia! if she could persuade,
Would ask thy presence, might she ask a maid."
Here cheerful quires for three auspicious nights
With songs prolong the pleasurable rites:
Here crowds in measures lightly-decent rove,
Or seek by pairs the covert of the grove,
Where meeting greens for arbours arch above,
And mingling flowerets strew the scenes of love.

Sed tamen nimfæ cavete, quod Cupido pulcher est:
Totus est inermis idem, quando nudus est Amor.
Cras amet, qui numquam amavit; quique amavit, cras amet.

Compari Venus pudore mittit ad te virgines:
Una res est quam rogamus: cede virgo Delia;
Ut nemus sit incruentum de ferinis stragibus.
Ipsa vellet ut venires, si deceret virginem:
Jam tribus choros videres feriatos noctibus,
Congreges inter catervas, ire per saltus tuos,

Here dancing Ceres shakes her golden sheaves:
Here Bacchus revels, deck'd with viny leaves:
Here wit's enchanting God in laurel crown'd
Wakes all the ravish'd Hours with silver sound.
Ye fields, ye forests, own Dione's reign,
And, Delia, huntress Delia, shun the plain.
Let those love now, who never lov'd before;
Let those who always lov'd, now love the more.

Gay with the bloom of all her opening year,
The Queen at Hybla bids her throne appear;
And there presides; and there the favourite band,
Her smiling Graces, share the great command.
Now, beauteous Hybla, dress thy flowery beds
With all the pride the lavish season sheds;
Now all thy colours, all thy fragrance yield,
And rival Enna's aromatic field.

Floreas inter coronas, myrteas inter casas.
Nec Ceres, nec Bacchus absunt, nec poetarum Deus;
Decinent, et tota nox est pervigila cantibus.
Regnet in silvis Dione: tu recede Delia.
Cras amet, qui numquam amavit; quique amavit, cras amet.

Jussit Hyblæis tribunal stare diva floribus;
Præsens ipsa jura dicit, adsederunt Gratiæ.
Hybla totos funde flores, quidquid annus adtulit,
Hybla florum rumpe vestem, quantus Ænnæ campus est.

To fill the presence of the gentle court
From every quarter rural nymphs resort,
From woods, from mountains, from their humble vales,
From waters curling with the wanton gales.
Pleas'd with the joyful train, the laughing Queen
In circles seats them round the bank of green;
And "lovely girls," she whispers, "guard your hearts;
My boy, though stript of arms, abounds in arts."
Let those love now, who never lov'd before;
Let those who always lov'd, now love the more.

Let tender grass in shaded alleys spread,
Let early flowers erect their painted head.
To-morrow's glory be to-morrow seen,
That day old Ether wedded Earth in green.

Ruris hic erunt puellæ, vel puellæ montium,
Quæque silvas, quæque lucos, quæque montes incolunt.
Jussit omnis adsidere pueri mater alitis,
Jussit et nudo puellas nil Amori credere.
Cras amet, qui numquam amavit; quique amavit, cras amet.

Et recentibus virentes ducat umbras floribus:
Cras erit qui primus æther copulavit nuptias
Ut pater roris crearet vernis annum nubibus,

The Vernal Father bid the spring appear,
In clouds he coupled to produce the year;
The sap descending o'er her bosom ran,
And all the various sorts of soul began.
By wheels unknown to sight, by secret veins
Distilling life, the fruitful goddess reigns,
Through all the lovely realms of native day,
Through all the circled land, the circling sea;
With fertile seed she fill'd the pervious earth,
And ever fix'd the mystic ways of birth.
Let those love now, who never lov'd before;
Let those who always lov'd, now love the more.

'Twas she the parent, to the Latian shore
Through various dangers Troy's remainder bore:

In sinum maritus imber fluxit almæ conjugis,
Ut fœtus immixtus omnis aleret magno corpore.
Ipsa venas atque mentem permeante spiritu
Intus occultis gubernat procreatrix viribus,
Perque cœlum, perque terras, perque pontum subditum,
Pervium sui tenorem seminali tramite
Imbuit, jussitque mundum nosse nascendi vias.
Cras amet, qui numquam amavit; quique amavit, cras amet.

Ipsa Trojanos nepotes in Latino transtulit;
Ipsa Laurentem puellam conjugem nato dedit;

She won Lavinia for her warlike son,
And winning her, the Latian empire won.
She gave to Mars the maid, whose honour'd womb
Swell'd with the founder of immortal Rome:
Decoy'd by shows the Sabine dames she led,
And taught our vigorous youth the means to wed.
Hence sprung the Romans, hence the race divine,
Through which great Cæsar draws his Julian line.
Let those love now, who never lov'd before;
Let those who always lov'd, now love the more.

In rural seats the soul of Pleasure reigns;
The life of Beauty fills the rural scenes;
E'en Love, if fame the truth of Love declare,
Drew first the breathings of a rural air.
Some pleasing meadow pregnant Beauty prest,
She laid her infant on its flowery breast;
From nature's sweets he sipp'd the fragrant dew.

Moxque Marti de sacello dat pudicam virginem;
Romuleas ipsa fecit cum Sabinis nuptias;
Unde Ramnes et Quirites, proque prole posterum
Romuli matrem crearet et nepotem Cæsarem.
Cras amet, qui numquam amavit; quique amavit, cras amet.

Rura fœcundat voluptas: rura Venerem sentiunt.
Ipse Amor puer Dionæ rure natus dicitur.
Hunc ager, cum parturiret ipsa, suscepit sinu;

He smil'd, he kiss'd them, and by kissing grew.
Let those love now, who never lov'd before;
Let those who always lov'd, now love the more.

Now bulls o'er stalks of broom extend their sides,
Secure of favours from their lowing brides.
Now stately rams their fleecy consorts lead,
Who bleating follow through the wandering shade.
And now the Goddess bids the birds appear,
Raise all their music, and salute the year.
Then deep the swan begins, and deep the song
Runs o'er the water where he sails along;
While Philomela tunes a treble strain,
And from the poplar charms the listening plain.
We fancy love express'd at every note,

Ipsa florum delicatis educavit osculis.
Cras amet, qui numquam amavit; quique amavit, cras amet.

Ecce, jam super genistas explicant tauri latus!
Quisque tuus quo tenetur conjugali fœdere.
Subter umbras cum maritis ecce balantum greges:
Et canoras non tacere diva jussit alites.
Jam loquaces ore rauco stagna cygni perstrepunt:
Adsonat Terei puella subter umbram populi;
Ut putas motus amoris ore dici musico,
Et neges queri sororem de marito barbaro.

It melts, it warbles, in her liquid throat:
Of barbarous Tereus she complains no more,
But sings for pleasure, as for grief before;
And still her graces rise, her airs extend,
And all is silence till the Siren end.

How long in coming is my lovely spring?
And when shall I, and when the swallow sing?
Sweet Philomela, cease; or here I sit,
And silent lose my rapturous hour of wit:
'Tis gone, the fit retires, the flames decay,
My tuneful Phœbus flies averse away.
His own Amycle thus, as stories run,
But once was silent, and that once undone.
Let those love now, who never lov'd before;
Let those who always lov'd, now love the more.

Illa cantat: nos tacemus. Quando ver venit meum?
Quando faciam ut celidon, ut tacere desinam?
Perdidi musam tacendo, nec me Phœbus respicit.
Sic Amyclas, cum tacerent, perdidit silentium.
Cras amet, qui numquam amavit; quique amavit, cras amet.

HOMER'S BATRACHOMUOMACHIA;

OR, THE

BATTLE OF THE FROGS AND MICE.

NAMES OF THE MICE.

PSYCARPAX, *one who plunders granaries.*
Troxartes, *a bread-eater.*
Lychomyle, *a licker of meal.*
Pternotroctas, *a bacon-eater.*
Lychopinax, *a licker of dishes.*
Embasichytros, *a creeper into pots.*
Lychenor, *a name from licking.*
Troglodytes, *one who runs into holes.*
Artophagus, *who feeds on bread.*
Tyroglyphus, *a cheese scooper.*
Pternoglyphus, *a bacon-scooper.*
Pternophagus, *a bacon-eater.*
Cnissodioctes, *one who follows the steam of kitchens.*
Sitophagus, *an eater of wheat.*
Meridarpax, *one who plunders his share.*

NAMES OF THE FROGS.

PHYSIGNATHUS, *one who swells his cheeks*
Peleus, *a name from mud.*
Hydromeduse, *a ruler in the waters.*
Hypsiboas, *a loud bawler.*
Pelion, *from mud.*
Seutlæus, *called from the beets.*
Polyphonus, *a great babbler.*
Lymnocharis, *one who loves the lake.*
Crambophagus, *a cabbage-eater.*
Lymnisius, *called from the lake.*
Calaminthius, *from the herb.*
Hydrocharis, *who loves the water.*
Borborocates, *who lies in the mud.*
Prassophagus, *an eater of garlick.*
Pelusius, *from mud.*
Pelobates, *who walks in the dirt.*
Prassæus, *called from garlick.*
Craugasides, *from croaking.*

HOMER'S BATTLE OF THE FROGS, ETC.

BOOK I.

To fill my rising song with sacred fire,
Ye tuneful Nine, ye sweet celestial quire!
From helicon's embowering height repair,
Attend my labours, and reward my prayer.
The dreadful toils of raging Mars I write,
The springs of contest, and the fields of fight;
How threatening mice advanc'd with warlike grace,
And wag'd dire combats with the croaking race.
Not louder tumults shook Olympus' towers,
When earth-born giants dar'd immortal powers.
These equal acts an equal glory claim,
And thus the Muse records the tale of fame.

Once on a time, fatigu'd and out of breath,
And just escap'd the stretching claws of death,
A gentle mouse, whom cats pursu'd in vain,
Fled swift of foot across the neighb'ring plain,
Hung o'er a brink, his eager thirst to cool,
And dipt his whiskers in the standing pool;
When near a courteous frog advanc'd his head
And from the water's, hoarse-resounding, said,

What art thou, stranger? What the line you boast?
What chance has cast thee panting on our coast?
With strictest truth let all thy words agree,
Nor let me find a faithless mouse in thee.
If worthy friendship, proffer'd friendship take,
And entering view the pleasurable lake:
Range o'er my palace, in my bounty share,
And glad return from hospitable fare.
This silver realm extends beneath my sway,
And me, their monach, all its frogs obey.
Great Physignathus I, from Peleus' race,
Begot in fair Hydromeduse' embrace,
Where by the nuptial bank that paints his side,
The swift Eridanus delights to glide.
Thee too, thy form, thy strength, and port proclaim
A sceptred king; a son of martial fame;
Then trace thy line, and aid my guessing eyes.
Thus ceas'd the frog, and thus the mouse replies.

Known to the gods, the men, the birds that fly
Through wild expanses of the midway sky,
My name resounds; and if unknown to thee,
The soul of great Psycarpax lives in me,
Of brave Troxartes' line, whose sleeky down
In love compress'd Lychomile the brown.
My mother she, and princess of the plains
Where'er her father Pternotroctes reigns:
Born where a cabin lifts its airy shed,
With figs, with nuts, with varied dainties fed.
But since our natures nought in common know,

From what foundation can a friendship grow?
These curling waters o'er thy palace roll;
But man's high food supports my princely soul.
In vain the circled loaves attempt to lie
Conceal'd in flaskets from my curious eye;
In vain the tripe that boasts the whitest hue,
In vain the gilded bacon shuns my view;
In vain the cheeses, offspring of the pail,
Or honey'd cakes, which gods themselves regale.
And as in arts I shine, in arms I fight,
Mix'd with the bravest, and unknown to flight,
Though large to mine the human form appear,
Not man himself can smite my soul with fear:
Sly to the bed with silent steps I go,
Attempt his finger, or attack his toe,
And fix indented wounds with dext'rous skill;
Sleeping he feels and only seems to feel.
Yet have we foes which direful dangers cause,
Grim owls with talons arm'd, and cats with claws,
And that false trap, the den of silent fate,
Where death his ambush plants around the bait:
All dreaded these, and dreadful o'er the rest
The potent warriors of the tabby vest:
If to the dark we fly, the dark they trace,
And rend our heroes of the nibbling race.
But me, nor stalks, nor watrish herbs delight,
Nor can the crimson radish charm my sight,
The lake-resounding frog's selected fare,
Which not a mouse of any taste can bear.

As thus the downy prince his mind express'd,
His answer thus the croaking king address'd.

Thy words luxuriant on thy dainties rove,
And, stranger, we can boast of bounteous Jove:
We sport in water, or we dance on land,
And born amphibious, food from both command.
But trust thyself where wonders ask thy view,
And safely tempt those seas, I'll bear the through:
Ascend my shoulders, firmly keep thy seat,
And reach my marshy court, and feast in state.

He said, and bent his back; with nimble bound
Leaps the light mouse, and clasps his arms around;
Then wondering floats, and sees with glad survey
The winding banks resembling ports at sea.
But when aloft the curling water rides,
And wets with azure wave his downy sides,
His thoughts grow conscious of approaching woe,
His idle tears with vain repentance flow;
His locks he rends, his trembling feet he rears,
Thick beats his heart with unaccustom'd fears;
He sighs, and chill'd with danger, longs for shore:
His tail extended forms a fruitless oar,
Half drench'd in liquid death his prayers he spake,
And thus bemoan'd him from the dreadful lake.

So pass'd Europa through the rapid sea,
Trembling and fainting all the venturous way;

With oary feet the bull triumphant row'd,
And safe in Crete depos'd his lovely load.
Ah safe at last! may thus the frog support
My trembling limbs to reach his ample court.

As thus he sorrows, death ambiguous grows,
Lo! from the deep a water-hydra rose;
He rolls his sanguin'd eyes, his bosom heaves,
And darts with active rage along the waves.
Confus'd the monarch sees his hissing foe,
And dives, to shun the sable fates, below.
Forgetful frog! The friend thy shoulders bore,
Unskill'd in swimming, floats remote from shore.
He grasps with fruitless hands to find relief,
Supinely falls, and grinds his teeth with grief;
Plunging he sinks, and struggling mounts again,
And sinks, and strives, but strives with fate in vain.
The weighty moisture clogs his hairy vest,
And thus the prince his dying rage express'd.

Nor thou, that fling'st me floundering from thy back,
As from hard rocks rebounds the shattering wrack,
Nor thou shalt 'scape thy due, perfidious king!
Pursu'd by vengeance on the swiftest wing:
At land thy strength could never equal mine,
At sea to conquer, and by craft, was thine.
But heaven has gods, and gods have searching eyes:
Ye mice, ye mice, my great avengers, rise!

This said, he sighing gasp'd, and gasping died.
His death the young Lychopinax espied,
As on the flowery brink he pass'd the day,
Bask'd in the beams, and loiter'd life away.
Loud shrieks the mouse, his shrieks the shores repeat;
The nibbling nation learn their hero's fate;
Grief, dismal grief ensues; deep murmurs sound,
And shriller fury fills the deafen'd ground.
From lodge to lodge the sacred heralds run,
To fix their council with the rising sun;
Where great Troxartes crown'd in glory reigns,
And winds his lengthening court beneath the plains:
Psycarpax' father, father now no more!
For poor Psycarpax lies remote from shore;
Supine he lies! the silent waters stand,
And no kind billow wafts the dead to land!

HOMER'S BATTLE OF THE FROGS AND MICE.

BOOK II.

When rosy-finger'd morn had ting'd the clouds
Around their monach-mouse the nation crowds;
Slow rose the sovereign, heav'd his anxious breast,
And thus, the council fill'd with rage, address'd.

For lost Psycarpax much my soul endures,
'Tis mine the private grief, the public, yours.
Three warlike sons adorn'd my nuptial bed,
Three sons, alas! before their father dead!
Our eldest perish'd by the ravening cat,
As near my court the prince unheedful sat.
Our next, an engine fraught with danger drew,
The portal gap'd, the bait was hung in view,
Dire arts assist the trap, the fates decoy,
And men unpitying kill'd my gallant boy.
The last, his country's hope, his parents' pride,
Plung'd in the lake by Physignathus, died.
Rouse all the war, my friends! avenge the deed,
And bleed that monarch, and his nation bleed.

His words in every breast inspir'd alarms,
And careful Mars supplied their host with arms.

In verdant hulls despoil'd of all their beans,
The buskin'd warriors stalk'd along the plains:
Quills aptly bound, their bracing corselet made,
Fac'd with the plunder of a cat they flay'd;
The lamp's round boss affords their ample shield;
Large shells of nuts their covering helmet yield;
And o'er the region with reflected rays,
Tall groves of needles for their lances blaze.
Dreadful in arms the marching mice appear;
The wondering frogs perceive the tumult near,
Forsake the waters, thickening form a ring,
And ask and hearken, whence the noises spring.
When near the crowd, disclos'd to public view,
The valiant chief Embasichytros drew:
The sacred herald's sceptre grac'd his hand,
And thus his words express'd his king's command.

Ye frogs! the mice, with vengeance fir'd, advance,
And deck'd in armour shake the shining lance:
Their hapless prince by Physignathus slain,
Extends incumbent on the watery plain.
Then arm your host, the doubtful battle try;
Lead forth those frogs that have the soul to die.

The chief retires, the crowd the challenge hear,
And proudly-swelling yet perplex'd appear:
Much they resent, yet much their monarch blame,
Who rising, spoke to clear his tainted fame.

O friends, I never forc'd the mouse to death,

Nor saw the gasping of his latest breath.
He, vain of youth, our art of swimming tried,
And venturous, in the lake the wanton died.
To vengeance now by false appearance led,
They point their anger at my guiltless head.
But wage the rising war by deep device,
And turn its fury on the crafty mice.
Your king directs the way; my thoughts elate
With hopes of conquest, form designs of fate.
Where high the banks their verdant surface heave,
And the steep sides confine the sleeping wave,
There, near the margin, clad in armour bright,
Sustain the first impetuous shocks of fight:
Then, where the dancing feather joins the crest,
Let each brave frog his obvious mouse arrest;
Each strongly grasping, headlong plunge a foe,
Till countless circles whirl the lake below;
Down sink the mice in yielding waters drown'd;
Loud flash the waters; and the shores resound:
The frogs triumphant tread the conquer'd plain,
And raise their glorious trophies of the slain.

He spake no more: his prudent scheme imparts
Redoubling ardour to the boldest hearts.
Green was the suit his arming heroes chose,
Around their legs the greaves of mallows close;
Green were the beets about their shoulders laid,
And green the colewort, which the target made;
Form'd of the varied shells the waters yield,
Their glossy helmets glisten'd o'er the field;

And tapering sea-reeds for the polish'd spear,
With upright order pierc'd the ambient air.
Thus dress'd for war, they take th' appointed height,
Poise the long arms, and urge the promis'd fight.

But now, where Jove's irradiate spires arise,
With stars surrounded in ethereal skies,
(A Solemn council call'd) the brazen gates
Unbar; the gods assume their golden seats;
The sire superior leans, and points to show
What wond'rous combats mortals wage below:
How strong, how large, the numerous heroes stride;
What length of lance they shake with warlike pride;
What eager fire, their rapid march reveals;
So the fierce Centaurs ravag'd o'er the dales;
And so confirm'd, the daring Titans rose,
Heap'd hills on hills, and bid the gods be foes.

This seen, the power his sacred visage rears,
He casts a pitying smile on worldly cares,
And asks what heavenly guardians take the list,
Or who the mice, or who the frogs assist?

Then thus to Pallas. If my daughter's mind
Have join'd the mice, why stays she still behind?
Drawn forth by savoury steams they wind their way,
And sure attendance round thine altar pay,
Where while the victims gratify their taste,
They sport to please the goddess of the feast.
Thus spake the ruler of the spacious skies;

But thus, resolv'd, the blue-ey'd maid replies.
In vain, my father! all their dangers plead;
To such, thy Pallas never grants her aid.
My flowery wreaths they petulantly spoil,
And rob my crystal lamps of feeding oil,
Ills following ills: but what afflicts me more,
My veil, that idle race profanely tore.
The web was curious, wrought with art divine;
Relentless wretches! all the work was mine;
Along the loom the purple warp I spread,
Cast the light shoot, and cross'd the silver thread.
In this their teeth a thousand breaches tear;
The thousand breaches skilful hands repair;
For which vile earthly duns thy daughter grieve:
The gods, that use no coin, have none to give;
And learning's goddess never less can owe:
Neglected learning gains no wealth below
Nor let the frogs to win my succour sue,
Those clamorous fools have lost my favour too.
For late, when all the conflict ceas'd at night,
When my stretch'd sinews work'd with eager fight;
When spent with glorious toil, I left the field,
And sunk for slumber on my swelling shield;
Lo from the deep, repelling sweet repose,
With noisy croakings half the nation rose:
Devoid of rest, with aching brows I lay,
Till cocks proclaim'd the crimson dawn of day.
Let all, like me, from either host forbear,
Nor tempt the flying furies of the spear;
Let heavenly blood, or what for blood may flow,

Adorn the conquest of a meaner foe.
Some daring mouse may meet the wondrous odds,
Though gods oppose, and brave the wounded gods.
O'er gilded clouds reclin'd, the danger view,
And be the wars of mortals scenes for you.

So mov'd the blue-ey'd queen ; her words persuade,
Great Jove assented, and the rest obey'd.

HOMER'S BATTLE OF THE FROGS AND MICE.

BOOK III.

Now front to front the marching armies shine,
Halt ere they meet, and form the lengthening line:
The chiefs conspicuous seen and heard afar,
Give the loud signal to the rushing war;
Their dreadful trumpets deep-mouth'd hornets sound,
The sounded charge remurmurs o'er the ground;
E'en Jove proclaims a field of horror nigh,
And rolls low thunder through the troubled sky.

First to the fight the large Hypsiboas flew,
And brave Lychenor with a javelin slew.
The luckless warrior fill'd with generous flame,
Stood foremost glittering in the post of fame;
When in his liver struck, the javelin hung;
The mouse fell thundering, and the target rung;
Prone to the ground he sinks his closing eye,
And soil'd in dust his lovely tresses lie.

A spear at Pelion Troglodytes cast,
The missive spear within the bosom past;
Death's sable shades the fainting frog surround,
And life's red tide runs ebbing from the wound.

Embasichytros felt Seutlæus' dart
Transfix and quiver in his panting heart;
But great Artophagus aveng'd the slain,
And big Seutlæus tumbling loads the plain,
And Polyphonus dies, a frog renown'd
For boastful speech and turbulence of sound;
Deep through the belly pierc'd, supine he lay,
And breath'd his soul against the face of day.

The strong Lymnocharis, who view'd with ire
A victor triumph, and a friend expire;
With heaving arms a rocky fragment caught,
And fiercely flung where Troglodytes fought;
A warrior vers'd in arts, of sure retreat,
But arts in vain elude impending fate;
Full on his sinewy neck the fragment fell,
And o'er his eyelids clouds eternal dwell.
Lychenor, second of the glorious name,
Striding advanc'd, and took no wandering aim;
Through all the frog the shining javelin flies,
And near the vanquish'd mouse the victor dies.

The dreadful stroke Crambophagus affrights,
Long bred to banquets, less inur'd to fights;
Heedless he runs, and stumbles o'er the steep,
And wildly floundering flashes up the deep:
Lychenor following with a downward blow,
Reach'd in the lake his unrecover'd foe;
Gasping he rolls, a purple stream of blood
Distains the surface of the silver flood;

Through the wide wound the rushing entrails throng,
And slow the breathless carcass floats along.

Lymnisius good Tyroglyphus assails,
Prince of the mice that haunt the flowery vales,
Lost to the milky fares and rural seat,
He came to perish on the bank of fate.

The dread Pternoglyphus demands the fight,
Which tender Calaminthius shuns by flight,
Drops the green target, springing quits the foe,
Glides through the lake, and safely dives below.
But dire Pternophagus divides his way
Through breaking ranks, and leads the dreadful day.
No nibbling prince excell'd in fierceness more,
His parents fed him on the savage boar;
But where his lance the field with blood imbru'd,
Swift as he mov'd, Hydrocharis pursu'd,
Till fallen in death he lies; a shattering stone
Sounds on the neck, and crushes all the bone;
His blood pollutes the verdure of the plain,
And from his nostrils bursts the gushing brain.

Lychopinax with Borb'rocœtes fights,
A blameless frog whom humbler life delights;
The fatal javelin unrelenting flies,
And darkness seals the gentle croaker's eyes.

Incens'd Prassophagus, with sprightly bound,
Bears Cnissodioctes off the rising ground,

Then drags him o'er the lake depriv'd of breath,
And downward plunging, sinks his soul to death.
But now the great Psycarpax shines afar,
(Scarce he so great whose loss provok'd the war,)
Swift to revenge his fatal javelin fled,
And through the liver struck Pelusius dead;
His freckled corpse before the victor fell,
His soul indignant sought the shades of hell.

This saw Pelobates, and from the flood
Heav'd with both hands a monstrous mass of mud:
The cloud obscene o'er all the hero flies,
Dishonours his brown face, and blots his eyes.
Enrag'd, and wildly spluttering, from the shore
A stone immense of size the warrior bore,
A load for labouring earth, whose bulk to raise,
Asks ten degenerate mice of modern days:
Full on the leg arrives the crushing wound;
The frog supportless writhes upon the ground.

Thus flush'd, the victor wars with matchless force,
Till loud Craugasides arrests his course:
Hoarse-croaking threats precede; with fatal speed
Deep through the belly ran the pointed reed,
Then strongly tugg'd, return'd imbru'd with gore;
And on the pile his reeking entrails bore.

The lame Sitophagus, oppress'd with pain,
Creeps from the desperate dangers of the plain;
And where the ditches rising weeds supply

To spread their lowly shades beneath the sky,
There lurks the silent mouse reliev'd from heat,
And safe embower'd, avoids the chance of fate.

But here Troxartes, Physignathus there,
Whirl the dire furies of the pointed spear:
But where the foot around its ankle plies,
Troxartes wounds, and Physignathus flies,
Halts to the pool a safe retreat to find,
And trails a dangling length of leg behind.
The mouse still urges, still the frog retires,
And half in anguish of the flight expires.

Then pious ardour young Prassæus brings,
Betwixt the fortunes of contending kings:
Lank, harmless frog! with forces hardly grown,
He darts the reed in combats not his own,
Which faintly tinkling on Troxartes' shield,
Hangs at the point, and drops upon the field.

Now nobly towering o'er the rest appears
A gallant prince that far transcends his years,
Pride of his sire, and glory of his house,
And more a Mars in combat than a mouse;
His action bold, robust his ample frame,
And Meridarpax his resounding name.
The warrior singled from the fighting crowd,
Boasts the dire honours of his arms aloud;
Then strutting near the lake, with looks elate,
To all its nations threats approaching fate.

And such his strength, the silver lakes around
Might roll their waters o'er unpeopled ground;
But powerful Jove, who shows no less his grace
To frogs that perish, than to human race,
Felt soft compassion rising in his soul,
And shook his sacred head, that shook the pole.
Then thus to all the gazing powers began
The sire of gods, and frogs, and Mice, and man.

What seas of blood I view! what worlds of slain!
An Iliad rising from a day's campaign!
How fierce his javelin o'er the trembling lakes
The black-furr'd hero Meridarpax shakes!
Unless some favouring deity descend,
Soon will the frogs' loquacious empire end.
Let dreadful Pallas wing'd with pity fly,
And make her ægis blaze before his eye:
While Mars refulgent on his rattling car,
Arrests his raging rival of the war.

He ceas'd, reclining with attentive head,
When thus the glorious god of combats said.
Nor Pallas, Jove! though Pallas take the field,
With all the terrors of her hissing shield,
Nor Mars himself, though Mars in armour bright
Ascend his car, and wheel amidst the fight;
Not these can drive the desperate mouse afar,
Or change the fortunes of the bleeding war.
Let all go forth, all heaven in arms arise;
Or launch thy own red thunder from the skies;

Such ardent bolts as flew that wondrous day,
When heaps of Titans mix'd with mountains lay,
When all the giant race enormous fell,
And huge Enceladus was hurl'd to hell."

'Twas thus th' armipotent advis'd the gods,
When from his throne the cloud-compeller nods;
Deep lengthening thunders run from pole to pole,
Olympus trembles as the thunders roll.
Then swift he whirls the brandish'd bolt around
And headlong darts it at the distant ground;
The bolt discharg'd inwrapp'd with lightning flies,
And rends its flaming passage through the skies:
Then earth's inhabitants, the nibblers, shake,
And frogs, the dwellers in the waters, quake.
Yet still the mice advance their dread design,
And the last danger threats the croaking line,
Till Jove, that inly mourn'd the loss they bore,
With strange assistants fill'd the frighted shore.

Pour'd from the neighb'ring strand, deform'd to [view,
They march, a sudden unexpected crew!
Strong suits of armour round their bodies close,
Which, like thick anvils, blunt the force of blows;
In wheeling marches turn'd, oblique they go!
With harpy claws their limbs divide below;
Fell shears the passage to their mouth command;
From out the flesh their bones by nature stand;
Broad spread their backs, their shining shoulders rise;

Unnumber'd joints distort their lengthen'd thighs;
With nervous cords their hands are firmly brac'd;
Their round black eyeballs in their bosom plac'd;
On eight long feet the wondrous warriors tread;
And either end alike supplies a head.
These, mortal wits to call the crabs agree,
The gods have other names for things than we.

Now where the jointures from their loins depend,
The heroes' tails with severing grasps they rend.
Here, short of feet, depriv'd the power to fly,
There, without hands, upon the field they lie,
Wrench'd from their holds, and scatter'd all around,
The bended lances heap the cumber'd ground.
Helpless amazement, fear pursuing fear,
And mad confusion through their host appear:
O'er the wild waste with headlong flight they go,
Or creep conceal'd in vaulted holes below.

But down Olympus to the western seas
Far-shooting Phœbus drove with fainter rays;
And a whole war (so Jove ordain'd) begun,
Was fought, and ceas'd, in one revolving sun.

TO MR. POPE.

To praise, yet still with due respect to praise,
A bard triumphant in immortal bays,
The learn'd to show, the sensible commend,
Yet still preserve the province of the friend,
What life, what vigour, must the lines require!
What music tune them! what affection fire!

O might thy genius in my bosom shine!
Thou shouldst not fail of numbers worthy thine,
The brightest ancients might at once agree
To sing within my lays, and sing of thee.

Horace himself would own thou dost excel
In candid arts to play the critic well.

Ovid himself might wish to sing the dame
Whom Windsor forest sees a gliding stream;
On silver feet, with annual osier crown'd,
She runs forever through poetic ground.

How flame the glories of Belinda's hair,
Made by thy Muse the envy of the fair.
Less shone the tresses Egypt's princess wore,
Which sweet Callimachus so sung before,
Here courtly trifles set the world at odds,

Belles war with beaux, and whims descend for gods.
The new machines in names of ridicule,
Mock the grave frenzy of the chymic fool:
But know, ye fair, a point conceal'd with art,
The Sylphs and Gnomes are but a woman's heart:
The Graces stand in sight; a Satyr train
Peep o'er their heads, and laugh behind the scene.

In Fame's fair temple, o'er the boldest wits
Inshrin'd on high the sacred Virgil sits,
And sits in measures, such as Virgil's Muse
To place thee near him might be fond to choose.
How might he tune th' alternate reed with thee,
Perhaps a Strephon thou, a Daphnis he,
While some old Damon o'er the vulgar wise,
Thinks he deserves, and thou deserv'st the prize!
Rapt with the thought my fancy seeks the plains,
And turns me shepherd while I hear the strains.
Indulgent nurse of every tender gale,
Parent of flowerets, old Arcadia, hail!
Here in the cool my limbs at ease I spread,
Here let thy poplars whisper o'er my head;
Still slide thy waters soft among the trees,
Thy aspins quiver in a breathing breeze;
Smile all thy valleys in eternal spring,
Be hush'd, ye winds! while Pope and Virgil sing.

In English lays, and all sublimely great,
Thy Homer warms with all his ancient heat;
He shines in council, thunders in the fight,

And flames with every sense of great delight.
Long has that poet reign'd, and long unknown,
Like monarchs sparkling on a distant throne;
In all the majesty of Greek retir'd,
Himself unknown, his mighty name admir'd;
His language failing, wrapp'd him round with night
Thine, rais'd by thee, recalls the work to light.
So wealthy mines, that ages long before
Fed the large realms around with golden ore,
When chok'd by sinking banks, no more appear,
And shepherds only say, the mines were here!
Should some rich youth, if nature warm his heart,
And all his projects stand inform'd with art,
Here clear the caves, there ope the leading vein;
The mines detected flame with gold again.

How vast, how copious are thy new designs!
How every music varies in thy lines!
Still as I read, I feel my bosom beat,
And rise in raptures by another's heat.
Thus in the wood, when summer dress'd the days,
When Windsor lent us tuneful hours of ease,
Our ears the lark, the thrush, the turtle blest,
And Philomela, sweetest o'er the rest:
The shades resound with song—O softly tread!
While a whole season warbles round my head.

This to my friend—and when a friend inspires,
My silent harp its master's hand requires,

Shakes off the dust, and makes these rocks resound,
For fortune plac'd me in unfertile ground;
Far from the joys that with my soul agree,
From wit, from learning,—far, O far from thee!
Here moss-grown trees expand the smallest leaf,
Here half an acre's corn is half a sheaf;
Here hills with naked heads the tempest meet,
Rocks at their side, and torrents at their feet;
Or lazy lakes, unconscious of a flood,
Whose dull brown Naiads ever sleep in mud.

Yet here content can dwell, and learned ease,
A friend delight me, and an author please;
Even here I sing, while Pope supplies the theme,
Show my own love, though not increase his fame.

A TRANSLATION OF PART OF THE FIRST CANTO OF THE RAPE OF THE LOCK.

INTO LEONINE VERSE, AFTER THE MANNER OF THE ANCIENT MONKS.

Et nunc dilectum speculum, pro more retectum,
Emicat in mensâ, quæ splendet pyxide densâ.
Tum primum lymphâ se purgat candida nympha;
Jamque sine mendâ, cœlestis imago videnda,
Nuda caput, bellos retinet, regit, implet, ocellos.
Hâc stupet explorans, seu cultûs numen adorans.
Inferior claram Pythonissa apparet ad aram,
Fertque tibi cautè, dicatque superbia! lautè,

PART OF THE FIRST CANTO OF THE RAPE OF THE LOCK.

And now unveil'd the toilet stands display'd,
Each silver vase in mystic order laid,
First rob'd in white, the nymph intent adores,
With head uncover'd, the cosmetic powers.
A heavenly image in the glass appears,
To that she bends, to that her eyes she rears:
Th' inferior priestess, at her altar's side,
Trembling, begins the sacred rites of pride.

Dona venusta ; oris, quæ cunctis, plena laboris,
Excerpta explorat, dominamque deamque decorat.
Pyxide devotâ, se pandit hic India tota,
Et tota ex istâ transpirat Arabia cistâ.
Testudo hic flectit dum se mea Lesbia pectit ;
Atque elephas lentè te pectit, Lesbia, dente ;
Hunc maculis nôris, nivei jacet ille coloris.
Hic jacet et mundè mundus muliebris abundè ;
Spinula resplendens æris longo ordine pendens,
Pulvis suavis odore, et epistola suavis amore.
Induit arma ergo Veneris pulcherrima virgo,
Pulchrior in præsens tempus de tempore crescens ;
Jam reparat risus, jam surgit gratia visûs,
Jam promit cultu miracula latentia vultu ;

Unnumber'd treasures ope at once, and here
The various offerings of the world appear ;
From each she nicely culls with curious toil,
And decks the goddess with the glittering spoil.
This casket India's glowing gems unlocks,
And all Arabia breathes from yonder box.
The tortoise here and elephant unite,
Transform'd to combs, the speckled and the white.
Here files of pins extend their shining rows,
Puffs, powders, patches, Bibles, billet doux.
Now awful beauty puts on all its arms,
The fair each moment rises in her charms,
Repàirs her smiles, awakens every grace,

Pigmina jam miscet, quo plus sua purpura gliscet,
Et geminans bellis splendet magè fulgor ocellis.
Stant Lemures muti, nymphæ intentique saluti,
Hic figit zonam, capiti locat ille coronam,
Hæc manicis formam, plicis dat et altera normam ;
Et tibi vel Betty, tibi vel nitidissima Letty !
Gloria factorum temerè conceditur horum.

And calls forth all the wonders of her face ;
Sees by degrees a purer blush arise,
And keener lightnings quicken in her eyes.
The busy sylphs surround their darling care ;
These set the head, and those divide the hair,
Some fold the sleeve, while others plait the gown,
And Betty 's prais'd for labours not her own.

HEALTH. AN ECLOGUE.

Now early shepherds o'er the meadow pass,
And print long footsteps in the glittering grass;
The cows neglectful of their pasture stand,
By turns obsequious to the milker's hand.

When Damon softly trod the shaven lawn,
Damon, a youth from city cares withdrawn;
Long was the pleasing walk he wander'd through,
A cover'd arbour clos'd the distant view; [throng
There rests the youth, and, while the feather'd
Raise their wild music, thus contrives a song.

Here, wafted o'er by mild Etesian air,
Thou country goddess, beauteous Health, repair!
Here let my breast through quivering trees inhale
Thy rosy blessings with the morning gale.
What are the fields, or flowers, or all I see?
Ah! tasteless all, if not enjoy'd with thee.

Joy to my soul! I feel the Goddess nigh,
The face of nature cheers as well as I;
O'er the flat green refreshing breezes run,
The smiling daisies blow beneath the sun,
The brooks run purling down with silver waves,
The planted lanes rejoice with dancing leaves,

The chirping birds from all the compass rove
To tempt the tuneful echoes of the grove:
High sunny summits, deeply shaded dales,
Thick mossy banks, and flowery winding vales,
With various prospect gratify the sight,
And scatter fix'd attention in delight.

Come, country Goddess, come! nor thou suffice,
But bring thy mountain-sister, Exercise.
Call'd by thy lively voice, she turns her pace,
Her winding horn proclaims the finish'd chase;
She mounts the rocks, she skims the level plain,
Dogs, hawks, and horses, crowd her early train;
Her hardy face repels the tanning wind,
And lines and meshes loosely float behind.
All these as means of toil the feeble see,
But these are helps to pleasure join'd with thee.

Let Sloth lie softening till high noon in down,
Or lolling fan her in the sultry town,
Unnerv'd with rest; and turn her own disease,
Or foster others in luxurious ease:
I mount the courser, call the deep-mouth'd hounds,
The fox unkennell'd flies to covert grounds;
I lead where stags through tangled thickets tread,
And shake the saplings with their branching head;
I make the falcons wing their airy way,
And soar to seize, or stooping strike their prey;
To snare the fish I fix the luring bait;
To wound the fowl I load the gun with fate.

'Tis thus through change of exercise I range,
And strength and pleasure rise from every change.
  Here, beauteous Health, for all the year remain;
  When the next comes, I'll charm thee thus again.

O come, thou Goddess of my rural song,
And bring thy daughter, calm Content, along!
Dame of the ruddy cheek and laughing eye,
From whose bright presence clouds of sorrow fly:
For her I mow my walks, I plat my bowers,
Clip my low hedges, and support my flowers;
To welcome her, this summer seat I drest,
And here I court her when she comes to rest;
When she from exercise to learned ease
Shall change again, and teach the change to please.

Now friends conversing my soft hours refine,
And Tully's Tusculum revives in mine:
Now to grave books I bid the mind retreat,
And such as make me rather good than great;
Or o'er the works of easy fancy rove,
Where flutes and innocence amuse the grove;
The native bard that on Sicilian plains
First sung the lowly manners of the swains,
Or Maro's Muse, that in the fairest light
Paints rural prospects and the charms of sight:
These soft amusements bring content along,
And fancy, void of sorrow, turns to song.
  Here, beauteous Health, for all the year remain;
  When the next comes, I'll charm thee thus again;

THE FLIES. AN ECLOGUE.

When in the river cows for coolness stand,
And sheep for breezes seek the lofty land,
A youth, whom Æsop taught that every tree,
Each bird and insect, spoke as well as he,
Walk'd calmly musing in a shaded way,
Where flowering hawthorn broke the sunny ray,
And thus instructs his moral pen to draw
A scene that obvious in the field he saw.

Near a low ditch, where shallow waters meet,
Which never learnt to glide with liquid feet,
Whose Naiads never prattle as they play,
But screen'd with hedges slumber out the day,
There stands a slender fern's aspiring shade,
Whose answering branches regularly laid
Put forth their answering.boughs, and proudly rise
Three stories upward, in the nether skies.

For shelter here, to shun the noonday heat,
An airy nation of the flies retreat;
Some in soft air their silken pinions ply,
And some from bough to bough delighted fly,
Some rise, and circling light to perch again;
A pleasing murmur hums along the plain.
So, when a stage invites to pageant shows,
If great and small are like, appear the beaux;

In boxes some with spruce pretension sit,
Some change from seat to seat within the pit,
Some roam the scenes, or turning cease to roam;
Preluding music fills the lofty dome.

When thus a fly (if what a fly can say
Deserves attention) rais'd the rural lay.

Where late Amintor made a nymph a bride,
Joyful I flew by young Favonia's side,
Who, mindless of the feasting, went to sip
The balmy pleasure of the shepherd's lip.
I saw the wanton, where I stoop'd to sup,
And half resolv'd to drown me in the cup;
Till brush'd by careless hands, she soar'd above;
Cease, beauty, cease to vex a tender love.
Thus ends the youth, the buzzing meadow rung,
And thus the rival of his music sung.

When suns by thousands shone in orbs of dew,
I wafted soft with Zephyretta flew;
Saw the clean pail, and sought the milky cheer,
While little Daphne seiz'd my roving dear.
Wretch that I was! I might have warn'd the dame,
Yet sat indulging as the danger came.
But the kind huntress left her free to soar:
Ah! guard, ye lovers, guard a mistress more.

Thus from the fern, whose high-projecting arms,
The fleeting nation bent with dusky swarms,

The swains their love in easy music breathe,
When tongues and tumult stun the field beneath.
Black ants in teams come darkening all the road,
Some call to march, and some to lift the load;
They strain, they labour with incessant pains,
Press'd by the cumbrous weight of single grains.
The flies, struck silent, gaze with wonder down:
The busy burghers reach their earthy town,
Where lay the burthens of a wintry store,
And thence unwearied part in search of more.
Yet one grave sage a moment's space attends,
And the small city's loftiest point ascends,
Wipes the salt dew that trickles down his face,
And thus harangues them with the gravest grace.

Ye foolish nurslings of the summer air,
These gentle tunes and whining songs forbear;
Your trees and whispering breeze, your grove and love,
Your Cupid's quiver, and his mother's dove.
Let bards to business bend their vigorous wing,
And sing but seldom, if they love to sing:
Else, when the flowerets of the season fail,
And this your ferny shade forsakes the vale,
Though one would save ye, not one grain of wheat
Should pay such songsters idling at my gate.

He ceas'd: the flies, incorrigibly vain,
Heard the mayor's speech, and fell to sing again.

AN ELEGY, TO AN OLD BEAUTY.

In vain, poor nymph, to please our youthful sight
You sleep in cream and frontlets all the night,
Your face with patches soil, with paint repair,
Dress with gay gowns, and shade with foreign hair.
If truth, in spite of manners, must be told,
Why really fifty-five is something old.

Once you were young; or one, whose life 's so long
She might have borne my mother, tells me wrong;
And once, since envy 's dead before you die,
The women own, you play'd a sparkling eye,
Taught the light foot a modish little trip,
And pouted with the prettiest purple lip.

To some new charmer are the roses fled,
Which blew, to damask all thy cheek with red;
Youth calls the Graces there to fix their reign,
And airs by thousands fill their easy train.
So parting summer bids her flowery prime
Attend the sun to dress some foreign clime,
While withering seasons in succession, here,
Strip the gay gardens, and deform the year.

But thou, since nature bids, the world resign;
'Tis now thy daughter's daughter's time to shine.

With more address, or such as pleases more,
She runs her female exercises o'er,
Unfurls or closes, raps or turns the fan,
And smiles, or blushes at the creature man.
With quicker life, as gilded coaches pass,
In sideling courtesy she drops the glass.
With better strength, on visit-days, she bears
To mount her fifty flights of ample stairs.
Her mien, her shape, her temper, eyes, and tongue,
Are sure to conquer,—for the rogue is young;
And all that 's madly wild, or oddly gay,
We call it only pretty Fanny's way.

Let time, that makes you homely, make you sage;
The sphere of wisdom is the sphere of age.
'Tis true, when beauty dawns with early fire,
And hears the flattering tongues of soft desire,
If not from virtue, from its gravest ways
The soul with pleasing avocation strays:
But beauty gone, 'tis easier to be wise;
As harpers better, by the loss of eyes.

Henceforth retire, reduce your roving airs,
Haunt less the plays, and more the public prayers,
Reject the Mechlin head, and gold brocade,
Go pray, in sober Norwich crape array'd.
Thy pendant diamonds let thy Fanny take,
(Their trembling lustre shows how much you shake;)

Or bid her wear thy necklace row'd with pearl,
You 'll find your Fanny an obedient girl.
So for the rest, with less incumbrance hung,
You walk through life, unmingled with the young;
And view the shade and substance, as you pass,
With joint endeavour trifling at the glass,
Or Folly drest, and rambling all her days,
To meet her counterpart, and grow by praise:
Yet still sedate yourself, and gravely plain,
You neither fret, nor envy at the vain.

'Twas thus, if man with woman we compare,
The wise Athenian cross'd a glittering fair.
Unmov'd by tongues and sights, he walk'd the place,
Through tape, toys, tinsel, gimp, perfume, and lace;
Then bends from Mars's hill his awful eyes,
And—'What a world I never want!' he cries;
But cries unheard; for Folly will be free.
So parts the buzzing gaudy crowd, and he:
As careless he for them, as they for him;
He wrapt in wisdom, and they whirl'd by whim.

THE BOOK-WORM.

Come hither, boy, we 'll hunt to-day
The book-worm, ravening beast of prey,
Produc'd by parent Earth, at odds,
As fame reports it, with the gods.
Him frantic hunger wildly drives
Against a thousand authors' lives :
Through all the fields of wit he flies ;
Dreadful his head with clustering eyes,
With horns without, and tusks within,
And scales to serve him for a skin.
Observe him nearly, lest he climb
To wound the bards of ancient time,
Or down the vale of fancy go
To tear some modern wretch below.
On every corner fix thine eye,
Or ten to one he slips thee by.

See where his teeth a passage eat :
We 'll rouse him from the deep retreat.
But who the shelter 's forc'd to give ?
'Tis sacred Virgil, as I live !
From leaf to leaf, from song to song,
He draws the tadpole form along,
He mounts the gilded edge before,
He 's up, he scuds the cover o'er,

He turns, he doubles, there he past,
And here we have him, caught at last.

Insatiate brute, whose teeth abuse
The sweetest servants of the Muse—
Nay, never offer to deny,
I took thee in the fact to fly.
His roses nipt in every page,
My poor Anacreon mourns thy rage;
By thee my Ovid wounded lies;
By thee my Lesbia's Sparrow dies;
Thy rabid teeth have half destroy'd
The work of love in Biddy Floyd;
They rent Belinda's locks away,
And spoil'd the Blouzelind of Gay.
For all, for every single deed,
Relentless justice bids thee bleed:
Then fall a victim to the Nine,
Myself the priest, my desk the shrine.

Bring Homer, Virgil, Tasso near,
To pile a sacred altar here:
Hold, boy, thy hand outruns thy wit,
You reach'd the plays that Dennis writ;
You reach'd me Philips' rustic strain;
Pray take your mortal bards again.

Come, bind the victim,—there he lies,
And here between his numerous eyes

This venerable dust I lay,
From manuscripts just swept away.

The goblet in my hand I take,
For the libation 's yet to make:
A health to poets! all their days,
May they have bread, as well as praise;
Sense may they seek, and less engage
In papers fill'd with party rage.
But if their riches spoil their vein,
Ye Muses, make them poor again.

Now bring the weapon, yonder blade,
With which my tuneful pens are made.
I strike the scales that arm thee round,
And twice and thrice I print the wound;
The sacred altar floats with red,
And now he dies, and now he 's dead.

How like the son of Jove I stand,
This Hydra stretch'd beneath the hand!
Lay bare the monster's entrails here,
To see what dangers threat the year:
Ye gods! what sonnet on a wench!
What lean translations out of French!
'Tis plain, this lobe is so unsound,
S—— prints, before the months go round.

But hold, before I close the scene,
The sacred altar should be clean.

O had I Shadwell's second bays,
Or, Tate, thy pert and humble lays!
(Ye pair, forgive me, when I vow
I never miss'd your works till now,)
I'd tear the leaves to wipe the shrine,
That only way you please the Nine:
But since I chance to want these two,
I'll make the songs of Durfey do.

Rent from the corps, on yonder pin,
I hang the scales that brac'd it in;
I hang my studious morning gown,
And write my own inscription down.

'This trophy from the Python won,
This robe, in which the deed was done,
These, Parnell, glorying in the feat,
Hung on these shelves, the Muses' seat.
Here Ignorance and Hunger found
Large realms of wit to ravage round;
Here Ignorance and Hunger fell;
Two foes in one I sent to hell.
Ye poets who my labours see,
Come share the triumph all with me!
Ye critics, born to vex the Muse,
Go mourn the grand ally you lose!'

AN ALLEGORY ON MAN.

A THOUGHTFUL being, long and spare,
Our race of mortals call him Care,
(Were Homer living, well he knew
What name the gods have call'd him too,)
With fine mechanic genius wrought,
And lov'd to work, though no one bought.

This being, by a model bred
In Jove's eternal sable head,
Contriv'd a shape impower'd to breathe,
And be the worldling here beneath.

The man rose staring, like a stake;
Wondering to see himself awake!
Then look'd so wise, before he knew
The business he was made to do;
That, pleas'd to see with what a grace
He gravely show'd his forward face,
Jove talk'd of breeding him on high,
An under-something of the sky.

But ere he gave the mighty nod,
Which ever binds a poet's god:
(For which his curls ambrosial shake,
And mother Earth 's oblig'd to quake,)

He saw old mother Earth arise,
She stood confess'd before his eyes;
But not with what we read she wore,
A castle for a crown before,
Nor with long streets and longer roads
Dangling behind her, like commodes;
As yet with wreaths älone she drest,
And trail'd a landskip-painted vest.
Then thrice she rais'd, as Ovid said,
And thrice she bow'd her weighty head.

Her honours made, great Jove, she cried,
This thing was fashion'd from my side;
His hands, his heart, his head, are mine;
Then what hast thou to call him thine?

Nay rather ask, the monarch said,
What boots his hand, his heart, his head,
Were what I gave remov'd away?
Thy part 's an idle shape of clay.

Halves, more than halves, cried honest Care
Your pleas would make your titles fair,
You claim the body, you the soul,
But I who join'd them, claim the whole.

Thus with the gods debate began,
On such a trivial cause, as man.
And can celestial tempers rage?
Quoth Virgil in a later age.

As thus they wrangled, Time came by;
(There 's none that paint him such as I,
For what the fabling ancients sung
Makes Saturn old, when Time was young.)
As yet his winters had not shed
Their silver honours on his head;
He just had got his pinions free
From his old sire Eternity.
A serpent girdled round he wore,
The tail within the mouth, before;
By which our almanacks are clear
That learned Egypt meant the year.
A staff he carried, where on high
A glass was fix'd to measure by,
As amber boxes made a show
For heads of canes an age ago.
His vest, for day, and night, was py'd;
A bending sickle arm'd his side;
And spring's new months his train adorn;
The other seasons were unborn.

Known by the gods, as near he draws,
They make him umpire of the cause.
O'er a low trunk his arm he laid,
Where since his hours a dial made;
Then leaning heard the nice debate,
And thus pronounc'd the words of fate.

Since body from the parent Earth,
And soul from Jove receiv'd a birth,

Return they where they first began;
But since their union makes the man,
Till Jove and Earth shall part these two,
To Care, who join'd them, man is due.

He said, and sprung with swift career
To trace a circle for the year;
Where ever since the seasons wheel,
And tread on one another's heel.

'Tis well, said Jove; and for consent
Thundering he shook the firmament:
Our umpire Time shall have his way,
With Care I let the creature stay.
Let business vex him, avarice blind,
Let doubt and knowledge rack his mind,
Let error act, opinion speak,
And want afflict, and sickness break,
And anger burn, dejection chill,
And joy distract, and sorrow kill;
Till, arm'd by Care, and taught to mow,
Time draws the long destructive blow;
And wasted man, whose quick decay
Comes hurrying on before his day,
Shall only find by this decree,
The soul flies sooner back to me.

AN IMITATION OF SOME FRENCH VERSES.

Relentless Time! destroying power,
  Whom stone and brass obey,
Who giv'st to every flying hour
  To work some new decay;
Unheard, unheeded, and unseen,
  Thy secret saps prevail,
And ruin man, a nice machine,
  By nature form'd to fail.
My change arrives; the change I meet,
  Before I thought it nigh:
My spring, my years of pleasure fleet,
  And all their beauties die.
In age I search, and only find
  A poor unfruitful gain,
Grave Wisdom stalking slow behind,
  Oppress'd with loads of pain.
My ignorance could once beguile,
  And fancied joys inspire;
My errors cherish'd Hope to smile
  On newly-born Desire.
But now experience shews the bliss
  For which I fondly sought,
Not worth the long impatient wish,
  And ardour of the thought.
My youth met Fortune fair array'd,
  (In all her pomp she shone,)

And might, perhaps, have well essay'd
  To make her gifts my own:
But when I saw the blessings shower
  On some unworthy mind,
I left the chase, and own'd the power
  Was justly painted blind,
I pass'd the glories which adorn
  The splendid courts of kings,
And while the persons mov'd my scorn,
  I rose to scorn the things.
My manhood felt a vigorous fire,
  By love increas'd the more;
But years with coming years conspire
  To break the chains I wore.
In weakness safe, the sex I see
  With idle lustre shine;
For what are all their joys to me,
  Which cannot now be mine?
But hold—I feel my gout decrease,
  My troubles laid to rest,
And truths, which would disturb my peace,
  Are painful truths at best.
Vainly the time I have to roll
  In sad reflection flies;
Ye fondling passions of my soul!
  Ye sweet deceits! arise.
I wisely change the scene within,
  To things that us'd to please;
In pain, philosophy is spleen,
  In health, 'tis only ease.

A NIGHT-PIECE ON DEATH.

By the blue taper's trembling light,
No more I waste the wakeful night,
Intent with endless view to pore
The schoolmen and the sages o'er;
Their books from wisdom widely stray,
Or point at best the longest way.
I'll seek a readier path, and go
Where wisdom 's surely taught below.

How deep yon azure dyes the sky,
Where orbs of gold unnumber'd lie,
While through their ranks in silver pride
The nether crescent seems to glide!
The slumbering breeze forgets to breathe,
The lake is smooth and clear beneath,
Where once again the spangled show
Descends to meet our eyes below.
The grounds which on the right aspire,
In dimness from the view retire:
The left presents a place of graves,
Whose wall the silent water laves.
That steeple guides thy doubtful sight
Among the livid gleams of night.
There pass, with melancholy state.
By all the solemn heaps of fate,

And think, as softly-sad you tread
Above the venerable dead,
'Time was, like thee they life possest,
And time shall be, that thou shalt rest.'

Those graves, with bending osier bound,
That nameless heave the crumbled ground,
Quick to the glancing thought disclose,
Where toil and poverty repose.

The flat smooth stones that bear a name,
The chisel's slender help to fame,
(Which ere our set of friends decay
Their frequent steps may wear away,)
A middle race of mortals own,
Men, half ambitious, all unknown.

The marble tombs that rise on high,
Whose dead in vaulted arches lie,
Whose pillars swell with sculptur'd stones,
Arms, angels, epitaphs, and bones.
These, all the poor remains of state,
Adorn the rich, or praise the great;
Who while on earth in fame they live,
Are senseless of the fame they give.

Hah! while I gaze, pale Cynthia fades,
The bursting earth unveils the shades!
All slow, and wan, and wrapp'd with shrouds,
They rise in visionary crowds,

And all with sober accent cry,
'Think, mortal, what it is to die.

Now from yon black and funeral yew,
That bathes the charnel-house with dew,
Methinks I hear a voice begin;
(Ye ravens, cease your croaking din,
Ye tolling clocks, no time resound
O'er the long lake and midnight ground!
It sends a peal of hollow groans,
Thus speaking from among the bones.

'When men my scythe and darts supply,
How great a king of fears am I!
They view me like the last of things:
They make, and then they dread, my stings.
Fools! if you less provok'd your fears,
No more my spectre form appears.
Death 's but a path that must be trod,
If man would ever pass to God;
A port of calms, a state of ease
From the rough rage of swelling seas.

Why then thy flowing sable stoles,
Deep pendant cypress, mourning poles,
Loose scarfs to fall athwart thy weeds,
Long palls, drawn hearses, cover'd steeds,
And plumes of black, that, as they tread,
Nod o'er the scutcheons of the dead?
'Nor can the parted body know,
Nor wants the soul, these forms of woe.

As men who long in prison dwell,
With lamps that glimmer round the cell,
Whene'er their suffering years are run,
Spring forth to greet the glittering sun:
Such joy, though far transcending sense,
Have pious souls at parting hence.
On earth, and in the body plac'd,
A few, and evil years they waste;
But when their chains are cast aside,
See the glad scene unfolding wide,
Clap the glad wing, and tower away
And mingle with the blaze of day.

A HYMN TO CONTENTMENT.

Lovely, lasting peace of mind!
Sweet delight of human-kind!
Heavenly-born and bred on high,
To crown the favourites of the sky
With more of happiness below,
Than victors in a triumph know!
Whither, O whither art thou fled,
To lay thy meek, contented head;
What happy region dost thou please
To make the seat of calms and ease!

Ambition searches all its sphere
Of pomp and state, to meet thee there.
Encreasing Avarice would find
Thy presence in its gold enshrin'd.
The bold adventurer ploughs his way
Through rocks amidst the foaming sea,
To gain thy love; and then perceives
Thou wert not in the rocks and waves.
The silent heart, which grief assails,
Treads soft and lonesome o'er the vales,
Sees daisies open, rivers run,
And seeks, as I have vainly done,
Amusing thought; but learns to know

That solitude 's the nurse of woe,
No real happiness is found
In trailing purple o'er the ground;
Or in a soul exalted high,
To range the circuit of the sky,
Converse with stars above, and know
All nature in its forms below;
The rest it seeks, in seeking dies,
And doubts at last, for knowledge, rise.

Lovely, lasting peace, appear!
This world itself, if thou art here,
Is once again with Eden blest,
And man contains it in his breast.

'Twas thus, as under shade I stood,
I sung my wishes to the wood,
And lost in thought, no more perceiv'd
The branches whisper as they wav'd:
It seem'd, as all the quiet place
Confess'd the presence of the Grace.
When thus she spoke—" Go rule thy will,
Bid thy wild passions all be still,
Know God—and bring thy heart to know
The joys which from religion flow:
Then every Grace shall prove its guest,
And I 'll be there to crown the rest.

Oh! by yonder mossy seat,
In my hours of sweet retreat,

Might I thus my soul employ,
With sense of gratitude and joy!
Rais'd as ancient prophets were,
In heavenly vision, praise, and prayer;
Pleasing all men, hurting none,
Pleas'd and bless'd with God alone:
Then while the gardens take my sight,
With all the colours of delight;
While silver waters glide along,
To please my ear, and court my song;
I'll lift my voice, and tune my string,
And thee, great source of nature, sing.

The sun that walks his airy way,
To light the world, and give the day;
The moon that shines with borrow'd light;
The stars that gild the gloomy night;
The seas that roll unnumber'd waves;
The wood that spreads its shady leaves;
The field whose ears conceal the grain,
The yellow treasure of the plain;
All of these, and all I see,
Should be sung, and sung by me:
They speak their maker as they can,
But want and ask the tongue of man.

Go search among your idle dreams,
Your busy or your vain extremes;
And find a life of equal bliss,
Or own the next begun in this.

THE HERMIT.

FAR in a wild, unknown to public view,
From youth to age a reverend hermit grew;
The moss his bed, the cave his humble cell,
His food the fruits, his drink the crystal well:
Remote from man, with God he pass'd the days,
Prayer all his business, all his pleasure praise.

A life so sacred, such serene repose,
Seem'd heaven itself, till one suggestion rose;
That vice should triumph, virtue vice obey,
This sprung some doubt of Providence's sway:
His hopes no more a certain prospect boast,
And all the tenour of his soul is lost.
So when a smooth expanse receives imprest
Calm nature's image on its watery breast,
Down bend the banks, the trees depending grow,
And skies beneath with answering colours glow:
But if a stone the gentle scene divide,
Swift ruffling circles curl on every side,
And glimmering fragments of a broken sun,
Banks, trees, and skies, in thick disorder run.

To clear this doubt, to know the world by sight,
To find if books, or swains, report it right,
(For yet by swains alone the world he knew,
Whose feet came wandering o'er the nightly dew,)

He quits his cell; the pilgrim-staff he bore,
And fix'd the scallop in his hat before;
Then with the sun a rising journey went,
Sedate to think, and watching each event.

The morn was wasted in the pathless grass,
And long and lonesome was the wild to pass;
But when the southern sun had warm'd the day,
A youth came posting o'er a crossing way;
His raiment decent, his complexion fair,
And soft in graceful ringlets wav'd his hair.
Then near approaching, "Father, hail!" he cried;
"And hail, my son," the reverend sire replied;
Words follow'd words, from question answer flow'd,
And talk of various kind deceiv'd the road;
Till each with other pleas'd, and loth to part,
While in their age they differ, join in heart:
Thus stands an aged elm in ivy bound,
Thus youthful ivy clasps an elm around.

Now sunk the sun; the closing hour of day
Came onward, mantled o'er with sober gray;
Nature in silence bid the world repose;
When near the road a stately palace rose:
There by the moon through ranks of trees they pass,
Whose verdure crown'd their sloping sides of grass.
It chanc'd the noble master of the dome
Still made his house the wandering stranger's home:
Yet still the kindness, from a thirst of praise,
Prov'd the vain flourish of expensive ease.

The pair arrive: the liveried servants wait;
Their lord receives them at the pompous gate.
The table groans with costly piles of food,
And all is more than hospitably good.
Then led to rest, the day's long toil they drown,
Deep sunk in sleep, and silk, and heaps of down.

At length 'tis morn, and at the dawn of day,
Along the wide canals the zephyrs play;
Fresh o'er the gay parterres the breezes creep,
And shake the neighbouring wood to banish
sleep.
Up rise the guests, obedient to the call:
An early banquet deck'd the splendid hall;
Rich luscious wine a golden goblet grac'd,
Which the kind master forc'd the guests to taste.
Then, pleas'd and thankful, from the porch they go;
And, but the landlord, none had cause of woe;
His cup was vanish'd; for in secret guise
The younger guest purloin'd the glittering prize.

As one who spies a serpent in his way,
Glistening and basking in the summer ray,
Disorder'd stops to shun the danger near,
Then walks with faintness on, and looks with fear;
So seem'd the sire; when far upon the road,
The shining spoil his wily partner show'd.
He stopp'd with silence, walk'd with trembling
heart,
And much he wish'd, but durst not ask to part:

Murmuring he lifts his eyes, and thinks it hard,
That generous actions meet a base reward.

While thus they pass, the sun his glory shrouds,
The changing skies hang out their sable clouds ;
A sound in air presag'd approaching rain,
And beasts to covert scud across the plain.
Warn'd by the signs, the wandering pair retreat,
To seek for shelter at a neighbouring seat.
'Twas built with turrets, on a rising ground,
And strong, and large, and unimprov'd around ;
Its owner's temper, timorous and severe,
Unkind and griping, caus'd a desert there.

As near the miser's heavy doors they drew,
Fierce rising gusts with sudden fury blew ;
The nimble lightning mix'd with showers began,
And o'er their heads loud rolling thunder ran.
Here long they knock, but knock or call in vain,
Driven by the wind, and batter'd by the rain.
At length some pity warm'd the master's breast,
('Twas then, his threshold first receiv'd a guest,)
Slow creaking turns the door with jealous care,
And half he welcomes in the shivering pair ;
One frugal fagot lights the naked walls,
And nature's fervour through their limbs recalls:
Bread of the coarsest sort, with eager wine,
Each hardly granted, serv'd them both to dine ;
And when the tempest first appear'd to cease,
A ready warning bid them part in peace.

With still remark the pondering hermit view'd
In one so rich, a life so poor and rude;
And why should such, within himself he cried,
Lock the lost wealth a thousand want beside?
But what new marks of wonder soon took place
In every settling feature of his face,
When from his vest the young companion bore
That cup, the generous landlord own'd before,
And paid profusely with the precious bowl
The stinted kindness of this churlish soul!

But now the clouds in airy tumult fly;
The sun emerging opes an azure sky;
A fresher green the smelling leaves display,
And, glittering as they tremble, cheer the day:
The weather courts them from the poor retreat,
And the glad master bolts the wary gate.
[wrought
While hence they walk, the pilgrim's bosom
With all the travel of uncertain thought;
His partner's acts without their cause appear,
'Twas there a vice, and seem'd a madness here:
Detesting that, and pitying this, he goes,
Lost and confounded with the various shows.

Now night's dim shades again involve the sky,
Again the wanderers want a place to lie,
Again they search, and find a lodging nigh:
The soil improv'd around, the mansion neat,
And neither poorly low, nor idly great:

It seem'd to speak its master's turn of mind,
Content, and not for praise, but virtue kind.

Hither the walkers turn with weary feet,
Then bless the mansion, and the master greet:
Their greeting fair bestow'd, with modest guise,
The courteous master hears, and thus replies:

"Without a vain, without a grudging heart,
To him who gives us all, I yield a part;
From him you come, for him accept it here,
A frank and sober, more than costly cheer."
He spoke, and bid the welcome table spread,
Then talk'd of virtue till the time of bed,
When the grave household round his hall repair,
Warn'd by a bell, and close the hours with prayer.

At length the world, renew'd by calm repose,
Was strong for toil, the dappled morn arose.
Before the pilgrims part, the younger crept
Near the clos'd cradle where an infant slept,
And writh'd his neck; the landlord's little pride,
O strange return! grew black, and gasp'd, and died.
Horror of horrors! what! his only son!
How look'd our hermit when the fact was done?
Not hell, though hell's black jaws in sunder part,
And breathe blue fire, could more assault his heart.

Confus'd, and struck with silence at the deed,
He flies, but, trembling, fails to fly with speed.

His steps the youth pursues; the country lay
Perplex'd with roads, a servant show'd the way;
A river cross'd the path; the passage o'er
Was nice to find; the servant trod before:
Long arms of oaks an open bridge supplied,
And deep the waves beneath the bending glide.
The youth, who seem'd to watch a time to sin,
Approach'd the careless guide, and thrust him in:
Plunging he falls, and rising lifts his head,
Then flashing turns, and sinks among the dead.

Wild, sparkling rage inflames the father's eyes.
He bursts the bands of fear, and madly cries,
"Detested wretch!"—but scarce his speech began,
When the strange partner seem'd no longer man:
His youthful face grew more serenely sweet;
His robe turn'd white, and flow'd upon his feet:
Fair rounds of radiant points invest his hair;
Celestial odours breathe through purpled air;
And wings, whose colours glitter'd on the day,
Wide at his back their gradual plumes display,
The form ethereal bursts upon his sight,
And moves in all the majesty of light.

Though loud at first the pilgrim's passion grew,
Sudden he gaz'd, and wist not what to do:
Surprise in secret chains his words suspends,
And in a calm his settling temper ends.
But silence here the beauteous angel broke,
The voice of music ravish'd as he spoke.

"Thy prayer, thy praise, thy life to vice unknown,
In sweet memorial rise before the throne:
These charms, success in our bright region find,
And force an angel down, to calm thy mind;
For this, commission'd, I forsook the sky,
Nay, cease to kneel—thy fellow-servant I.

"Then know the truth of government divine,
And let these scruples be no longer thine.

"The Maker justly claims that world he made
In this the right of Providence is laid;
Its sacred majesty through all depends
On using second means to work his ends:
'Tis thus, withdrawn in state from human eye,
The power exerts his attributes on high,
Your actions uses, nor controls your will,
And bids the doubting sons of men be still.

"What strange events can strike with more surprise
Than those which lately struck thy wondering eyes?
Yet taught by these, confess th' Almighty just,
And where you can't unriddle, learn to trust!

"The great, vain man, who far'd on costly food,
Whose life was too luxurious to be good;
Who made his ivory stands with goblets shine,
And forc'd his guests to morning draughts of wine,
Has, with the cup, the graceless custom lost,
And still he welcomes, but with less of cost.

"The mean, suspicious wretch, whose bolted door
Ne'er mov'd in duty to the wandering poor;
With him I left the cup, to teach his mind
That heaven can bless, if mortals will be kind.
Conscious of wanting worth, he views the bowl,
And feels compassion touch his grateful soul.
Thus artists melt the sullen ore of lead,
With heaping coals of fire upon its head;
In the kind warmth the metal learns to glow,
And loose from dross, the silver runs below.

"Long had our pious friend in virtue trod,
But now the child half-wean'd his heart from God;
Child of his age, for him he liv'd in pain,
And measur'd back his steps to earth again.
To what excesses had this dotage run!
But God, to save the father, took the son.
To all but thee, in fits he seem'd to go,
And 'twas my ministry to deal the blow.
The poor fond parent, humbled in the dust,
Now owns in tears the punishment was just.

"But how had all his fortune felt a wrack,
Had that false servant sped in safety back!
This night his treasur'd heaps he meant to steal,
And what a fund of charity would fail!

"Thus Heaven instructs thy mind: this trial o'er,
Depart in peace, resign, and sin no more"

On sounding pinions here the youth withdrew,
The sage stood wondering as the seraph flew.
Thus look'd Elisha, when, to mount on high,
His master took the chariot of the sky;
The fiery pomp ascending left the view;
The prophet gaz'd, and wish'd to follow too.

The bending hermit here a prayer begun,
"Lord! as in heaven, on earth thy will be done!"
Then gladly turning, sought his ancient place,
And pass'd a life of piety and peace.

PIETY: OR THE VISION.

'Twas when the night in silent sable fled,
When cheerful morning sprung with rising red,
When dreams and vapours leave to crowd the brain,
And best the vision draws its heavenly scene;
'Twas then, as slumbering on my couch I lay,
A sudden splendour seem'd to kindle day,
A breeze came breathing in a sweet perfume,
Blown from eternal gardens, fill'd the room;
And in a void of blue, that clouds invest,
Appear'd a daughter of the realms of rest;
Her head a ring of golden glory wore,
Her honour'd hand the sacred volume bore,
Her raiment glittering seem'd a silver white,
And all her sweet companions sons of light.

Straight as I gaz'd, my fear and wonder grew,
Fear barr'd my voice, and wonder fix'd my view;
When lo! a cherub of the shining crowd
That sail'd as guardian in her azure cloud,
Fann'd the soft air, and downwards seem'd to glide,
And to my lips a living coal applied.
Then while the warmth o'er all my pulses ran
Diffusing comfort, thus the maid began:

"Where glorious mansions are prepar'd above,
The seats of music, and the seats of love,

Thence I descend, and Piety my name,
To warm thy bosom with celestial flame,
To teach thee praises mix'd with humble prayers,
And tune thy soul to sing seraphic airs.
Be thou my bard." A vial here she caught,
(An angel's hand the crystal vial brought,)
And as with awful sound the word was said,
She pour'd a sacred unction on my head;
Then thus proceeded: "Be thy Muse thy zeal,
Dare to be good, and all my joys reveal.
While other pencils flattering forms create,
And paint the gaudy plumes that deck the great;
While other pens exalt the vain delight,
Whose wasteful revel wakes the depth of night;
Or others softly sing in idle lines
How Damon courts, or Amaryllis shines;
More wisely thou select a theme divine,
Fame is their recompense, 'tis heaven is thine.
Despise the raptures of discorded fire,
Where wine, or passion, or applause inspire
Low restless life, and ravings born of earth,
Whose meaner subjects speak their humble birth,
Like working seas, that, when loud winters blow,
Not made for rising, only rage below.
Mine is a warm and yet a lambent heat,
More lasting still, as more intensely great,
Produc'd where prayer, and praise, and pleasure breathe,
And ever mounting whence it shot beneath.
Unpaint the love, that, hovering over beds,

From glittering pinions guilty pleasure sheds;
Restore the colour to the golden mines
With which behind the feather'd idol shines;
To flowering greens give back their native care,
The rose and lily, never his to wear;
To sweet Arabia send the balmy breath;
Strip the fair flesh, and call the phantom Death;
His bow be sabled o'er, his shafts the same,
And fork and point them with eternal flame.

"But urge thy powers, thine utmost voice ad-
vance,
Make the loud strings against thy fingers dance;
'Tis love that angels praise and men adore,
'Tis love divine that asks it all and more.
Fling back the gates of ever-blazing day,
Pour floods of liquid light to gild the way;
And all in glory wrapt, through paths untrod,
Pursue the great unseen descent of God;
Hail the meek virgin, bid the child appear,
The child is God, and call him Jesus here.
He comes, but where to rest? A manger's nigh,
Make the great Being in a manger lie;
Fill the wide sky with angels on the wing,
Make thousands gaze, and make ten thousand
sing;
Let men afflict him, men he came to save,
And still afflict him till he reach the grave;
Make him resign'd, his loads of sorrow meet,
And me, like Mary, weep beneath his feet;

I 'll bathe my tresses there, my prayers rehearse,
And glide in flames of love along thy verse.

"Ah! while I speak, I feel my bosom swell,
My raptures smother what I long to tell.
'Tis God! a present God! through cleaving air
I see the throne, and see the Jesus there
Plac'd on the right. He shows the wounds he bore,
(My fervours oft have won him thus before);
How pleas'd he looks! my words have reach'd his
ear;
He bids the gates unbar; and calls me near."
[tread
She ceas'd. The cloud on which she seem'd to
Its curls unfolded, and around her spread;
Bright angels waft their wings to raise the cloud,
And sweep their ivory lutes, and sing aloud;
The scene moves off, while all its ambient sky
Is turn'd to wondrous music as they fly;
And soft the swelling sounds of music grow,
And faint their softness, till they fail below.

My downy sleep the warmth of Phœbus broke,
And while my thoughts were settling, thus I spoke.
"Thou beauteous vision! on the soul impress'd,
When most my reason would appear to rest,
'Twas sure with pencils dipt in various lights
Some curious angel limn'd thy sacred sights;
From blazing suns his radiant gold he drew,
While moons the silver gave, and air the blue.

I 'll mount the roving wind's expanded wing,
And seek the sacred hill, and light to sing;
('Tis known in Jewry well) I 'll make my lays,
Obedient to thy summons, sound with praise."

But still I fear, unwarm'd with holy flame,
I take for truth the flatteries of a dream;
And barely wish the wondrous gift I boast,
And faintly practise what deserves it most.

Indulgent Lord! whose gracious love displays
Joy in the light, and fills the dark with ease!
Be this, to bless my days, no dream of bliss;
Or be, to bless the nights, my dreams like this.

BACCHUS: OR, THE DRUNKEN METAMORPHOSIS.

As Bacchus, ranging at his leisure,
(Jolly Bacchus, king of pleasure!)
Charm'd the wide world with drink and dances
And all his thousand airy fancies,
Alas! he quite forgot the while
His favourite vines in Lesbos isle.

The god, returning ere they died,
"Ah! see my jolly Fauns," he cried,
"The leaves but hardly born are red,
And the bare arms for pity spread:
The beasts afford a rich manure;
Fly, my boys, to bring the cure;
Up the mountains, o'er the vales,
Through the woods, and down the dales;
For this, if full the clusters grow,
Your bowls shall doubly overflow."

So cheer'd, with more officious haste
They bring the dung of every beast;
The loads they wheel, the roots they bare,
They lay the rich manure with care;
While oft he calls to labour hard,
And names as oft the red reward.

The plants refresh'd, new leaves appear,
The thickening clusters load the year;
The season swiftly purple grew,
The grapes hung dangling deep with blue.

A vineyard ripe, a day serene
Now calls them all to work again.
The Fauns through every furrow shoot
To load their flaskets with the fruit;
And now the vintage early trod,
The wines invite the jovial god.

Strow the roses, raise the song,
See the master comes along;
Lusty Revel join'd with laughter,
Whim and Frolic follow after:
The Fauns aside the vats remain,
To show the work, and reap the gain.
All around, and all around,
They sit to riot on the ground;
A vessel stands amidst the ring,
And here they laugh, and there they sing
Or rise a jolly jolly band,
And dance about it hand in hand;
Dance about, and shout amain,
Then sit to laugh and sing again.
Thus they drink, and thus they play
The sun and all their wits away.

But, as an ancient author sung,
The vine manur'd with every dung,

From every creature strangely drew
A twang of brutal nature too;
'Twas hence in drinking on the lawns
New turns of humour seiz'd the Fauns.

Here one was crying out, "By Jove!"
Another, "Fight me in the grove;"
This wounds a friend, and that the trees;
The lion's temper reign'd in these.

Another grins, and leaps about,
And keeps a merry world of rout,
And talks impertinently free,
And twenty talk the same as he;
Chattering, idle, airy, kind;
These take the monkey's turn of mind.

Here one, that saw the Nymphs which stood
To peep upon them from the wood,
Skulks off to try if any maid
Be lagging late beneath the shade;
While loose discourse another raises
In naked nature's plainest phrases,
And every glass he drinks enjoys,
With change of nonsense, lust, and noise;
Mad and careless, hot and vain;
Such as these the goat retain.

Another drinks and casts it up,
And drinks, and wants another cup;

Solemn, silent, and sedate,
Ever long, and ever late,
Full of meats, and full of wine;
This takes his temper from the swine.

Here some who hardly seem to breathe,
Drink, and hang the jaw beneath.
Gaping, tender, apt to weep;
Their nature 's alter'd by the sheep.

'Twas thus one autumn all the crew,
(If what the poets say be true)
While Bacchus made the merry feast,
Inclin'd to one or other beast;
And since, 'tis said, for many a mile
He spread the vines of Lesbos isle.

DR. DONNE'S THIRD SATIRE VERSIFIED.

Compassion checks my spleen, yet scorn denies
The tears a passage through my swelling eyes:
To laugh or weep at sins, might idly show
Unheedful passion, or unfruitful woe.
Satire! arise, and try thy sharper ways,
If ever satire cur'd an old disease.
Is not religion (Heaven-descended dame)
As worthy all our soul's devoutest flame,
As moral Virtue in her early sway,
When the best Heathens saw by doubtful day?
Are not the joys, the promis'd joys above,
As great and strong to vanquish earthly love,
As earthly glory, fame, respect, and show,
As all rewards their virtue found below?
Alas! Religion proper means prepares,
These means are ours, and must its end be theirs?
And shall thy father's spirit meet the sight
Of heathen sages cloth'd in heavenly light,
Whose merit of strict life, severely suited
To reason's dictates, may be faith imputed,
Whilst thou, to whom he taught the nearer road,
Art ever banish'd from the blest abode?

Oh! if thy temper such a fear can find,
This fear were valour of the noblest kind.

Dar'st thou provoke, when rebel souls aspire,
Thy Maker's vengeance, and thy monarch's ire;
Or live entomb'd in ships, thy leader's prey,
Spoil of the war, the famine, or the sea;
In search of pearl, in depth of ocean breathe,
Or live, exil'd the sun, in mines beneath,
Or, where in tempests icy mountains roll,
Attempt a passage by the northern pole?
Or dar'st thou parch within the fires of Spain,
Or burn beneath the line, for Indian gain?
Or for some idol of thy fancy draw
Some loose-gown'd dame? O courage made of
straw!
Thus, desperate coward, wouldst thou bold appear,
Yet when thy God has plac'd thee sentry here,
To thy own foes, to his, ignoble yield,
And leave, for wars forbid, th' appointed field?

Know thy own foes; th' apostate angel; he
You strive to please, the foremost of the three;
He makes the pleasures of his realm the bait,
But can he give for love that acts in hate?
The world's thy second love, thy second foe,
The world, whose beauties perish as they blow,
They fly, she fades herself, and at the best,
You grasp a wither'd strumpet to your breast;
The flesh is next, which in fruition wastes,
High flush'd with all the sensual joys it tastes.
While men the fair, the goodly soul destroy,
From whence the flesh has power to taste a joy.

Seek thou Religion primitively sound—
Well, gentle friend, but where may she be found?

By faith implicit blind Ignaro led,
Thinks the bright seraph from his country fled,
And seeks her seat at Rome, because we know,
She there was seen a thousand years ago;
And loves her relic rags, as men obey
The foot-cloth where the prince sat yesterday.
These pageant forms are whining Obed's scorn,
Who seeks Religion at Geneva born,
A sullen thing, whose coarseness suits the crowd;
Though young, unhandsome; though unhandsome, proud;
Thus, with the wanton, some perversely judge
All girls unhealthy but the country drudge.

No foreign schemes make easy Cæpio roam,
The man contented takes his church at home;
Nay, should some preachers, servile bawds of gain,
Should some new laws, which like new fashions reign,
Command his faith to count salvation tied,
To visit his, and visit none beside;
He grants salvation centres in his own,
And grants it centres but in his alone;
From youth to age he grasps the proffer'd dame,
And they confer his faith, who give his name;
So from the guardian's hands the wards, who live
Enthrall'd to guardians, take the wives they give.

From all professions careless Airy flies,
" For all professions can't be good," he cries ;
And here a fault, and there another views,
And lives unfix'd for want of heart to choose ;
So men, who know what some loose girls have done,
For fear of marrying such, will marry none.
The charms of all obsequious Courtly strike ;
On each he dotes, on each attends alike ;
And thinks, as different countries deck the dame,
The dresses altering, and the sex the same :
So fares Religion, chang'd in outward show,
But, 'tis Religion still where'er we go :
This blindness springs from an excess of light,
And men embrace the wrong to choose the right.
But thou of force must one Religion own,
And only one, and that the right alone ;
To find that right one, ask thy reverend sire,
Let his of him, and him of his inquire ;
Though Truth and Falsehood seem as twins allied,
There 's eldership on Truth's delightful side ;
Her seek with heed—who seeks the soundest first,
Is not of no Religion, nor the worst.
T' adore, or scorn an image, or protest,
May all be bad ; doubt wisely for the best,
'Twere wrong to sleep, or headlong run astray ;
It is not wandering, to inquire the way.

On a large mountain, at the basis wide,
Steep to the top, and craggy at the side,
Sits Sacred Truth enthron'd ; and he who means

To reach the summit, mounts with weary pains,
Winds round and round, and every turn essays,
Where sudden breaks resist the shorter ways.
Yet labour so, that ere faint age arrive,
Thy searching soul possess her rest alive:
To work by twilight were to work too late,
And age is twilight to the night of fate.
To will alone, is but to mean delay,
To work at present is the use of day.
For man's employ much thought and deed remain,
High thoughts the soul, hard deeds the body strain,
And mysteries ask believing, which to view,
Like the fair Sun, are plain, but dazzling too.

Be Truth, so found, with sacred heed possest,
Not kings have power to tear it from thy breast.
By no blank charters harm they where they hate,
Nor are they vicars, but the hands of fate.
Ah! fool and wretch, who lett'st thy soul be tied
To human laws! or must it so be tried?
Or will it boot thee, at the latest day,
When Judgment sits, and Justice asks thy plea,
That Philip that, or Gregory taught thee this,
Or John or Martin? All may teach amiss:
For every contrary in each extreme
This holds alike, and each may plead the same.

Wouldst thou to power a proper duty show?
'Tis thy first task the bounds of power to know;
The bounds once pass'd, it holds the same no more,

Its nature alters, which it own'd before,
Nor were submission humbleness exprest,
But all a low idolatry at best.
Power from above, subordinately spread,
Streams like a fountain from th' eternal head;
There, calm and pure, the living waters flow,
But roars a torrent or a flood below;
Each flower ordain'd the margins to adorn,
Each native beauty, from its roots is torn,
And left on deserts, rocks and sands, are tost,
All the long travel, and in ocean lost.
So fares the soul, which more that power reveres,
Man claims from God, than what in God inheres.

ON BISHOP BURNET'S BEING SET ON FIRE IN HIS CLOSET.

FROM that dire era, bane to Sarum's pride,
Which broke his schemes, and laid his friends aside,
He talks and writes that popery will return,
And we, and he, and all his works will burn.
What touch'd himself was almost fairly prov'd:
Oh, far from Britain be the rest remov'd!
For, as of late he meant to bless the age,
With flagrant prefaces of party-rage,
O'erwrought with passion, and the subject's weight,
Lolling, he nodded in his elbow seat;
Down fell the candle; grease and zeal conspire,
Heat meets with heat, and pamphlets burn their sire.
Here crawls a preface on its half-burn'd maggots,
And there an introduction brings its fagots:
Then roars the prophet of the northern nation,
Scorch'd by a flaming speech on moderation.

Unwarn'd by this, go on, the realm to fright,
Thou Briton vaunting in thy second-sight!
In such a ministry you safely tell,
How much you'd suffer, if religion fell.

ON MRS. ARABELLA FERMOR LEAVING LONDON.

FROM town fair Arabella flies;
    The beaux unpowder'd grieve:
The rivers play before her eyes;
The breezes, softly breathing, rise;
    The spring begins to live.

Her lovers swore, they must expire,
    Yet quickly find their ease;
For as she goes, their flames retire;
Love thrives before a nearer fire,
    Esteem by distant rays.

Yet soon the fair one will return,
    When Summer quits the plain:
Ye rivers, pour the weeping urn;
Ye breezes, sadly sighing, mourn;
    Ye lovers, burn again!

'Tis constancy enough in love
    That nature's fairly shown:
To search for more, will fruitless prove;
Romances, and the turtle-dove,
    The virtue boast alone.

CHLORIS APPEARING IN A LOOKING-GLASS.

Oft have I seen a piece of art,
  Of light and shade the mixture fine,
Speak all the passions of the heart,
  And show true life in every line.

But what is this before my eyes,
  With every feature, every grace,
That strikes with love, and with surprise,
  And gives me all the vital face?

It is not Chloris: for, behold,
  The shifting phantom comes and goes;
And when 'tis here, 'tis pale and cold,
  Nor any female softness knows.

But 'tis her image, for I feel
  The very pains that Chloris gives;
Her charms are there, I know them well,
  I see what in my bosom lives.

Oh, could I but the picture save:
  'Tis drawn by her own matchless skill;
Nature the lively colours gave,
  And she need only look to kill.

Ah! fair one, will it not suffice,
 That I should once your victim lie;
Unless you multiply your eyes,
 And strive to make me doubly die?

THE

POETICAL WORKS

OF

THOMAS TICKELL.

WITH A LIFE,

BY DR. JOHNSON.

BOSTON:
LITTLE, BROWN AND COMPANY.
NEW YORK: EVANS AND DICKERSON.
PHILADELPHIA: LIPPINCOTT, GRAMBO AND CO.
M.DCCC.LIV.

RIVERSIDE, CAMBRIDGE:
PRINTED BY H. O. HOUGHTON AND COMPANY.

STEREOTYPED BY STONE AND SMART.

CONTENTS.

THE LIFE OF TICKELL,

BY DR. JOHNSON.

Thomas Tickell, the son of the Reverend Richard Tickell, was born in 1686, at Bridekirk, in Cumberland; and in April, 1701, became a member of Queen's College, in Oxford; in 1708, he was made master of arts; and, two years afterwards, was chosen fellow; for which, as he did not comply with the statutes by taking orders, he obtained a dispensation from the Crown. He held his fellowship till 1726, and then vacated it, by marrying, in that year, at Dublin.

Tickell was not one of those scholars who wear away their lives in closets; he entered early into the world, and was long busy in public affairs; in which he was initiated under the patronage of Addison, whose notice he is said to have gained by his verses in praise of Rosamond.

To those verses it would not have been just to deny regard; for they contain some of the most elegant encomiastic strains; and, among the innumerable poems of the same kind, it will be hard to find one with which they need to fear a comparison. It may deserve observation, that when Pope wrote long afterwards in praise of Addison, he has copied, at least has resembled, Tickell.

Let joy salute fair Rosamonda's shade,
And wreaths of myrtle crown the lovely maid.
While now perhaps with Dido's ghost she roves,
And hears and tells the story of their loves,
Alike they mourn, alike they bless their fate,
Since Love, which made them wretched, makes them great.
Nor longer that relentless doom bemoan,
Which gain'd a Virgil and an Addison.

TICKELL.

Then future ages with delight shall see
How Plato's, Bacon's, Newton's looks agree;
Or in fair series laurell'd bards be shown,
A Virgil there, and here an Addison.

POPE.

He produced another piece of the same kind at the appearance of Cato, with equal skill, but not equal happiness.

When the ministers of Queen Anne were negotiating with France, Tickell published The Prospect of Peace, a poem, of which the tendency was to reclaim the nation from the pride of conquest to the pleasures of tranquillity. How far Tickell, whom Swift afterwards mentioned as Whiggissimus, had then connected himself with any party, I know not; this poem certainly did not flatter the practices, or promote the opinions, of the men by whom he was afterwards befriended.

Mr. Addison, however he hated the men then

in power, suffered his friendship to prevail over his public spirit, and gave in the Spectator such praises of Tickell's poem, that when, after having long wished to peruse it, I laid hold on it at last, I thought it unequal to the honours which it had received, and found it a piece to be approved rather than admired. But the hope excited by a work of genius, being general and indefinite, is rarely gratified. It was read at that time with so much favour, that six editions were sold.

At the arrival of King George he sung The Royal Progress; which, being inserted in the Spectator, is well known; and of which it is just to say, that it is neither high nor low.

The poetical incident of most importance in Tickell's life was his publication of the first book of the Iliad, as translated by himself, an apparent opposition to Pope's Homer, of which the first part made its entrance into the world at the same time.

Addison declared that the rival versions were both good; but that Tickell's was the best that ever was made; and with Addison, the wits, his adherents and followers, were certain to concur. Pope does not appear to have been much dismayed; "for," says he, "I have the town, that is, the mob on my side." But he remarks, "that it is common for the smaller party to make up in diligence what they want in numbers; he appeals to the people as his proper judges; and, if they are not inclined to condemn him, he is in little care about the high-flyers at Button's."

Pope did not long think Addison an impartial judge; for he considered him as the writer of Tickell's version. The reasons for his suspicion I will literally transcribe from Mr. Spence's Collection.

"There had been a coldness (said Mr. Pope) between Mr. Addison and me for some time; and we had not been in company together, for a good while, any where but at Button's coffee-house, where I used to see him almost every day. On his meeting me there, one day in particular, he took me aside, and said he should be glad to dine with me, at such a tavern, if I staid till those people were gone, (Budgell and Philips.) We went accordingly; and after dinner Mr. Addison said, 'That he had wanted for some time to talk with me; that his friend Tickell had formerly, whilst at Oxford, translated the first book of the Iliad; that he designed to print it, and had desired him to look it over; that he must therefore beg that I would not desire him to look over my first book, because, if he did, it would have the air of double-dealing. I assured him, that I did not at all take it ill of Mr. Tickell that he was going to publish his translation; that he certainly had as much right to translate any author as myself; and that publishing both was entering on a fair stage. I then added, that I would not desire him to look over my first book of the Iliad, because he had looked over Mr. Tickell's; but could wish to have the benefit of his observations on the second, which I had then finished, and which Mr. Tickell had not touched upon. Accordingly I sent him the second book the next morning; and Mr. Addison a few days after returned it, with very high commendations. Soon after it was generally known that Mr. Tickell was publishing the first book of the Iliad, I met Dr. Young in the street; and upon our falling into that subject, the Doctor expressed a great deal of surprise at Tickell's having had such a translation so long by him. He said, that it was inconceivable to him, and that there must be some mistake in the matter; that each used to communicate to the other whatever verses they wrote, even to the least things; that Tickell could not have been busied in so long a work there without his knowing something of the matter; and that he had never heard a single word of it till on this occasion. The surprise of Dr. Young, together with what Steele has said against Tickell in relation to this affair, make it highly probable that there was some underhand dealing in that business; and indeed Tickell himself, who is a very fair worthy man, has since, in a manner as good as owned it to me. When it was introduced into a conversation between Mr. Tickell and Mr. Pope, by a third person, Tickell did not deny it; which, considering his honour and zeal for his departed friend, was the same as owning it."

Upon these suspicions, with which Dr. Warburton hints that other circumstances concurred, Pope always, in his Art of Sinking, quotes this book as the work of Addison.

To compare the two translations would be tedious; the palm is now given universally to Pope; but I think the first lines of Tickell's were rather to be preferred; and Pope seems to have since borrowed something from them in the correction of his own.

When the Hanover succession was disputed, Tickell gave what assistance his pen would supply. His letter to Avignon stands high among party-poems; it expresses contempt without coarseness, and superiority without insolence. It had the success which it deserved, being five times printed.

He was now intimately united to Mr. Addison, who, when he went into Ireland as secretary to the lord Sunderland, took him thither and employed him in public business; and when (1717) afterwards he rose to be secretary of state, made him under-secretary. Their friendship seems to have continued without abatement; for when Addison died, he left him the charge of publishing his works, with a solemn recommendation to the patronage of Craggs.

To these works he prefixed an elegy on the author, which could owe none of its beauties to the assistance which might be suspected to have strengthened or embellished his earlier compositions; but neither he nor Addison ever produced nobler lines than are contained in the third and fourth paragraphs; nor is a more sublime or more elegant funeral-poem to be found in the whole compass of English literature.

He was afterwards (about 1725) made secretary to the Lords Justices of Ireland, a place of great honour; in which he continued till 1740, when he died on the twenty-third of April, at Bath.

Of the poems yet unmentioned the longest is Kensington Gardens, of which the versification is smooth and elegant, but the fiction unskilfully compounded of Grecian deities and Gothic fairies. Neither species of those exploded beings could have done much; and, when they are brought together, they only make each other contemptible. To Tickell, however, cannot be refused a high place among the minor poets; nor should it be forgotten that he was one of the contributors to the Spectator. With respect to his personal character, he is said to have been a man of gay conversation, at least a temperate lover of wine and company, and in his domestic relations without censure.

POEMS.

ON QUEEN CAROLINE'S

REBUILDING THE LODGINGS OF THE BLACK PRINCE, AND HENRY V. AT QUEEN'S COLLEGE, OXFORD.

Where bold and graceful soars, secure of fame,
The pile, now worthy great Philippa's name,
Mark that old ruin, gothic and uncouth,
Where the Black Edward pass'd his beardless youth;
And the Fifth Henry, for his first renown,
Outstripp'd each rival in a student's gown.
In that coarse age were princes fond to dwell
With meagre monks, and haunt the silent cell:
Sent from the monarch's to the Muse's court,
Their meals were frugal, and their sleeps were short;
To couch at curfew time they thought no scorn,
And froze at matins every winter-morn;
They read, an early book, the starry frame,
And lisped each constellation by its name;

Art after art still dawning to their view,
And their mind opening as their stature grew.
Yet, whose ripe manhood spread our fame so far,
Sages in peace, and demi-gods in war!
Who, stern in fight, made echoing Cressi ring,
And, mild in conquest, serv'd his captive king!
Who gain'd, at Agincourt, the victor's bays;
Nor took himself, but gave good Heaven, the praise!
Thy nurslings, ancient dome! to virtue form'd;
To mercy listening, whilst in fields they storm'd:
Fierce to the fierce; and warm the opprest to save;
Through life rever'd, and worshipp'd in the grave!
In tenfold pride the mouldering roofs shall shine,
The stately work of bounteous Caroline;
And blest Philippa, with unenvious eyes,
From Heaven behold her rival's fabric rise.
If still, bright saint, this spot deserves thy care,
Incline thee to the ambitious Muse's prayer:
O, could'st thou win young William's bloom to grace
His mother's walls, and fill thy Edward's place,
How would that genius whose propitious wings
Have here twice hover'd o'er the sons of kings,
Descend triumphant to his ancient seat,
And take in charge a third Plantagenet!

TO THE SUPPOSED

AUTHOR OF THE SPECTATOR.

In courts licentious, and a shameless stage,
How long the war shall wit with virtue wage?
Enchanted by this prostituted fair,
Our youth run headlong in the fatal snare;
In height of rapture clasp unheeded pains,
And suck pollution through their tingling veins?
Thy spotless thoughts unshock'd the priest may hear;
And the pure vestal in her bosom wear.
To conscious blushes and diminished pride,
Thy glass betrays what treacherous love would hide;
Nor harsh thy precepts, but infus'd by stealth,
Pleas'd while they cure, and cheat us into health.
Thy works in Chloe's toilet gain a part,
And with his tailor share the fopling's heart:
Lash'd in thy satire, the penurious cit
Laughs at himself, and finds no harm in wit:
From felon gamesters the raw squire is free,
And Britain owes her rescued oaks to thee.
His miss the frolic viscount dreads to toast,
Or his third cure the shallow Templar boast;

And the rash fool, who scorn'd the beaten road,
Dares quake at thunder, and confess his God.
The brainless stripling, who, expell'd the town,
Damn'd the stiff college and pedantic gown,
Aw'd by thy name, is dumb, and thrice a week
Spells uncouth Latin, and pretends to Greek.
A sauntering tribe! such, born to wide estates;
With yea and no in senates hold debates:
At length despised each to his fields retires,
First with the dogs, and king amidst the squires;
From pert to stupid, sinks supinely down,
In youth a coxcomb, and in age a clown.
Such readers scorn'd, thou wing'st thy daring flight,
Above the stars, and tread'st the fields of light;
Fame, Heaven and Hell, are thy exalted theme,
And visions such as Jove himself might dream;
Man sunk to slavery, though to glory born,
Heaven's pride when upright, and deprav'd his scorn.
Such hints alone could British Virgil lend,
And thou alone deserve from such a friend;
A debt so borrow'd is illustrious shame,
And fame, when shar'd with him, is double fame.
So, flush'd with sweets by Beauty's queen bestow'd,
With more than mortal charms Æneas glow'd:
Such generous strifes Eugene and Marlborough try,
And as in glory, so in friendship, vie.

Permit these lines by thee to live—nor blame
A Muse that pants and languishes for fame;
That fears to sink when humbler themes she sings,
Lost in the mass of mean forgotten things:
Receiv'd by thee, I prophesy my rhymes,
The praise of virgins in succeeding times:
Mix'd with thy works, their life no bounds shall see,
But stand protected, as inspir'd, by thee.
So some weak shoot, which else would poorly rise,
Jove's tree adopts, and lifts him to the skies;
Through the new pupil fostering juices flow,
Thrust forth the gems, and give the flowers to blow
Aloft; immortal reigns the plant unknown,
With borrow'd life, and vigour not his own.

A POEM,

TO HIS EXCELLENCY, THE LORD PRIVY SEAL,

ON THE PROSPECT OF PEACE.

......Sacerdos
Fronde super mitram, et felici comptus oliva.

VIRG.

TO THE LORD PRIVY SEAL.

CONTENDING kings, and fields of death, too long
Have been the subject of the British song.
Who hath not read of fam'd Ramillia's plain,
Bavaria's fall, and Danube choak'd with slain!
Exhausted themes! a gentler note I raise,
And sing returning peace in softer lays.
Their fury quell'd, and martial rage allay'd,
I wait our heroes in the sylvan shade:
Disbanding hosts are imag'd to my mind,
And warring powers in friendly leagues combin'd,
While ease and pleasure make the nations smile,
And Heaven and Anna bless Britannia's isle.
Well sends our queen her mitred Bristol forth,
For early counsels fam'd, and long-tried worth;
Who, thirty rolling years, had oft withheld
The Swede and Saxon from the dusty field;

Completely form'd to heal the Christian wounds,
To name the kings, and give each kingdom bounds;
The face of ravag'd Nature to repair,
By leagues to soften earth, and Heaven by prayer,
To gain by love, where rage and slaughter fail,
And make the crosier o'er the sword prevail.
So when great Moses, with Jehovah's wand,
Had scatter'd plagues o'er stubborn Pharaoh's land,
Now spread an host of locusts round the shore,
Now turn'd Nile's fattening streams to putrid gore;
Plenty and gladness mark'd the priest of God,
And sudden almonds shot from Aaron's rod.
O thou from whom these bounteous blessings flow,
To whom, as chief, the hopes of peace we owe,
(For next to thee, the man whom kings contend
To style companion, and to make their friend,
Great Strafford, rich in every courtly grace,
With joyful pride accepts the second place,)
From Britain's isle, and Isis' sacred spring,
One hour, oh! listen while the Muses sing.
Though ministers of mighty monarchs wait,
With beating hearts to learn their master's fate,
One hour forbear to speak thy queen's commands,
Nor think the world, thy charge, neglected stands;
The blissful prospects, in my verse display'd
May lure the stubborn, the deceiv'd persuade:
Ev'n thou to peace shalt speedier urge the way,
And more be hasten'd by this short delay.

ON THE PROSPECT OF PEACE.

The haughty Gaul, in ten campaigns o'erthrown,
Now ceas'd to think the western world his own.
Oft had he mourn'd his boasting leaders bound,
And his proud bulwarks smoking on the ground:
In vain with powers renew'd he fill'd the plain,
Made timorous vows, and brib'd the saints in vain;
As oft his legions did the fight decline,
Lurk'd in the trench, and skulk'd behind the line.
Before his eyes the fancied javelin gleams,
At feasts he starts, and seems dethron'd in dreams;
On glory past reflects with secret pain,
On mines exhausted, and on millions slain.
To Britain's queen the scepter'd suppliant bends,
To her his crowns and infant race commends,
Who grieves her fame with Christian blood to buy,
Nor asks for glory at a price so high.
At her decree, the war suspended stands,
And Britain's heroes hold their lifted hands,
Their open brows no threatening frowns disguise,
But gentler passions sparkle in their eyes.
The Gauls, who never in their courts could find
Such temper'd fire with manly beauty join'd,
Doubt if they're those, whom, dreadful to the view,
In forms so fierce their fearful fancies drew;
At whose dire names ten thousand widows prest
Their helpless orphans clinging to the breast.

In silent rapture each his foe surveys:
They vow firm friendship, and give mutual praise.
Brave minds, howe'er at war, are secret friends;
Their generous discord with the battle ends;
In peace they wonder whence dissension rose,
And ask how souls so like could e'er be foes.
Methinks I hear more friendly shouts rebound,
And social clarions mix their sprightly sound.
The British flags are furl'd, her troops disband,
And scatter'd armies seek their native land.
The hardy veteran, proud of many a scar,
The manly charms and honours of the war,
Who hop'd to share his friends' illustrious doom,
And in the battle find a soldier's tomb,
Leans on his spear to take his farewell view,
And, sighing, bids the glorious camp adieu.
Ye generous fair, receive the brave with smiles,
O'erpay their sleepless nights, and crown their toils;
Soft beauty is the gallant soldier's due,
For you they conquer, and they bleed for you.
In vain proud Gaul with boastful Spain conspires,
When English valour English beauty fires;
The nations dread your eyes, and kings despair
Of chiefs so brave, till they have nymphs so fair.
See the fond wife in tears of transport drown'd,
Hugs her rough lord, and weeps o'er every wound,
Hangs on the lips that fields of blood relate,
And smiles, or trembles, at his various fate.
Near the full bowl he draws the fancied line,
And marks feign'd trenches in the flowing wine,

Then sets the invested fort before his eyes,
And mines, that whirl'd battalions to the skies:
His little listening progeny turn pale,
And beg again to hear the dreadful tale.
Such dire achievements sings the bard that tells
Of palfrey'd dames, bold knights, and magic spells,
Where whole brigades one champion's arms o'erthrow,
And cleave a giant at a random blow,
Slay paynims vile, that force the fair, and tame
The goblin's fury, and the dragon's flame.
Our eager youth to distant nations run,
To visit fields, their valiant fathers won;
From Flandria's shore their country's fame they trace,
Till far Germania shows her blasted face.
The exulting Briton asks his mournful guide,
Where his hard fate the lost Bavaria tried:
Where Stepney grav'd the stone to Anna's fame,
He points to Blenheim, once a vulgar name;
Here fled the Household, there did Tallard yield,
Here Marlborough turn'd the fortune of the field,
On those steep banks, near Danube's raging flood;
The Gauls thrice started back, and trembling stood:
When, Churchill's arm perceiv'd, they stood not long,
But plung'd amidst the waves, a desperate throng,
Crowds whelm'd on crowds dash'd wide the watery bed,
And drove the current to its distant head.

As, when by Raphael's, or by Kneller's hands
A warlike courser on the canvas stands,
Such as on Landen bleeding Ormond bore,
Or set young Ammon on the Granic shore;
If chance a generous steed the work behold,
He snorts, he neighs, he champs the foamy gold:
So, Hocstet seen, tumultuous passions roll,
And hints of glory fire the Briton's soul,
In fancy'd fights he sees the troops engage,
And all the tempest of the battle rage.
Charm me, ye powers, with scenes less nobly bright,
Far humbler thoughts th' inglorious Muse delight,
Content to see the honours of the field
By ploughshares levell'd, or in flowers conceal'd.
O'er shatter'd walls may creeping ivy twine,
And grass luxuriant clothe the harmless mine.
Tame flocks ascend the breach without a wound,
Or crop the bastion, now a fruitful ground;
While shepherds sleep, along the rampard laid,
Or pipe beneath the formidable shade.
Who was the man? Oblivion blast his name,
Torn out, and blotted from the list of Fame!
Who, fond of lawless rule, and proudly brave,
First sunk the filial subject to a slave,
His neighbour's realms by frauds unkingly gain'd,
In guiltless blood the sacred ermine stain'd,
Laid schemes for death, to slaughter turn'd his heart,
And fitted murder to the rules of art.

Ah! curst Ambition, to thy lures we owe
All the great ills, that mortals bear below.
Curst by the hind, when to the spoil he yields
His year's whole sweat, and vainly ripen'd fields;
Curst by the maid, torn from her lover's side,
When left a widow, though not yet a bride;
By mothers curst, when floods of tears they shed,
And scatter useless roses on the dead.
Oh, sacred Bristol! then, what dangers prove
The arts, thou smil'st on with paternal love?
Then, mixt with rubbish by the brutal foes,
In vain the marble breathes, the canvas glows;
To shades obscure the glittering sword pursues
The gentle poet, and defenceless Muse.
A voice like thine, alone, might then assuage
The warrior's fury, and control his rage;
To hear thee speak, might the fierce Vandal stand,
And fling the brandish'd sabre from his hand.
Far hence be driven to Scythia's stormy shore
The drum's harsh music, and the cannon's roar;
Let grim Bellona haunt the lawless plain,
Where Tartar clans and grizzly Cossacks reign;
Let the steel'd Turk be deaf to matrons' cries,
See virgins ravish'd with relentless eyes,
To death gray heads and smiling infants doom,
Nor spare the promise of the pregnant womb,
O'er wasted kingdoms spread his wide command,
The savage lord of an unpeopled land.

Her guiltless glory just Britannia draws
From pure religion, and impartial laws,
To Europe's wounds a mother's aid she brings,
And holds in equal scales the rival kings:
Her generous sons in choicest gifts abound,
Alike in arms, alike in arts renown'd.
As when sweet Venus (so the fable sings)
Awak'd by Nereids, from the ocean springs,
With smiles she sees the threatening billows rise,
Spreads smooth the surge, and clears the louring skies.
Light, o'er the deep, with fluttering Cupids crown'd,
The pearly couch and silver turtles bound;
Her tresses shed ambrosial odours round.
Amidst the world of waves so stands serene
Britannia's isle, the ocean's stately queen;
In vain the nations have conspired her fall,
Her trench the sea, and fleets her floating wall:
Defenceless barks, her powerful navy near,
Have only waves and hurricanes to fear.
What bold invader, or what land opprest,
Hath not her anger quell'd, her aid redrest!
Say, where have e'er her union-crosses sail'd,
But much her arms, her justice more prevail'd!
Her labours are, to plead th' Almighty's cause,
Her pride to teach th' untam'd barbarian laws:
Who conquers wins by brutal strength the prize;
But 'tis a godlike work to civilize.

Have we forgot how from great Russia's throne
The king, whose power half Europe's regions own,
Whose sceptre waving, with one shout rush forth
In swarms the harness'd millions of the north,
Through realms of ice pursued his tedious way
To court our friendship, and our fame survey!
Hence the rich prize of useful arts he bore,
And round his empire spread the learned store:
(T' adorn old realms is more than new to raise,
His country's parent is a monarch's praise.)
His bands now march in just array to war,
And Caspian gulfs unusual navies bear;
With Runick lays Smolensko's forests ring,
And wondering Volga hears the Muses sing.
Did not the painted kings of India greet
Our queen, and lay their sceptres at her feet?
Chiefs who full bowls of hostile blood had quaff'd,
Fam'd for the javelin, and envenom'd shaft,
Whose haughty brows made savages adore,
Nor bow'd to less than stars or sun before.
Her pitying smile accepts their suppliant claim,
And adds four monarchs to the Christian name.
Blest use of power! O virtuous pride in kings!
And like his bounty, whence dominion springs!
Which o'er new worlds makes Heaven's indulgence shine,
And ranges myriads under laws divine!
Well bought with all that those sweet regions hold,
With groves of spices, and with mines of gold.

Fearless our merchant now pursues his gain,
And roams securely o'er the boundless main.
Now o'er his head the polar Bear he spies,
And freezing spangles of the Lapland skies;
Now swells his canvas to the sultry line,
With glittering spoils where Indian grottos shine,
Where fumes of incense glad the southern seas,
And wafted citron scents the balmy breeze.
Here nearer suns prepare the ripening gem,
To grace great Anne's imperial diadem,
And here the ore, whose melted mass shall yield
On faithful coins each memorable field,
Which, mix'd with medals of immortal Rome,
May clear disputes, and teach the times to come.
In circling beams shall godlike Anna glow,
And Churchill's sword hang o'er the prostrate foe;
In comely wounds shall bleeding worthies stand,
Webb's firm platoon, and Lumley's faithful band.
Bold Mordaunt in Iberian trophies drest,
And Campbell's dragon on his dauntless breast,
Great Ormond's deeds on Vigo's spoils enroll'd,
And Guiscard's knife on Harley's Chili gold.
And if the Muse, O Bristol, might decree,
Here Granville noted by the lyre should be,
The lyre for Granville, and the cross for thee.
Such are the honours grateful Britain pays;
So patriots merit, and so monarchs praise.
O'er distant times such records shall prevail,
When English numbers, antiquated, fail:

A trifling song the Muse can only yield,
And soothe her soldiers panting from the field.
To sweet retirements see them safe convey'd,
And raise their battles in the rural shade.
From fields of death to Woodstock's peaceful glooms,
(The poet's haunt) Britannia's hero comes—
Begin my Muse, and softly touch the string:
Here Henry lov'd; and Chaucer learn'd to sing.
Hail, fabled grotto! hail, Elysian soil!
Thou fairest spot of fair Britannia's isle!
Where kings of old, conceal'd, forgot the throne,
And beauty was content to shine unknown;
Where Love and War by turns pavilions rear,
And Henry's bowers near Blenheim's dome appear;
The weary'd champion lull in soft alcoves,
The noblest boast of thy romantic groves.
Oft, if the Muse presage, shall be seen
By Rosamonda fleeting o'er the green,
In dreams be hail'd by heroes' mighty shades,
And hear old Chaucer warble through the glades,
O'er the fam'd echoing vaults his name shall bound,
And hill to hill reflect the favourite sound.
Here, here at least thy love for arms give o'er,
Nor, one world conquer'd, fondly wish for more.
Vice of great souls alone! O thirst of fame!
The Muse admires it, while she strives to blame.
Thy toils be now to chase the bounding deer,
Or view the coursers stretch in wild career.

This lovely scene shall soothe thy soul to rest,
And wear each dreadful image from thy breast.
With pleasure, by thy conquests shalt thou see
Thy queen triumphant, and all Europe free.
No cares henceforth shall thy repose destroy,
But what thou giv'st the world, thyself enjoy.
Sweet Solitude! when life's gay hours are past
Howe'er we range, in thee we fix at last:
Tost through tempestuous seas (the voyage o'er)
Pale we look back, and bless thy friendly shore.
Our own strict judges, our past life we scan,
And ask if glory hath enlarg'd the span:
If bright the prospect, we the grave defy,
Trust future ages, and contented die.
When strangers from far distant climes shall come,
To view the pomp of this triumphant dome,
Where, rear'd aloft, dissembled trophies stand,
And breathing labours of the sculptor's hand,
Where Kneller's art shall paint the flying Gaul,
And Bourbon's woes shall fill the story'd wall;
Heirs of thy blood shall o'er their bounteous board
Fix Europe's guard, thy monumental sword,
Banners that oft have wav'd on conquer'd walls,
And trumps, that drown'd the groans of gasping Gauls.
Fair dames shall oft, with curious eye, explore
The costly robes that slaughter'd generals wore,
Rich trappings from the Danube's whirlpools brought,
(Hesperian nuns the gorgeous broidery wrought,)

Belts stiff with gold, the Boian horseman's pride,
And Gaul's fair flowers, in human crimson dy'd.
Of Churchill's race perhaps some lovely boy
Shall mark the burnish'd steel that hangs on high,
Shall gaze transported on its glittering charms,
And reach it struggling with unequal arms,
By signs the drum's tumultuous sound request,
Then seek, in starts, the hushing mother's breast.
So in the painter's animated frame,
Where Mars embraces the soft Paphian dame,
The little Loves in sport his fauchion wield,
Or join their strength to heave his ponderous shield:
One strokes the plume in Tytion's gore embrued,
And one the spear, that reeks with Typhon's blood:
Another's infant brows the helm sustain,
He nods his crest, and frights the shrieking train.
Thus, the rude tempest of the field o'erblown,
Shall whiter rounds of smiling years roll on,
Our victors, blest in peace, forget their wars,
Enjoy past dangers, and absolve the stars.
But, oh! what sorrows shall bedew your urns,
Ye honour'd shades, whom widow'd Albion mourns!
If your thin forms yet discontented moan,
And haunt the mangled mansions, once your own;
Behold what flowers the pious Muses strow,
And tears, which in the midst of triumph flow;

Cypress and bays your envy'd brows surround,
Your names the tender matron's heart shall wound,
And the soft maid grow pensive at the sound.
Accept, great Anne, the tears their memory draws,
Who nobly perish'd in their sovereign's cause:
For thou in pity bid'st the war give o'er,
Mourn'st thy slain heroes, nor wilt venture more.
Vast price of blood on each victorious day!
(But Europe's freedom doth that price repay.)
Lamented triumphs! when one breath must tell
That Marlborough conquer'd, and that Dormer fell.
Great queen! whose name strikes haughty monarchs pale,
On whose just sceptre hangs Europa's scale,
Whose arm like Mercy wounds, decides like Fate,
On whose decree the nations anxious wait:
From Albion's cliffs thy wide-extended hand
Shall o'er the main to far Peru command;
So vast a tract whose wide domain shall run,
Its circling skies shall see no setting sun.
Thee, thee an hundred languages shall claim,
And savage Indians swear by Anna's name;
The line and poles shall own thy rightful sway,
And thy commands the sever'd globe obey.
Round the vast ball thy new dominions chain
The watery kingdoms, and control the main;
Magellan's straits to Gibraltar they join,
Across the seas a formidable line;

The sight of adverse Gaul we fear no more,
But pleas'd see Dunkirk, now a guiltless shore,
In vain great Neptune tore the narrow ground,
And meant his waters for Britannia's bound;
Her giant genius takes a mighty stride,
And sets his foot beyond the encroaching tide;
On either bank the land its master knows,
And in the midst the subject ocean flows.
So near proud Rhodes, across the raging flood,
Stupendous form! the vast Colossus stood,
(While at one foot their thronging galleys ride,
A whole hour's sail scarce reach the further side,)
Betwixt his brazen thighs, in loose array,
Ten thousand streamers on the billows play.
By Harley's counsels, Dunkirk, now restor'd
To Britain's empire, owns her ancient lord.
In him transfus'd his godlike father reigns,
Rich in the blood which swell'd that patriot's veins,
Who, boldly faithful, met his sovereign's frown,
And scorn'd for gold to yield th' important town.
His son was born the ravish'd prey to claim,
And France still trembles at an Harley's name.
A fort so dreadful to our English shore,
Our fleets scarce fear'd the sands or tempests more,
Whose vast expenses to such sums amount,
That the tax'd Gaul scarce furnish'd out th' account,
Whose walls such bulwarks, such vast towers restrain,
Its weakest ramparts are the rocks and main,

His boast great Louis yields, and cheaply buys
Thy friendship, Anna, with the mighty prize.
Holland repining, and in grief cast down,
Sees the new glories of the British crown:
Ah! may they ne'er provoke thee to the fight,
Nor foes, more dreadful than the Gaul, invite.
Soon may they hold the olive, soon assuage
Their secret murmurs, nor call forth thy rage
To rend their banks, and pour, at one command,
Thy realm, the sea, o'er their precarious land.
Henceforth be thine, vicegerent of the skies,
Scorn'd worth to raise, and vice in robes chastise
To dry the orphan's tears, and from the bar
Chase the brib'd judge, and hush the wordy war,
Deny the curst blasphemer's tongue to rage,
And turn God's fury from an impious age.
Blest change! the soldier's late destroying hand
Shall rear new temples in his native land;
Mistaken zealots shall with fear behold,
And beg admittance in our sacred fold:
On her own works the pious queen shall smile,
And turn her cares upon her favourite isle.
So the keen bolt a warrior angel aims,
Array'd in clouds, and wrapt in mantling flames;
He bears a tempest on his sounding wings,
And his red arm the forky vengeance flings;
At length, Heaven's wrath appeas'd, he quits the war,
To roll his orb, and guide his destin'd star,

To shed kind fate, and lucky hours bestow,
And smile propitious on the world below.
Around thy throne shall faithful nobles wait,
These guard the church, and those direct the state.
To Bristol, graceful in maternal tears,
The church her towery forehead gently rears;
She begs her pious son t' assert her cause,
Defend her rights, and reënforce her laws,
With holy zeal the sacred work begin,
To bend the stubborn, and the meek to win.
Our Oxford's earl in careful thought shall stand,
To raise his queen, and save a sinking land.
The wealthiest glebe to ravenous Spaniards known
He marks, and makes the golden world our own,
Content with hands unsoil'd to guard the prize,
And keep the store with undesiring eyes.
So round the tree, that bore Hesperian gold,
The sacred watch lay curl'd in many a fold,
His eyes uprearing to th' untasted prey,
The sleepless guardian wasted life away.
Beneath the peaceful olives, rais'd by you,
Her ancient pride, shall every art renew,
(The arts with you fam'd Harcourt shall defend,
And courtly Bolingbroke, the Muse's friend.)
With piercing eye some search where Nature plays,
And trace the wanton through her darksome maze,
Whence health from herbs; from seeds how groves begun,
How vital streams in circling eddies run.

Some teach why round the Sun the spheres advance,
In the fix'd measures of their mystic dance,
How tides, when heav'd by pressing moons, o'erflow,
And sun-born Iris paints her showery bow.
In happy chains our daring language bound,
Shall sport no more in arbitrary sound,
But buskin'd bards henceforth shall wisely rage,
And Grecian plans reform Britannia's stage:
Till Congreve bids her smile, Augusta stands
And longs to weep when flowing Rowe commands.
Britain's Spectators shall their strength combine
To mend our morals and our taste refine,
Fight virtue's cause, stand up in wit's defence,
Win us from vice, and laugh us into sense.
Nor, Prior, hast thou hush'd the trump in vain,
Thy lyre shall now revive her mirthful strain,
New tales shall now be told; if right I see,
The soul of Chaucer is restor'd in thee.
Garth, in majestic numbers, to the stars
Shall raise mock heroes, and fantastic wars;
Like the young spreading laurel, Pope, thy name
Shoots up with strength, and rises into fame;
With Philips shall the peaceful valleys ring,
And Britain hear a second Spenser sing.
That much-lov'd youth, whom Utrecht's walls confine,
To Bristol's praises shall his Strafford's join:

He too, from whom attentive Oxford draws
Rules for just thinking, and poetic laws,
To growing bards his learned aid shall lend,
The strictest critic and the kindest friend.
Ev'n mine, a bashful Muse, whose rude essays
Scarce hope for pardon, not aspire to praise,
Cherish'd by you, in time may grow to fame,
And mine survive with Bristol's glorious name.
  Fir'd with the views this glittering scene displays,
And smit with passion for my country's praise,
My artless reed attempts this lofty theme,
Where sacred Isis rolls her ancient stream;
In cloister'd domes, the great Philippa's pride,
Where Learning blooms, while Fame and Worth preside,
Where the fifth Henry arts and arms was taught,
And Edward form'd his Cressy, yet unfought,
Where laurell'd bards have struck the warbling strings,
The seat of sages, and the nurse of kings.
Here thy commands, O Lancaster, inflame
My eager breast to raise the British name,
Urge on my soul, with no ignoble pride,
To woo the Muse, whom Addison enjoy'd,
See that bold swan to Heaven sublimely soar,
Pursue at distance, and his steps adore.

TO MR. ADDISON.

ON HIS OPERA OF ROSAMOND.

...... Ne fortè pudori
Sit tibi Musa lyræ solers, et cantor Apollo.

THE Opera first Italian masters taught,
Enrich'd with songs, but innocent of thought;
Britannia's learned theatre disdains
Melodious trifles, and enervate strains;
And blushes on her injur'd stage to see
Nonsense well-tun'd, and sweet stupidity.
No charms are wanting to thy artful song,
Soft as Corelli, and as Virgil strong.
From words so sweet new grace the notes receive,
And Music borrows helps, she us'd to give.
Thy style hath match'd what ancient Romans knew,
Thy flowing numbers far excel the new.
Their cadence in such easy sound convey'd,
The height of thought may seem superfluous aid;
Yet in such charms the noble thoughts abound,
That needless seem the sweets of easy sound.
Landscapes how gay the bowery grotto yields,
Which thought creates, and lavish fancy builds!

What art can trace the visionary scenes,
The flowery groves, and everlasting greens,
The babbling sounds that mimic echo plays,
The fairy shade, and its eternal maze?
Nature and Art in all their charms combin'd,
And all Elysium to one view confin'd!
No further could imagination roam,
Till Vanbrugh fram'd, and Marlborough rais'd the
dome.
Ten thousand pangs my anxious bosom tear,
When drown'd in tears I see th' imploring fair;
When bards less soft the moving words supply,
A seeming justice dooms the nymph to die;
But here she begs, nor can she beg in vain
(In dirges thus expiring swans complain;)
Each verse so swells expressive of her woes,
And every tear in lines so mournful flows;
We, spite of fame, her fate revers'd believe,
O'erlook her crimes, and think she ought to live.
Let joy salute fair Rosamonda's shade,
And wreaths of myrtle crown the lovely maid,
While now perhaps with Dido's ghost she roves,
And hears and tells the story of their loves,
Alike they mourn, alike they bless their fate,
Since Love, which made them wretched, makes
them great.
Nor longer that relentless doom bemoan,
Which gain'd a Virgil, and an Addison.
Accept, great monarch of the British lays,
The tribute song an humble subject pays.

So tries the artless lark her early flight,
And soars, to hail the god of verse and light.
Unrivall'd, as unmatch'd, be still thy fame,
And thy own laurels shade thy envy'd name:
Thy name, the boast of all the tuneful quire,
Shall tremble on the strings of every lyre;
While the charm'd reader with thy thought complies,
Feels corresponding joys or sorrows rise,
And views thy Rosamond with Henry's eyes.

TO THE SAME;

ON HIS TRAGEDY OF CATO.

Too long hath love engross'd Britannia's stage,
And sunk to softness all our tragic rage:
By that alone did empires fall or rise,
And fate depended on a fair-one's eyes:
The sweet infection, mixt with dangerous art,
Debas'd our manhood, while it sooth'd the heart,
You scorn to raise a grief thyself must blame,
Nor from our weakness steal a vulgar fame:
A patriot's fall may justly melt the mind,
And tears flow nobly, shed for all mankind.
How do our souls with generous pleasure glow!
Our hearts exulting, while our eyes o'erflow,

When thy firm hero stands beneath the weight
Of all his sufferings venerably great;
Rome's poor remains still sheltering by his side,
With conscious virtue, and becoming pride!
  The aged oak thus rears his head in air,
His sap exhausted, and his branches bare;
'Midst storms and earthquakes, he maintains his state,
Fixt deep in earth, and fasten'd by his weight:
His naked boughs still lend the shepherds aid,
And his old trunk projects an awful shade.
  Amidst the joys triumphant peace bestows,
Our patriots sadden at his glorious woes;
Awhile they let the world's great business wait,
Anxious for Rome, and sigh for Cato's fate.
Here taught how ancient heroes rose to fame,
Our Britons crowd, and catch the Roman flame,
Where states and senates well might lend an ear,
And kings and priests without a blush appear.
  France boasts no more, but, fearful to engage,
Now first pays homage to her rival's stage,
Hastes to learn thee, and learning shall submit
Alike to British arms, and British wit:
No more she'll wonder, forc'd to do us right,
Who think like Romans, could like Romans fight.
  Thy Oxford smiles this glorious work to see,
And fondly triumphs in a son like thee.
The senates, consuls, and the gods of Rome,
Like old acquaintance at their native home,

In thee we find: each deed, each word exprest,
And every thought that swell'd a Roman breast,
We trace each hint that could thy soul inspire
With Virgil's judgment, and with Lucan's fire;
We know thy worth, and, give us leave to boast,
We most admire, because we know thee most.

THE ROYAL PROGRESS.

When Brunswick first appear'd, each honest heart,
Intent on verse, disdain'd the rules of art;
For him the songsters, in unmeasur'd odes,
Debas'd Alcides, and dethron'd the gods,
In golden chains the kings of India led,
Or rent the turban from the sultan's head.
One, in old fables, and the pagan strain,
With nymphs and tritons, wafts him o'er the main;
Another draws fierce Lucifer in arms
And fills th' infernal region with alarms;
A third awakes some druid, to foretell
Each future triumph, from his dreary cell.
Exploded fancies! that in vain deceive,
While the mind nauseates what she can't believe.
My Muse th' expected hero shall pursue
From clime to clime, and keep him still in view;

His shining march describe in faithful lays
Content to paint him, nor presume to praise;
Their charms, if charms they have, the truth supplies,
And from the theme unlabour'd beauties rise.
By longing nations for the throne design'd,
And call'd to guard the rights of human-kind;
With secret grief his god-like soul repines,
And Britain's crown with joyless lustre shines,
While prayers and tears his destin'd progress stay,
And crowds of mourners choke their sovereign's way.
Not so he march'd, when hostile squadrons stood
In scenes of death, and fir'd his generous blood;
When his hot courser paw'd th' Hungarian plain,
And adverse legions stood the shock in vain.
His frontiers past, the Belgian bounds he views,
And cross the level fields his march pursues.
Here, pleas'd the land of freedom to survey,
He greatly scorns the thirst of boundless sway.
O'er the thin soil, with silent joy, he spies
Transplanted woods, and borrow'd verdure rise;
Where every meadow, won with toil and blood
From haughty tyrants and the raging flood,
With fruit and flowers the careful hind supplies,
And clothes the marshes in a rich disguise.
Such wealth for frugal hands doth Heaven decree,
And such thy gifts, celestial Liberty!
Through stately towns, and many a fertile plain,
The pomp advances to the neighbouring main,

Whole nations crowd around with joyful cries,
And view the hero with insatiate eyes.
In Haga's towers he waits till eastern gales
Propitious rise to swell the British sails.
Hither the fame of England's monarch brings
The vows and friendships of the neighbouring kings;
Mature in wisdom, his extensive mind
Takes in the blended interests of mankind,
The world's great patriot. Calm thy anxious breast,
Secure in him, O Europe, take thy rest;
Henceforth thy kingdoms shall remain confin'd
By rocks or streams, the mounds which Heaven design'd;
The Alps their new-made monarch shall restrain,
Nor shall thy hills, Pirene, rise in vain.
But see! to Britain's isle the squadrons stand,
And leave the sinking towers, and lessening land.
The royal bark bounds o'er the floating plain,
Breaks through the billows, and divides the main.
O'er the vast deep, great monarch, dart thine eyes,
A watery prospect bounded by the skies:
Ten thousand vessels, from ten thousand shores,
Bring gums and gold, and either India's stores:
Behold the tributes hastening to thy throne,
And see the wide horizon all thy own.
Still is it thine; though now the cheerful crew
Hail Albion's cliffs; just whitening to the view.

Before the wind with swelling sails they ride,
Till Thames receives them in his opening tide.
The monarch hears the thundering peals around,
From trembling woods and echoing hills rebound,
Nor misses yet, amid the deafening train,
The roarings of the hoarse-resounding main.
  As in the flood he sails, from either side
He views his kingdom in his rural pride;
A various scene the wide-spread landscape yields,
O'er rich enclosures and luxuriant fields;
A lowing herd each fertile pasture fills,
And distant flocks stray o'er a thousand hills.
Fair Greenwich, hid in woods, with new delight,
Shade above shade, now rises to the sight;
His woods ordain'd to visit every shore,
And guard the island which they grac'd before.
  The sun now rolling down the western way,
A blaze of fires renews the fading day;
Unnumber'd barks the regal barge infold,
Brightening the twilight with its beamy gold;
Less thick the finny shoals, a countless fry,
Before the whale or kingly dolphin fly.
In one vast shout he seeks the crowded strand,
And in a peal of thunder gains the land.
  Welcome, great stranger, to our longing eyes,
Oh! king desir'd, adopted Albion cries.
For thee the East breath'd out a prosperous breeze,
Bright were the suns, and gently swell'd the seas.
Thy presence did each doubtful heart compose,
And factions wonder'd that they once were foes.

That joyful day they lost each hostile name,
The same their aspect, and their voice the same.
So two fair twins, whose features were design'd
At one soft moment in the mother's mind,
Show each the other with reflected grace,
And the same beauties bloom in either face;
The puzzled strangers which is which inquire;
Delusion grateful to the smiling sire.
From that fair hill,[1] where hoary sages boast
To name the stars, and count the heavenly host,
By the next dawn doth great Augusta rise,
Proud town! the noblest scene beneath the skies.
O'er Thames her thousand spires their lustre shed,
And a vast navy hides his ample bed,
A floating forest. From the distant strand
A line of golden cars strikes o'er the land:
Britannia's peers in pomp and rich array,
Before their king triumphant, lead the way.
Far as the eye can reach, the gaudy train,
A bright procession, shines along the plain.
So, haply through the heaven's wide pathless ways
A comet draws a long extended blaze;
From east to west burns through the ethereal frame,
And half heaven's convex glitters with the flame.
Now to the regal towers securely brought,
He plans Britannia's glories in his thought;

[1] Mr. Flamstead's house.

Resumes the delegated power he gave,
Rewards the faithful, and restores the brave.
Whom shall the Muse from out the shining throng,
Select, to heighten and adorn her song?
Thee, Halifax. To thy capacious mind,
O man approv'd, is Britain's wealth consign'd.
Her coin, while Nassau fought, debas'd and rude,
By thee in beauty and in truth renew'd,
An arduous work! again thy charge we see,
And thy own care once more returns to thee.
O! form'd in every scene to awe and please,
Mix wit with pomp, and dignity with ease:
Though call'd to shine aloft, thou wilt not scorn
To smile on arts thyself did once adorn:
For this thy name succeeding time shall praise,
And envy less thy garter, than thy bays.
  The Muse, if fir'd with thy enlivening beams,
Perhaps shall aim at more exalted themes,
Record our monarch in a nobler strain,
And sing the opening wonders of his reign;
Bright Carolina's heavenly beauties trace,
Her valiant consort, and his blooming race.
A train of kings their fruitful love supplies,
A glorious scene to Albion's ravish'd eyes;
Who sees by Brunswick's hand her sceptre sway'd,
And through his line from age to age convey'd.

AN IMITATION OF THE PROPHECY OF NEREUS.

FROM HORACE. BOOK II. ODE XV.

Dicam insigne, recens, adhuc
  Indictum ore alio: non secus in jugis
Ex somnis stupet Euias
  Hebrum prospiciens, et nive candidam
Thracen, ac pede barbaro
  Lustratam Rhodopen. HOR.

As Mar his round one morning took,
(Whom some call earl, and some call duke,)
And his new brethren of the blade,
Shivering with fear and frost, survey'd,
On Perth's bleak hills he chanc'd to spy
An aged wizard six foot high,
With bristled hair and visage blighted,
Wall-ey'd, bare-haunch'd, and second-sighted.
  The grizzly sage, in thought profound
Beheld the chief with back so round,
Then roll'd his eye-balls to and fro
O'er his paternal hills of snow,
And into these tremendous speeches
Broke forth the prophet without breeches.

"Into what ills betray'd, by thee,
This ancient kingdom do I see!
Her realms unpeopled and forlorn!
Wae's me! that ever thou wert born!
Proud English loons (our clans o'ercome)
On Scottish pads shall amble home;
I see them drest in bonnets blue;
(The spoils of thy rebellious crew;)
I see the target cast away,
And chequer'd plaid become their prey,
The chequer'd plaid to make a gown
For many a lass in London town.
"In vain thy hungry mountaineers
Come forth in all thy warlike geers,
The shield, the pistol, dirk, and dagger,
In which they daily wont to swagger,
And oft have sally'd out to pillage
The hen-roosts of some peaceful village,
Or, while their neighbours were asleep,
Have carry'd off a low-land sheep.
"What boots thy high-born host of beggars,
Mac-leans, Mac-kenzies, and Mac-gregors,
With popish cutthroats, perjur'd ruffians,
And Foster's troop of ragamuffins?
"In vain thy lads around thee bandy,
Inflam'd with bagpipe and with brandy,
Doth not bold Sutherland the trusty,
With heart so true, and voice so rusty,
(A loyal soul,) thy troops affright,
While hoarsely he demands the fight?

Dost thou not generous Ilay dread,
The bravest hand, the wisest head?
Undaunted dost thou hear th' alarms
Of hoary Athol sheath'd in arms?
"Douglass, who draws his lineage down
From Thanes and peers of high renown,
Fiery, and young, and uncontroll'd,
With knights, and squires, and barons bold,
(His noble household-band) advances,
And on the milk-white courser prances.
Thee Forfar to the combat dares,
Grown swarthy in Iberian wars;
And Monroe, kindled into rage,
Sourly defies thee to engage;
He'll rout thy foot, though ne'er so many,
And horse to boot—if thou hadst any.
"But see Argyll, with watchful eyes,
Lodg'd in his deep entrenchments lies,
Couch'd like a lion in thy way,
He waits to spring upon his prey;
While, like a herd of timorous deer,
Thy army shakes and pants with fear,
Led by their doughty general's skill,
From frith to frith, from hill to hill.
"Is thus thy haughty promise paid
That to the Chevalier was made,
When thou didst oaths and duty barter,
For dukedom, generalship, and garter?
Three moons thy Jemmy shall command,
With Highland sceptre in his hand,

Too good for his pretended birth,
..Then down shall fall the king of Perth.
"'Tis so decreed: for George shall reign,
And traitors be forsworn in vain.
Heaven shall for ever on him smile,
And bless him still with an Argyll.
While thou, pursued by vengeful foes,
Condemn'd to barren rocks and snows,
And hinder'd passing Inverlocky,
Shall burn the clan, and curse poor Jocky."

AN EPISTLE

FROM A LADY IN ENGLAND TO A GENTLEMAN AT AVIGNON.

To thee, dear rover, and thy vanquish'd friends,
The health, she wants, thy gentle Chloe sends.
Though much you suffer, think I suffer more,
Worse than an exile on my native shore.
Companions in your master's flight you roam,
Unenvy'd by your haughty foes at home;
For ever near the royal outlaw's side
You share his fortunes, and his hopes divide,
On glorious schemes, and thoughts of empire dwell,
And with imaginary titles swell.

Say, for thou know'st I own his sacred line,
The passive doctrine, and the right divine,
Say, what new succours does the chief prepare?
The strength of armies? or the force of prayer?
Does he from Heaven or Earth his hopes derive?
From saints departed, or from priests alive?
Nor saints nor priests can Brunswick's troops withstand,
And beads drop useless through the zealot's hand;
Heaven to our vows may future kingdoms owe,
But skill and courage win the crowns below.
Ere to thy cause, and thee, my heart inclin'd,
Or love to party had seduc'd my mind,
In female joys I took a dull delight,
Slept all the morn, and punted half the night:
But now, with fears and public cares possest,
The church, the church, for ever breaks my rest.
The postboy on my pillow I explore,
And sift the news of every foreign shore,
Studious to find new friends, and new allies;
What armies march from Sweden in disguise;
How Spain prepares her banners to unfold,
And Rome deals out her blessings, and her gold:
Then o'er the map my finger, taught to stray,
Cross many a region marks the winding way;
From sea to sea, from realm to realm I rove,
And grow a mere geographer by love:
But still Avignon, and the pleasing coast
That holds thee banish'd, claims my care the most:

Oft on the well-known spot I fix my eyes,
And span the distance that between us lies.
Let not our James, though foil'd in arms, despair,
Whilst on his side he reckons half the fair:
In Britain's lovely isle a shining throng
War in his cause, a thousand beauties strong.
Th' unthinking victors vainly boast their powers;
Be theirs the musket, while the tongue is ours.
We reason with such fluency and fire,
The beaux we baffle, and the learned tire,
Against her prelates plead the church's cause,
And from our judges vindicate the laws.
Then mourn not, hapless prince, thy kingdoms lost;
A crown, though late, thy sacred brows may boast;
Heaven seems through us thy empire to decree;
Those who win hearts, have given their hearts to thee.
Hast thou not heard that when, profusely gay,
Our well-drest rivals grac'd their sovereign's day,
We stubborn damsels met the public view
In loathsome wormwood, and repenting rue?
What Whig but trembled, when our spotless band
In virgin roses whiten'd half the land!
Who can forget what fears the foe possest,
When oaken-boughs mark'd every loyal breast!
Less scar'd than Medway's stream the Norman stood,
When cross the plain he spy'd a marching wood,
Till, near at hand, a gleam of swords betray'd
The youth of Kent beneath its wandering shade?

Those who the succours of the fair despise,
May find that we have nails as well as eyes.
Thy female bards, O prince by fortune crost,
At least more courage than thy men can boast:
Our sex has dar'd the mug-house chiefs to meet,
And purchas'd fame in many a well-fought street.
From Drury-Lane, the region of renown,
The land of love, the Paphos of the town,
Fair patriots sallying oft have put to flight
With all their poles the guardians of the night,
And bore, with screams of triumph, to their side
The leader's staff in all its painted pride.
Nor fears the hawker in her warbling note
To vend the discontented statesman's thought,
Though red with stripes, and recent from the thong,
Sore smitten for the love of sacred song,
The tuneful sisters still pursue their trade,
Like Philomela darkling in the shade.
Poor Trott attends, forgetful of a fare,
And hums in concert o'er his easy chair.

Meanwhile, regardless of the royal cause,
His sword for James no brother sovereign draws
The pope himself, surrounded with alarms,
To France his bulls, to Corfu sends his arms,
And though he hears his darling son's complaint,
Can hardly spare one tutelary saint,
But lists them all to guard his own abodes,
And into ready money coins his gods.
The dauntless Swede, pursued by vengeful foes,
Scarce keeps his own hereditary snows;

Nor must the friendly roof of kind Lorrain
With feasts regale our garter'd youth again.
Safe, Bar-le-Duc, within thy silent grove
The pheasant now may perch, the hare may rove:
The knight, who aims unerring from afar,
Th' adventurous knight, now quits the sylvan war:
Thy brinded boars may slumber undismay'd,
Or grunt secure beneath the chestnut shade.
Inconstant Orleans (still we mourn the day,
That trusted Orleans with imperial sway)
Far o'er the Alps our helpless monarch sends,
Far from the call of his desponding friends.
Such are the terms, to gain Britannia's grace!
And such the terrors of the Brunswick race!
Was it for this the Sun's whole lustre fail'd,
And sudden midnight o'er the Moon prevail'd!
For this did Heaven display to mortal eyes
Aërial knights and combats in the skies!
Was it for this Northumbrian streams look'd red!
And Thames driv'n backward show'd his secret bed!
False auguries! th' insulting victor's scorn!
Ev'n our own prodigies against us turn!
O portents construed on our side in vain!
Let never Tory trust eclipse again!
Run clear, ye fountains! be at peace, ye skies!
And, Thames, henceforth to thy green borders rise!
To Rome then must the royal wanderer go,
And fall a suppliant at the papal toe?

His life in sloth inglorious must he wear,
One half in luxury, and one in prayer?
His mind perhaps at length debauch'd with ease,
The proffer'd purple and the hat may please.
Shall he, whose ancient patriarchal race
To mighty Nimrod in one line we trace,
In solemn conclave sit, devoid of thought,
And poll for points of faith his trusty vote!
Be summon'd to his stall in time of need,
And with his casting suffrage fix a creed!
Shall he in robes on stated days appear,
And English heretics curse once a year!
Garnet and Faux shall he with prayers invoke,
And beg that Smithfield piles once more may smoke!
Forbid it, Heaven! my soul, to fury wrought,
Turns almost Hanoverian at the thought.
From James and Rome I feel my heart decline,
And fear, O Brunswick, 'twill be wholly thine;
Yet still his share thy rival will contest,
And still the double claim divides my breast.
The fate of James with pitying eyes I view,
And wish my homage were not Brunswick's due:
To James my passion and my weakness guide,
But reason sways me to the victor's side.
Though griev'd I speak it, let the truth appear!
You know my language, and my heart, sincere.
In vain did falsehood his fair fame disgrace?
What force had falsehood, when he show'd his face!

In vain to war our boastful clans were led;
Heaps driv'n on heaps, in the dire shock they fled:
France shuns his wrath, nor raises to our shame
A second Dunkirk in another name:
In Britain's funds their wealth all Europe throws:
And up the Thames the world's abundance flows:
Spite of feign'd fears and artificial cries,
The pious town sees fifty churches rise:
The hero triumphs as his worth is known,
And sits more firmly on his shaken throne.
To my sad thought no beam of hope appears
Through the long prospect of succeeding years.
The son, aspiring to his father's fame,
Shows all his sire: another and the same.
He, blest in lovely Carolina's arms,
To future ages propagates her charms:
With pain and joy at strife, I often trace
The mingled parents in each daughter's face;
Half sickening at the sight, too well I spy
The father's spirit through the mother's eye:
In vain new thoughts of rage I entertain,
And strive to hate their innocence in vain.
O princess! happy by thy foes confest!
Blest in thy husband! in thy children blest!
As they from thee, from them new beauties born,
While Europe lasts, shall Europe's thrones adorn.
Transplanted to each court, in times to come,
Thy smile celestial and unfading bloom,
Great Austria's sons with softer lines shall grace,
And smooth the frowns of Bourbon's haughty race.

The fair descendants of thy sacred bed,
Wide-branching o'er the western world shall spread,
Like the fam'd Banian tree, whose pliant shoot
To earthward bending of itself takes root,
Till, like their mother plant, ten thousand stand
In verdant arches on the fertile land;
Beneath her shade the tawny Indians rove,
Or hunt, at large, through the wide echoing grove.
O thou, to whom these mournful lines I send,
My promis'd husband, and my dearest friend;
Since Heaven appoints this favour'd race to reign,
And blood has drench'd the Scottish fields in vain;
Must I be wretched, and thy flight partake?
Or wilt not thou, for thy lov'd Chloe's sake,
Tir'd out at length, submit to fate's decree?
If not to Brunswick, O return to me!
Prostrate before the victor's mercy bend:
What spares whole thousands, may to thee extend.
Should blinded friends thy doubtful conduct blame,
Great Brunswick's virtue shall secure thy fame:
Say these invite thee to approach his throne,
And own the monarch, Heaven vouchsafes to own:
The world, convinc'd thy reasons will approve;
Say this to them; but swear to me 'twas love.

AN ODE,

OCCASIONED BY HIS EXCELLENCY THE EARL OF STANHOPE'S VOYAGE TO FRANCE, 1718.

Idem
Pacis eras mediusque belli. HOR.

FAIR daughter once of Windsor's woods!
In safety o'er the rolling floods,
Britannia's boast and darling care,
Big with the fate of Europe, bear.
May winds propitious on his way
The minister of peace convey;
Nor rebel wave, nor rising storm,
Great George's liquid realms deform.

Our vows are heard. Thy crowded sails
Already swell with western gales;
Already Albion's coast retires,
And Calais multiplies her spires:
At length has royal Orleans prest,
With open arms, the well-known guest;
Before in sacred friendship join'd,
And now in counsels for mankind:

Whilst his clear schemes our patriot shows,
And plans the threaten'd world's repose,
They fix each haughty monarch's doom,
And bless whole ages yet to come.
Henceforth great Brunswick shall decree
What flag must awe the Tyrrhene sea;
From whom the Tuscan grape shall glow,
And fruitful Arethusa flow.

See in firm leagues with Thames combine
The Seine, the Maese, and distant Rhine!
Nor, Ebro, let thy single rage
With half the warring world engage.
Oh! call to mind thy thousands slain,
And Almanara's fatal plain;
While yet the Gallic terrours sleep,
Nor Britain thunders from the deep.

PROLOGUE

TO THE UNIVERSITY OF OXFORD, 1713.

WHAT kings henceforth shall reign, what states be free,
Is fixt at length by Anna's just decree:
Whose brows the Muse's sacred wreath shall fit
Is left to you, the arbiters of wit.

With beating hearts the rival poets wait,
Till you, Athenians, shall decide their fate;
Secure, when to these learned seats they come,
Of equal judgment, and impartial doom.
  Poor is the player's fame, whose whole renown
Is but the praise of a capricious town;
While, with mock-majesty, and fancy'd power,
He struts in robes, the monarch of an hour.
Oft wide of nature must he act a part,
Make love in tropes, in bombast break his heart:
In turn and simile resign his breath,
And rhyme and quibble in the pangs of death.
We blush, when plays like these receive applause;
And laugh, in secret, at the tears we cause;
With honest scorn our own success disdain,
A worthless honour, and in glorious gain.
  No trifling scenes at Oxford shall appear;
Well, what we blush to act, may you to hear.
To you our fam'd, our standard plays we bring,
The work of poets, whom you taught to sing:
Though crown'd with fame, they dare not think it
Nor take the laurel till bestow'd by you. [due,
Great Cato's self, the glory of the stage,
Who charms, corrects, exalts, and fires the age,
Begs here he may be try'd by Roman laws;
To you, O fathers, he submits his cause;
He rests not in the people's general voice,
Till you, the senate, have confirm'd his choice.
  Fine is the secret, delicate the art,
To wind the passions, and command the heart;

For fancy'd ills to force our tears to flow,
And make the generous soul in love with woe;
To raise the shades of heroes to our view;
Rebuild fall'n empires, and old time renew.
How hard the task! how rare the godlike rage!
None should presume to dictate for the stage,
But such as boast a great extensive mind,
Enrich'd by Nature, and by Art refin'd;
Who from the ancient stores their knowledge bring,
And tasted early of the Muses' spring.
May none pretend upon her throne to sit,
But such as, sprung from you, are born to wit:
Chosen by the mob, their lawless claim we slight:
Yours is the old hereditary right.

THOUGHTS

OCCASIONED BY THE SIGHT OF AN ORIGINAL PICTURE OF KING CHARLES I. TAKEN AT THE TIME OF HIS TRIAL.

INSCRIBED TO GEORGE CLARKE, ESQ.

. . . . Animum pictura pascit inani
Multa gemens, largoque humectat flumine vultum.

VIRG.

CAN this be he! could Charles, the good, the great,
Be sunk by Heaven to such a dismal state!
How meagre, pale, neglected, worn with care!
What steady sadness, and august despair!
In those sunk eyes the grief of years I trace,
And sorrow seems acquainted with that face.
Tears, which his heart disdain'd, from me o'erflow,
Thus to survey God's substitute below,
In solemn anguish, and majestic woe.
When spoil'd of empire by unhallow'd hands,
Sold by his slaves, and held in impious bands;
Rent from, what oft had sweeten'd anxious life,
His helpless children, and his bosom wife;
Doom'd for the faith, plebeian rage to stand,
And fall a victim for the guilty land;

Then thus was seen, abandon'd and forlorn,
The king, the father, and the saint to mourn.—
How could'st thou, artist, then thy skill display?
Thy steady hands thy savage heart betray:
Near thy bold work the stunn'd spectators faint,
Nor see unmov'd, what thou unmov'd could'st paint.
What brings to mind each various scene of woe,
Th' insulting judge, the solemn-mocking show,
The horrid sentence, and accursed blow.
Where then, just Heaven, was thy unactive hand,
Thy idle thunder, and thy lingering brand!
Thy adamantine shield, thy angel wings,
And the great genii of anointed kings!
Treason and fraud shall thus the stars regard;
And injur'd virtue meet this sad reward!
So sad, none like, can Time's old records tell,
Though Pompey bled, and poor Darius fell.
All names but one too low—that one too high:
All parallels are wrongs, or blasphemy.
O Power Supreme! How secret are thy ways!
Yet man, vain man, would trace the mystic maze,
With foolish wisdom, arguing, charge his God,
His balance hold, and guide his angry rod;
New-mould the spheres, and mend the sky's design,
And sound th' immense with his short scanty line.
Do thou, my soul, the destin'd period wait,
When God shall solve the dark decrees of fate,
His now unequal dispensations clear,
And make all wise and beautiful appear;

When suffering saints aloft in beams shall glow,
And prosperous traitors gnash their teeth below.
Such boding thoughts did guilty conscience dart,
A pledge of Hell to dying Cromwell's heart:
Then this pale image seem'd t' invade his room,
Gaz'd him to stone, and warn'd him to the tomb.
While thunders roll, and nimble lightnings play,
And the storm wings his spotted soul away.
A blast more bounteous ne'er did Heaven command
To scatter blessings o'er the British land.
Not that more kind, which dash'd the pride of Spain,
And whirl'd her crush'd Armada round the main;
Not those more kind, which guide our floating towers,
Waft gums and gold, and made far India ours:
That only kinder, which to Britain's shore
Did mitres, crowns, and Stuart's race restore,
Renew'd the church, revers'd the kingdom's doom,
And brought with Charles an Anna yet to come.
O Clarke, to whom a Stuart trusts her reign
O'er Albion's fleets, and delegates the main;
Dear, as the faith thy loyal heart hath sworn,
Transmit this piece to ages yet unborn.
This sight shall damp the raging ruffian's breast,
The poison spill, and half-drawn sword arrest;
To soft compassion stubborn traitors bend,
And, one destroy'd, a thousand kings defend.

A FRAGMENT

OF A POEM ON HUNTING.

Dona cano divûm lætas venantibus artes,
Auspicio, Diana, tuo—— GRATIUS.

HORSES and hounds, their care, their various race,
The numerous beasts, that range the rural chase,
The huntsman's chosen scenes, his friendly stars,
The laws and glory of the sylvan wars,
I first in British verse presume to raise;
A venturous rival of the Roman praise.
Let me, chaste queen of woods, thy aid obtain,
Bring here thy light-foot nymphs, and sprightly train:
If oft, o'er lawns, thy care prevents the day
To rouse the foe, and press the bounding prey,
Woo thine own Phœbus in the task to join,
And grant me genius for the bold design.
In this soft shade, O soothe the warrior's fire,
And fit his bow-string to the trembling lyre;
And teach, while thus their arts and arms we sing,
The groves to echo, and the vales to ring.
* * * * * * * *
* * * * * * *

Thy care be first the various gifts to trace,
The minds and genius of the latrant race.
In powers distinct the different clans excel,
In sight, or swiftness, or sagacious smell;
By wiles ungenerous some surprise the prey,
And some by courage win the doubtful day.
Seest thou the gaze-hound! how with glance severe
From the close herd he marks the destin'd deer!
How every nerve the greyhound's stretch displays,
The hare preventing in her airy maze;
The luckless prey how treacherous tumblers gain,
And dauntless wolf-dogs shake the lion's mane;
O'er all, the bloodhound boasts superior skill,
To scent, to view, to turn, and boldly kill!
His fellows' vain alarms rejects with scorn,
True to the master's voice, and learned horn.
His nostrils oft, if ancient Fame sing true,
Trace the sly felon through the tainted dew;
Once snuff'd, he follows with unalter'd aim,
Nor odours lure him from the chosen game;
Deep mouth'd he thunders, and inflam'd he views,
Springs on relentless, and to death pursues.
Some hounds of manners vile, (nor less we find
Of fops in hounds, than in the reasoning kind,)
Puff'd with conceit run gladding o'er the plain,
And from the scent divert the wiser train;
For the foe's footsteps fondly snuff their own,
And mar the music with their senseless tone;

Start at the starting prey, or rustling wind,
And, hot at first, inglorious lag behind.
A sauntering tribe! may such my foes disgrace!
Give me, ye gods, to breed the nobler race.
Nor grieve thou to attend, while truths unknown
I sing, and make Athenian arts our own.
Dost thou in hounds aspire to deathless fame?
Learn well their lineage and their ancient stem.
Each tribe with joy old rustic heralds trace,
And sing the chosen worthies of their race;
How his sire's features in the son were spy'd,
When Die was made the vigorous Ringwood's bride.
Less sure thick lips the fate of Austria doom,
Or eagle noses rul'd almighty Rome.
Good shape to various kinds old bards confine,
Some praise the Greek, and some the Roman line;
And dogs to beauty make as differing claims,
As Albion's nymphs, and India's jetty dames.
Immense to name their lands, to mark their bounds,
And paint the thousand families of hounds:
First count the sands, the drops where oceans flow,
Or Gauls by Marlborough sent to shades below,
The task be mine, to teach Britannia's swains,
My much-lov'd country, and my native plains.
Such be the dog, I charge, thou mean'st to train,
His back is crooked, and his belly plain,
Of fillet stretch'd, and huge of haunch behind,
A tapering tail, that nimbly cuts the wind;

Truss-thigh'd, straight-ham'd, and fox-like form'd his paw,
Large-legg'd, dry sol'd, and of protended claw.
His flat, wide nostrils snuff the savoury steam,
And from his eyes he shoots pernicious gleam;
Middling his head, and prone to earth his view,
With ears and chest that dash the morning dew:
He best to stem the flood, to leap the bound,
And charm the Dryads with his voice profound;
To pay large tribute to his weary lord,
And crown the sylvan hero's plenteous board.
The matron bitch whose womb shall best produce
The hopes and fortune of th' illustrious house,
Deriv'd from noble, but from foreign seed,
For various nature loaths incestuous breed,
Is like the sire throughout. Nor yet displease
Large flanks, and ribs, to give the teemer ease.
In Spring let loose thy pairs. Then all things prove
The stings of pleasure, and the pangs of love:
Ethereal Jove then glads, with genial showers,
Earth's mighty womb, and strews her lap with flowers.
Hence juices mount, and buds, embolden'd, try
More kindly breezes, and a softer sky:
Kind Venus revels. Hark! on every bough,
In lulling strains the feather'd warblers woo.
Fell tigers soften in th' infectious flames,
And lions fawning, court their brinded dames:

Great Love pervades the deep; to please his mate,
The whale, in gambols, moves his monstrous weight,
Heav'd by his wayward mirth old Ocean roars,
And scatter'd navies bulge on distant shores.
All Nature smiles; come now, nor fear, my love,
To taste the odours of the woodbine grove,
To pass the evening glooms in harmless play,
And, sweetly swearing, languish life away.
An altar, bound with recent flowers, I rear
To thee, best season of the various year;
All hail! such days in beauteous order ran,
So swift, so sweet, when first the world began,
In Eden's bowers, when man's great sire assign'd
The names and natures of the brutal kind.
Then lamb and lion friendly walk'd their round,
And hares, undaunted, lick'd the fondling hound;
Wondrous to tell! but when, with luckless hand,
Our daring mother broke the sole command,
Then Want and Envy brought their meagre train,
Then Wrath came down, and Death had leave to reign:
Hence foxes earth'd, and wolves abhorr'd the day,
And hungry churls ensnar'd the nightly prey;
Rude arts at first; but witty Want refin'd
The huntsman's wiles, and Famine form'd the mind.
Bold Nimrod first the lion's trophies wore,
The panther bound, and lanc'd the bristling boar;
He taught to turn the hare, to bay the deer,
And wheel the courser in his mid career:

Ah! had he there restrain'd his tyrant hand!
Let me, ye powers, an humbler wreath demand.
No pomps I ask, which crowns and sceptres yield,
Nor dangerous laurels in the dusty field;
Fast by the forest, and the limpid spring,
Give me the warfare of the woods to sing,
To breed my whelps, and healthful press the game,
A mean, inglorious, but a guiltless name.
  And now thy female bears in ample womb
The bane of hares, and triumphs yet to come.
No sport, I ween, nor blast of sprightly horn,
Should tempt me then to hurt the whelps unborn.
Unlock'd, in covers let her freely run,
To range thy courts, and bask before the sun;
Near thy full table let the favourite stand,
Strok'd by thy son's, or blooming daughter's hand.
Caress, indulge, by arts the matron bride,
T' improve her breed, and teem a vigorous tribe.
  So, if small things may be compar'd with great,
And Nature's works the Muses imitate,
So stretch'd in shades, and lull'd by murmuring streams,
Great Maro's breast receiv'd the heavenly dreams.
Recluse, serene, the musing prophet lay,
Till thoughts in embryo, ripening, burst their way.
Hence bees in state, and foaming coursers come,
Heroes, and gods, and walls of lofty Rome.

* * * * * * * * * * * *

* * * * * * * * * * *

TO APOLLO MAKING LOVE.

FROM MONSIEUR FONTENELLE.

I AM, cry'd Apollo, when Daphne he woo'd,
And panting for breath, the coy virgin pursued,
When his wisdom, in manner most ample, exprest,
The long list of the graces his godship possest:

I'm the god of sweet song, and inspirer of lays;
Nor for lays, nor sweet song, the fair fugitive stays;
I'm the god of the harp—stop my fairest—in vain;
Nor the harp, nor the harper could fetch her again.

Every plant, every flower, and their virtues I know,
God of light I'm above, and of physic below:
At the dreadful word physic, the nymph fled more fast;
At the fatal word physic she doubled her haste.

Thou fond god of wisdom, then, alter thy phrase,
Bid her view the young bloom, and thy ravishing rays,
Tell her less of thy knowledge, and more of thy charms,
And, my life for't, the damsel will fly to thy arms.

THE FATAL CURIOSITY.

Much had I heard of fair Francelia's name,
The lavish praises of the babbler, Fame:
I thought them such, and went prepar'd to pry,
And trace the charmer, with a critic's eye;
Resolv'd to find some fault, before unspy'd,
And disappointed, if but satisfy'd.
  Love pierc'd the vassal heart, that durst rebel,
And where a judge was meant, a victim fell:
On those dear eyes, with sweet perdition gay,
I gaz'd, at once, my pride and soul away;
All o'er I felt the luscious poison run,
And, in a look, the hasty conquest won.
  Thus the fond moth around the taper plays,
And sports and flutters near the treacherous blaze;
Ravish'd with joy, he wings his eager flight,
Nor dreams of ruin in so clear a light;
He tempts his fate, and courts a glorious doom,
A bright destruction, and a shining tomb.

TO A LADY:

WITH A DESCRIPTION OF THE PHENIX.

Lavish of wit, and bold, appear the lines,
Where Claudian's genius in the Phenix shines;
A thousand ways each brilliant point is turn'd,
And the gay poem, like its theme, adorn'd:
A tale more strange ne'er grac'd the poet's art,
Nor e'er did fiction play so wild a part.
Each fabled charm in matchless Cælia meets,
The heavenly colours, and ambrosial sweets;
Her virgin bosom chaster fires supplies,
And beams more piercing guard her kindred eyes.
O'erflowing with th' imagin'd wonder drew,
But fertile fancy ne'er can reach the true.
Now buds your youth, your cheeks their bloom disclose,
The untainted lily, and unfolding rose;
Ease in your mien, and sweetness in your face,
You speak a Syren, and you move a Grace;
Nor time shall urge these beauties to decay,
While virtue gives, what years shall steal away:
The fair, whose youth can boast the worth of age,
In age shall with the charms of youth engage;
In every change still lovely, still the same,
A fairer Phenix in a purer flame.

A DESCRIPTION OF THE PHENIX.

FROM CLAUDIAN.

In utmost ocean lies a lovely isle,
Where Spring still blooms, and greens for ever smile,
Which sees the Sun put on his first array,
And hears his panting steeds bring on the day;
When, from the deep, they rush with rapid force,
And whirl aloft, to run their glorious course;
When first appear the ruddy streaks of light,
And glimmering beams dispel the parting night.
In these soft shades, unprest by human feet,
The happy Phenix keeps his balmy seat,
Far from the world disjoin'd; he reigns alone,
Alike the empire, and its king unknown.
A godlike bird! whose endless round of years
Outlasts the stars, and tires the circling spheres;
Not us'd like vulgar birds to eat his fill,
Or drink the crystal of the murmuring rill;
But fed with warmth from Titan's purer ray,
And slak'd by streams which eastern seas convey;
Still he renews his life in these abodes,
Contemns the power of Fate, and mates the gods.

His fiery eyes shoot forth a glittering ray,
And round his head ten thousand glories play;
High on his crest, a star celestial bright
Divides the darkness with its piercing light;
His legs are stain'd with purple's lively dye,
His azure wings the fleeting winds outfly;
Soft plumes of cheerful blue his limbs infold,
Enrich'd with spangles, and bedropt with gold.
Begot by none himself, begetting none,
Sire of himself he is, and of himself the son;
His life in fruitful death renews his date,
And kind destruction but prolongs his fate:
Ev'n in the grave new strength his limbs receive,
And on the funeral pile begin to live.
For when a thousand times the summer Sun
His bending race has on the zodiac run,
And when as oft the vernal signs have roll'd,
As oft the wintery brought the numbing cold;
Then drops the bird, worn out with aged cares,
And bends beneath the mighty load of years.
So falls the stately pine, that proudly grew,
The shade and glory of the mountain's brow.
When pierc'd by blasts, and spouting clouds o'er-
It, slowly sinking, nods its tottering head, [spread.
Part dies by winds, and part by sickly rains,
And wasting age destroys the poor remains.
Then, as the silver empress of the night,
O'erclouded, glimmers in a fainter light,
So froz'n with age, and shut from light's supplies,
In lazy rounds scarce roll his feeble eyes,

And those fleet wings, for strength and speed re-
nown'd,
Scarce rear th' inactive lumber from the ground.
Mysterious arts a second time create
The bird, prophetic of approaching fate.
Pil'd on a heap Sabæan herbs he lays,
Parch'd by his sire the Sun's intensest rays;
The pile design'd to form his funeral scene
He wraps in covers of a fragrant green,
And bids his spicy heap at once become
A grave destructive, and a teeming womb.
On the rich bed the dying wonder lies,
Imploring Phœbus with persuasive cries,
To dart upon him in collected rays,
And new-create him in a deadly blaze.
The god beholds the suppliant from afar,
And stops the progress of his heavenly car.
" O thou," says he,, " whom harmless fires shall
burn,
Thy age the flame to second youth shall turn,
An infant's cradle is thy funeral urn. [doom
Thou, on whom Heaven has fix'd th' ambiguous
To live by ruin, and by death to bloom,
Thy life, thy strength, thy lovely form renew,
And with fresh beauties doubly charm the
view."
Thus speaking, 'midst the aromatic bed
A golden beam he tosses from his head;
Swift as desire, the shining ruin flies,
And straight devours the willing sacrifice,

Who hastes to perish in the fertile fire,
Sink into strength, and into life expire.
In flames the circling odours mount on high,
Perfume the air, and glitter in the sky,
The Moon and Stars, amaz'd, retard their flight,
And Nature startles at the doubtful sight;
For, whilst the pregnant urn with fury glows,
The goddess labours with a mother's throes,
Yet joys to cherish, in the friendly flames,
The noblest product of the skill she claims.
Th' enlivening dust its head begins to rear,
And on the ashes sprouting plumes appear;
In the dead bird reviving vigour reigns,
And life returning revels in his veins:
A new-born Phenix starting from the flame,
Obtains at once a son's, and father's name;
And the great change of double life displays,
In the short moment of one transient blaze.
On his new pinions to the Nile he bends,
And to the gods his parent urn commends,
To Egypt bearing, with majestic pride,
The balmy nest, where first he liv'd and dy'd.
Birds of all kinds admire th' unusual sight,
And grace the triumph of his infant flight;
In crowds unnumber'd round their chief they fly,
Oppress the air, and cloud the spacious sky;
Nor dares the fiercest of the winged race
Obstruct his journey through th' ethereal space;
The hawk and eagle useless wars forbear,
Forego their courage, and consent to fear;

The feather'd nations humble homage bring,
And bless the gaudy flight of their ambrosial king.
Less glittering pomp does Parthia's monarch yield,
Commanding legions to the dusty field;
Though sparkling jewels on his helm abound,
And royal gold his awful head surround;
Though rich embroidery paint his purple vest,
And his steed bound in costly trappings drest,
Pleas'd in the battle's dreadful van to ride,
In graceful grandeur, and imperial pride.
Fam'd for the worship of the Sun, there stands
A sacred fane in Egypt's fruitful lands,
Hewn from the Theban mountain's rocky womb
An hundred columns rear the marble dome;
Hither, 'tis said, he brings the precious load,
A grateful offering to the beamy god;
Upon whose altar's consecrated blaze
The seeds and relics of himself he lays,
Whence flaming incense makes the temple shine,
And the glad altars breathe perfumes divine,
The wafted smell to far Pelusium flies,
To cheer old Ocean, and enrich the skies,
With nectar's sweets to make the nations smile,
And scent the seven-fold channels of the Nile.
Thrice happy Phenix! Heaven's peculiar care
Has made thyself thyself's surviving heir;
By Death thy deathless vigour is supply'd,
Which sinks to ruin all the world beside;

Thy age, not thee, assisting Phœbus burns,
And vital flames light up thy funeral urns.
Whate'er events have been, thy eyes survey,
And thou art fixt, while ages roll away;
Thou saw'st when raging Ocean burst his bed,
O'ertopp'd the mountains, and the earth o'er-
spread;
When the rash youth inflam'd the high abodes,
Scorch'd up the skies, and scar'd the deathless gods.
When Nature ceases, thou shalt still remain,
Nor second Chaos bound thy endless reign;
Fate's tyrant laws thy happier lot shall brave,
Baffle Destruction, and elude the Grave.

VERSES

TO MRS. LOWTHER ON HER MARRIAGE.

FROM MENAGE.

The greatest swain that treads th' Arcadian grove,
Our shepherds envy, and our virgins love,
His charming nymph, his softer fair obtains,
The bright Diana of our flowery plains;
He, 'midst the graceful, of superior grace,
And she the loveliest of the loveliest race.

Thy fruitful influence guardian Juno, shed,
And crown the pleasures of the genial bed:
Raise thence, their future joy, a smiling heir,
Brave as the father, as the mother fair.
Well may'st thou shower thy choicest gifts on those
Who boldly rival thy most hated foes;
The vigorous bridegroom with Alcides vies,
And the fair bride has Cytherea's eyes.

TO A LADY;

WITH A PRESENT OF FLOWERS.

The fragrant painting of our flowery fields,
The choicest stores that youthful summer yields,
Strephon to fair Elisa hath convey'd,
The sweetest garland to the sweetest maid.
O cheer the flowers, my fair, and let them rest
On the Elysium of thy snowy breast,
And there regale the smell, and charm the view,
With richer odours, and a lovelier hue.
Learn hence, nor fear a flatterer in the flower,
Thy form divine, and beauty's matchless power:
Faint, near thy cheeks, the bright carnation glows,
And thy ripe lips outblush the opening rose:

The lily's snow betrays less pure a light,
Lost in thy bosom's more unsullied white;
And wreaths of jasmine shed perfumes, beneath
Th' ambrosial incense of thy balmy breath.
  Ten thousand beauties grace the rival pair,
How fair the chaplet, and the nymph how fair!
But ah! too soon these fleeting charms decay,
The fading lustre of one hastening day.
This night shall see the gaudy wreath decline,
The roses wither, and the lilies pine.
  The garland's fate to thine shall be apply'd,
And what advance thy form, shall check thy pride:
Be wise, my fair, the present hour improve,
Let joy be now, and now a waste of love;
Each drooping bloom shall plead thy just excuse,
And that which show'd thy beauty, show its use.

ON A LADY'S PICTURE:

TO GILFRED LAWSON, ESQ.

As Damon Chloe's painted form survey'd,
He sigh'd, and languish'd for the jilting shade:
For Cupid taught the artist hand its grace,
And Venus wanton'd in the mimic face.

Now he laments a look so falsely fair,
And almost damns, what yet resembles her;
Now he devours it, with his longing eyes;
Now sated, from the lovely phantom flies,
Yet burns to look again, yet looks again, and dies.
Her ivory neck his lips presume to kiss,
And his bold hands the swelling bosom press;
The swain drinks in deep draughts of vain desire,
Melts without heat, and burns in fancy'd fire.
Strange power of paint! thou nice creator art!
What love inspires, may life itself impart.
Struck with like wounds, of old, Pygmalion pray'd,
And hugg'd to life his artificial maid;
Clasp, new Pygmalion, clasp the seeming charms,
Perhaps ev'n now th' enlivening image warms,
Destin'd to crown thy joys, and revel in thy arms:
Thy arms, which shall with fire so fierce invade,
That she at once shall be, and cease to be a maid.

PART OF THE FOURTH BOOK OF LUCAN.

Cæsar, having resolved to give battle to Petreius and Afranius, Pompey's lieutenants in Spain, encamped near the enemy in the same field. The behaviour of their soldiers, at their seeing and knowing one another, is the subject of the following verses.

THEIR ancient friends, as now they nearer drew,
Prepar'd for fight the wondering soldiers knew;
Brother with brother, in unnatural strife,
And the son arm'd against the father's life:
Curst civil war! then conscience first was felt,
And the tough veteran's heart began to melt.
Fix'd in dumb sorrow all at once they stand,
Then wave, a pledge of peace, the guiltless hand;
To vent ten thousand struggling passions move,
The stings of nature, and the pangs of love.
All order broken, wide their arms they throw,
And run, with transport, to the longing foe:
Here the long-lost acquaintance neighbours claim,
There an old friend recalls his comrade's name,
Youths, who in arts beneath one tutor grew,
Rome rent in twain, and kindred hosts they view.
  Tears wet their impious arms, a fond relief,
And kisses, broke by sobs, the words of grief;

Though yet no blood was spilt, each anxious mind
With horror thinks on what his rage design'd.
Ah! generous youths, why thus, with fruitless pain,
Beat ye those breasts? why gush those eyes in vain?
Why blame ye Heaven, and charge your guilt on Fate?
Why dread the tyrant, whom yourselves make great?
Bids he the trumpet sound? the trumpet slight.
Bids he the standards move? refuse the fight.
Your generals, left by you, will love again
A son and father, when they're private men.
Kind Concord, heavenly born! whose blissful reign
Holds this vast globe in one surrounding chain,
Whose laws the jarring elements control,
And knit each atom close from pole to pole;
Soul of the world! and love's eternal spring!
This lucky hour, thy aid fair goddess bring!
This lucky hour, ere aggravated crimes
Heap guilt on guilt, and doubly stain the times.
No veil henceforth for sin, for pardon none;
They know their duty, now their friends are known.
Vain wish! from blood short must the respite be,
New crimes, by love inhanc'd, this night shall see:
Such is the will of Fate, and such the hard decree.
'Twas peace. From either camp, now void of fear
The soldiers mingling cheerful feasts prepare:

On the green sod the friendly bowls were crown'd,
And hasty banquets pil'd upon the ground:
Around the fire they talk; one shows his scars,
One tells what chance first led him to the wars!
Their stories o'er the tedious night prevail,
And the mute circle listens to the tale, [hate,
They own they fought, but swear they ne'er could
Deny their guilt, and lay the blame on Fate;
Their love revives, to make them guiltier grow,
A short-liv'd blessing, but to heighten woe.
When to Petreius first the news was told,
The jealous general thought his legions sold.
Swift with the guards, his headstrong fury drew,
From out his camp he drives the hostile crew;
Cuts clasping friends asunder with his sword,
And stains with blood each hospitable board.
Then thus his wrath breaks out, "O! lost to
fame!
Oh! false to Pompey, and the Roman name!
Can ye not conquer, ye degenerate bands?
Oh! die at least; 'tis all that Rome demands.
What! will ye own, while ye can wield the sword,
A rebel standard, and usurping lord?
Shall he be sued to take you into place
Amongst his slaves, and grant you equal grace?
What? shall my life be begg'd? inglorious
thought?
And life abhorr'd, on such conditions bought!
The toils we bear, my friends, are not for life,
Too mean a prize in such a dreadful strife;

But peace would lead to servitude and shame,
A fair amusement, and a specious name.
Never had man explor'd the iron ore,
Mark'd out the trench, or rais'd the lofty tower,
Ne'er had the steed in harness sought the plain,
Or fleets encounter'd on th' unstable main;
Were life, were breath, with fame to be compar'd
Or peace to glorious liberty preferr'd.
By guilty oaths the hostile army bound,
Holds fast its impious faith, and stands its ground;
Are you perfidious, who espouse the laws,
And traitors only in a righteous cause?
Oh shame! in vain through nations far and
wide,
Thou call'st the crowding monarchs to thy side,
Fall'n Pompey! while thy legions here betray
Thy cheap-bought life, and treat thy fame away."
He ended fierce. The soldier's rage returns,
His blood flies upward, and his bosom burns.
So, haply tam'd, the tiger bears his bands,
Less grimly growls, and licks his keeper's hands;
But if by chance he tastes forbidden gore,
He yells amain, and makes his dungeon roar.
He glares, he foams, he aims a desperate bound,
And his pale master flies the dangerous ground.
Now deeds are done, which man might charge
aright
On stubborn Fate, or undiscerning Night,
Had not their guilt the lawless soldiers known,
And made the whole malignity their own.

The beds, the plenteous tables, float with gore,
And breasts are stabb'd, that were embrac'd
before:
Pity awhile their hands from slaughter kept;
Inward they groan'd, and, as they drew, they
wept;
But every blow their wavering rage assures,
In murder hardens, and to blood inures.
Crowds charge on crowds, nor friends their friends
descry,
But sires by sons, and sons by fathers die.
Black, monstrous rage! each, with victorious cries,
Drags his slain friend before the general's eyes,
Exults in guilt, that throws the only shame
On Pompey's cause, and blots the Roman name.

THE FIRST BOOK OF HOMER'S ILIAD.

THE DEDICATION.

When I first entered upon this translation, I was ambitious of dedicating it to the Earl of Halifax; but being prevented from doing myself that honour, by the unspeakable loss which our country hath sustained in the death of that extraordinary person, I hope I shall not be blamed for presuming to make a dedication of it to his memory. The greatness of his name will justify a practice altogether uncommon, and may gain favour towards a work, which (if it had deserved his patronage) is perhaps the only one inscribed to his lordship, that will escape being rewarded by him.

I might have one advantage from such a dedication, that nothing I could say in it would be suspected of flattery. Besides that the world would take a pleasure in hearing those things said of this great man, now he is dead, which he himself would have been offended at when living. But though I am sensible, so amiable and exalted a character would be very acceptable to the public, were I able to draw it in its full extent; I should be censured, very deservedly, should I venture upon an undertaking, to which I am by no means equal.

His consummate knowledge in all kinds of business, his winning eloquence in public assemblies, his active zeal for the good of his country, and the share he had in conveying the supreme power to an illustrious family famous for being friends to mankind, are subjects easy to be enlarged upon, but incapable of being exhausted. The nature of the following performance more directly leads me to lament the misfortune, which hath befallen the learned world, by the death of so generous and universal a patron.

He rested not in a barren admiration of the polite arts, wherein he himself was so great a master; but was acted by that humanity they naturally inspire: which gave rise to many excellent writers, who have cast a light upon the age in which he lived, and will distinguish it to posterity. It is well known, that very few celebrated pieces have been published for several years, but what were either promoted by his encouragement, or supported by his approbation, or recompensed by his bounty. And if the succession of men, who excel in most of the refined arts, should not continue; though some may impute it to a decay of genius in our countrymen; those who are unacquainted with his lordship's character, will know more justly how to account for it.

The cause of liberty will receive no small advantage in future times, when it shall be observed that the Earl of Halifax was one of the patriots who were at the head of it; and that most of those who were eminent in the several parts of polite or useful learning, were by his influence and example engaged in the same interest.

I hope, therefore, the public will excuse my ambition for thus intruding into the number of those applauded men who have paid him this kind of homage, especially since I am also prompted to it by gratitude, for the protection with which he had begun to honour me; and do it at a time when he cannot suffer by the importunity of my acknowledgments.

THE FIRST BOOK OF THE ILIAD.

TO THE READER.

I must inform the reader, that when I began this first book, I had some thoughts of translating the whole Iliad; but had the pleasure of being diverted from that design, by finding the work was fallen into a much abler hand. I would not therefore be thought to have any other view in publishing this small specimen of Homer's Iliad, than to bespeak, if possible, the favour of the public to a translation of Homer's Odysseis, wherein I have already made some progress.

Achilles' fatal wrath, whence discord rose,
That brought the sons of Greece unnumber'd woes,
O goddess, sing. Full many a hero's ghost
Was driven untimely to th' infernal coast,
While in promiscuous heaps their bodies lay,
A feast for dogs, and every bird of prey.
So did the sire of gods and men fulfil
His steadfast purpose, and almighty will;
What time the haughty chiefs their jars begun,
Atrides, king of men, and Peleus' godlike son.
What god in strife the princes did engage?
Apollo burning with vindictive rage

Against the scornful king, whose impious pride
His priest dishonour'd, and his power defy'd.
Hence swift contagion, by the god's commands,
Swept thro' the camp, and thinn'd the Grecian
bands.

For, wealth immense the holy Chryses bore,
(His daughter's ransom) to the tented shore:
His sceptre stretching forth, the golden rod,
Hung round with hallow'd garlands of his god,
Of all the host, of every princely chief,
But first of Atreus' sons he begg'd relief:

"Great Atreus' sons and warlike Greeks
attend.
So may th' immortal gods your cause befriend,
So may you Priam's lofty bulwarks burn,
And rich in gather'd spoils to Greece return,
As for these gifts my daughter you bestow,
And reverence due to great Apollo show,
Jove's favourite offspring, terrible in war,
Who sends his shafts unerring from afar."

Throughout the host consenting murmurs rise,
The priest to reverence, and give back the prize,
When the great king, incens'd, his silence broke
In words reproachful, and thus sternly spoke:

"Hence, dotard, from my sight. Nor ever more
Approach, I warn thee, this forbidden shore;
Lest thou stretch forth, my fury to restrain,
The wreaths and sceptre of thy god, in vain.
The captive maid I never will resign,
Till age o'ertakes her, I have vow'd her mine.

To distant Argos shall the fair be led:
She shall; to ply the loom, and grace my bed.
Begone, ere evil intercept thy way.
Hence on thy life: nor urge me by thy stay."
He ended frowning. Speechless and dismay'd,
The aged sire his stern command obey'd.
Silent he pass'd, amid the deafening roar
Of tumbling billows, on the lonely shore;
Far from the camp he pass'd: then suppliant stood;
And thus the hoary priest invok'd his god:
"Dread warrior with the silver bow, give ear.
Patron of Chrysa and of Cilla, hear.
To thee the guard of Tenedos belongs;
Propitious Smintheus! O! redress my wrongs.
If e'er within thy fane, with wreaths adorn'd,
The fat of bulls and well-fed goats I burn'd,
O! hear my prayer. Let Greece thy fury know,
And with thy shafts avenge thy servant's woe."
Apollo heard his injur'd suppliant's cry.
Down rush'd the vengeful warrior from the sky;
Across his breast the glittering bow he slung,
And at his back the well-stor'd quiver hung:
(His arrows rattled, as he urg'd his flight.)
In clouds he flew, conceal'd from mortal sight;
Then took his stand, the well-aim'd shaft to throw:
Fierce sprung the string, and twang'd the silver bow.
The dogs and mules his first keen arrow slew;
Amid the ranks the next more fatal flew,

A deathful dart. The funeral piles around
For ever blaz'd on the devoted ground.
Nine days entire he vex'd th' embattled host,
The tenth, Achilles through the winding coast
Summon'd a council, by the queen's command
Who wields Heaven's sceptre in her snowy hand:
She mourn'd her favourite Greeks, who now enclose
The hero, swiftly speaking as he rose:
"What now, O Atreus' son, remains in view,
But o'er the deep our wanderings to renew,
Doom'd to destruction, while our wasted powers
The sword and pestilence at once devours?
Why haste we not some prophet's skill to prove,
Or seek by dreams? (for dreams descend from Jove.)
What moves Apollo's rage let him explain,
What vow withheld, what hecatomb unslain:
And if the blood of lambs and goats can pay
The price for guilt, and turn this curse away?"
Thus he. And next the reverend Calchas rose,
Their guide to Ilion whom the Grecians chose;
The prince of augurs, whose enlighten'd eye
Could things past, present, and to come, descry:
Such wisdom Phœbus gave. He thus began,
His speech addressing to the godlike man:
"Me then command'st thou, lov'd of Jove, to show
What moves the god that bends the dreadful bow?

First plight thy faith thy ready help to lend,
By words to aid me, or by arms defend.
For I foresee his rage, whose ample sway
The Argian powers and sceptred chiefs obey.
The wrath of kings what subject can oppose?
Deep in their breasts the smother'd vengeance glows,
Still watchful to destroy. Swear, valiant youth,
Swear, wilt thou guard me, if I speak the truth?"
To this Achilles swift replies: "Be bold.
Disclose what Phœbus tells thee, uncontroll'd.
By him, who, listening to thy powerful prayer,
Reveals the secret, I devoutly swear,
That, while these eyes behold the light, no hand
Shall dare to wrong thee on this crowded strand.
Not Atreus' son: though now himself he boast
The king of men, and sovereign of the host."
Then boldly he. "Nor does the god complain
Of vows withheld, or hecatombs unslain.
Chryseïs to her awful sire refus'd,
The gifts rejected, and the priest abus'd,
Call down these judgments, and for more they call,
Just ready on th' exhausted camp to fall;
Till ransom-free the damsel is bestow'd,
And hecatombs are sent to soothe the god,
To Chrysa sent. Perhaps Apollo's rage
The gifts may expiate, and the priest assuage."
He spoke and sat. When, with an angry frown,
The chief of kings upstarted from his throne.

Disdain and vengeance in his bosom rise,
Lower in his brows, and sparkle in his eyes:
Full at the priest their fiery orbs he bent,
And all at once his fury found a vent.
"Augur of ills, (for never good to me
Did that most inauspicious voice decree)
For ever ready to denounce my woes,
When Greece is punish'd, I am still the cause;
And now when Phœbus spreads his plagues abroad,
And wastes our camp, 'tis I provoke the god,
Because my blooming captive I detain,
And the large ransom is produc'd in vain.
Fond of the maid, my queen in beauty's pride,
Ne'er charm'd me more, a virgin and a bride;
Not Clytæmnestra boasts a nobler race,
A sweeter temper, or a lovelier face,
In works of female skill hath more command,
Or guides the needle with a nicer hand.
Yet she shall go. The fair our peace shall buy:
Better I suffer, than my people die.
But mark me well. See instantly prepar'd
A full equivalent, a new reward.
Nor is it meet, while each enjoys his share,
Your chief should lose his portion of the war:
In vain your chief; whilst the dear prize, I boast,
Is wrested from me, and for ever lost."
To whom the swift pursuer quick reply'd:
"Oh sunk in avarice, and swoln with pride!
How shall the Greeks, though large of soul they be,
Collect their sever'd spoils, a heap for thee

To search anew, and cull the choicest share
Amid the mighty harvest of the war?
Then yield thy captive to the god resign'd,
Assur'd a tenfold recompense to find,
When Jove's decree shall throw proud Ilion down,
And give to plunder the devoted town."
"Think not," Atrides answer'd, "though thou shine,
Graceful in beauty, like the powers divine,
Think not, thy wiles, in specious words convey'd,
From its firm purpose shall my soul dissuade.
Must I alone bereft sit down with shame,
And thou insulting keep thy captive dame?
If, as I ask, the large-soul'd Greeks consent
Full recompense to give, I stand content.
If not, a prize I shall myself decree,
From him, or him, or else perhaps from thee.
While the proud prince, despoil'd, shall rage in vain.
But break we here. The rest let time explain.
Launch now a well-trimm'd galley from the shore,
With hands experienc'd at the bending oar:
Enclose the hecatomb; and then with care
To the high deck convey the captive fair.
The sacred bark let sage Ulysses guide,
Or Ajax, or Idomeneus, preside:
Or thou, O mighty man, the chief shalt be.
And who more fit to soothe the god than thee?"
"Shameless, and poor of soul," the prince replies,
And on the monarch casts his scornful eyes,

"What Greek henceforth will march at thy command
In search of danger on the doubtful strand?
Who in the face of day provoke the fight,
Or tempt the secret ambush of the night?
Not I, be sure. Henceforward I am free.
For ne'er was Priam's house a foe to me.
Far from their inroads, in my pastures feed
The lowing heifer, and the pamper'd steed,
On Phthia's hills our fruits securely grow,
And ripen careless of the distant foe,
Between whose realms and our Thessalian shore
Unnumber'd mountains rise, and billows roar.
For thine, and for thy baffled brother's fame,
Across those seas, disdainful man, I came;
Yet insolent! by arbitrary sway
Thou talk'st of seizing on my rightful prey,
The prize whose purchase toils and dangers cost,
And given by suffrage of the Grecian host.
What town, when sack'd by our victorious bands,
But still brought wealth to those rapacious hands?
To me, thus scorn'd, contented dost thou yield
My share of blood in the tumultuous field;
But still the flower of all the spoil is thine;
There claim'st thou most. Nor e'er did I repine.
Whate'er was giv'n I took, and thought it best,
With slaughter tir'd, and panting after rest.
To Phthia now, for I shall fight no more,
My ships their crooked prows shall turn from shore.

When I am scorn'd, I think I well foresee
What spoils and pillage will be won by thee."
"Hence!" cry'd the monarch, "hence! without delay."
Think not, vain man! my voice shall urge thy stay,
Others thou leav'st, to the great cause inclin'd,
A league of kings thou leav'st, and Jove behind.
Of all the chiefs dost thou oppose me most:
Outrage and uproar are thy only boast.
Discord and jars thy joy. But learn to know,
If thou art strong, 'tis Jove hath made thee so.
Go, at thy pleasure. None will stop thy way.
Go, bid thy base-born Myrmidons obey.
Thou, nor thy rage, shall my resolves subdue;
I fix my purpose, and my threats renew.
Since 'tis decreed I must the maid restore,
A ship shall waft her to th' offended power;
But fair Briseïs, thy allotted prize,
Myself will seize, and seize before thy eyes:
That thou and each audacious man may see,
How vain the rash attempt to cope with me."
Stung to the soul, tumultuous thoughts began
This way and that to rend the godlike man.
To force a passage with his falchion drawn,
And hurl th' imperial boaster from his throne,
He now resolves: and now resolves again
To quell his fury, and his arm restrain.
While thus by turns his rage and reason sway'd,
And half unsheath'd he held the glittering blade;

That moment, Juno, whose impartial eye
Watch'd o'er them both, sent Pallas from the sky:
She flew, and caught his yellow hair behind,
(To him alone the radiant goddess shin'd.)
Sudden he turn'd, and started with surprise;
Rage and revenge flash'd dreadful in his eyes.
Then thus with hasty words: "O! heavenly-born,
Com'st thou to see proud Agamemnon's scorn?
But thou shalt see (my sword shall make it good)
This glutted sand smoke with the tyrant's blood."
"To soothe thy soul," the blue-ey'd maid replies,
"(If thou obey my voice) I left the skies.
Heaven's queen, who favours both, gave this command!
Suppress thy wrath, and stay thy vengeful hand.
Be all thy rage in tauntful words exprest;
But guiltless let the thirsty falchion rest,
Mark what I speak. An hour is on its way,
When gifts tenfold for this affront shall pay.
Suppress thy wrath; and Heaven and me obey."
Then he: "I yield; though with reluctant mind.
Who yields to Heaven shall Heaven propitious find."
The silver hilt close-grasping, at the word,
Deep in the sheath he plung'd his mighty sword.
The goddess, turning, darted from his sight,
And reach'd Olympus in a moment's flight.
But fierce Achilles, in a thundering tone,
Throws out his wrath, and goes impetuous on:

"Valiant with wine, and furious from the bowl!
Thou fierce-look'd talker with a coward soul!
War's glorious peril ever slow to share:
Aloof thou view'st the field; for Death is there,
'Tis greater far this peaceful camp to sway,
And peel the Greeks, at will, who disobey:
A tyrant lord o'er slaves to earth debas'd;
For, had they souls, this outrage were thy last.
But, thou, my fix'd, my final purpose hear.
By this dread sceptre solemnly I swear:
By this (which, once from out the forest torn,
Nor leaf nor shade shall ever more adorn;
Which never more its verdure must renew,
Lopp'd from the vital stem, whence first it grew!
But given by Jove the sons of men to awe,
Now sways the nations, and confirms the law)
A day shall come, when for this hour's disdain
The Greeks shall wish for me, and wish in vain;
Nor thou, though griev'd, the wanted aid afford,
When heaps on heaps shall fall by Hector's sword:
Too late with anguish shall thy heart be torn,
That the first Greek was made the public scorn."

He said. And, mounting with a furious bound,
He dash'd his studded sceptre on the ground;
Then sat. Atrides, eager to reply,
On the fierce champion glanc'd a vengeful eye.

'Twas then, the madding monarchs to compose,
The Pylian prince, the smooth-speech'd Nestor rose.
His tongue dropp'd honey. Full of days was he;
Two ages past, he liv'd the third to see:
And his first race of subjects long decay'd,
O'er their sons' sons a peaceful sceptre sway'd.
"Alas for Greece!" he cries, "and with what joy
Shall Priam hear, and every son of Troy!
That you, the first in wisdom as in wars,
Waste your great souls in poor ignoble jars!
Go to! you both are young. Yet oft rever'd
Greater than you have the wise Nestor heard.
Their equals never shall these eyes behold:
Cæneus the just, Pirithous the bold,
Exadius, Dryas, born to high command,
Shepherds of men, and rulers of the land,
Theseus unrivall'd in his sire's abodes,
And mighty Polypheme, a match for gods.
They, greatest names that ancient story knows,
In mortal conflict met as dreadful foes:
Fearless thro' rocks and wilds their prey pursued,
And the huge double Centaur race subdued.
With them my early youth was pleas'd to roam
Through regions, far from my sweet native home;
They call'd me to the wars. No living hand
Could match their valour, or their strength withstand;
Yet wont they oft my sage advice to hear.
Then listen both, with an attentive ear.

Seize not thou, king of men, the beauteous slave,
Th' allotted prize the Grecian voices gave.
Nor thou, Pelides, in a threatening tone
Urge him to wrath, who fills that sacred throne,
The king of forty kings, and honour'd more
By mighty Jove, than e'er was king before.
Brave though thou art, and of a race divine,
Thou must obey a power more great than thine.
And thou, O king, forbear. Myself will sue
Great Thetis' son his vengeance to subdue:
Great Thetis' valiant son, our country's boast,
The shield and bulwark of the Grecian host."
"Wise are thy words, O sire," the king began,
"But what can satiate this aspiring man?
Unbounded power he claims o'er human-kind,
And hopes for slaves, I trust he ne'er shall find.
Shall we, because the gods have form'd him strong,
Bear the lewd language of his lawless tongue!"
"If aw'd by thee, the Greeks might well despise
My name," the prince, precipitate, replies,
"In vain thou nodd'st from thy imperial throne.
Thy vassals seek elsewhere; for I am none.
But break we here. The fair, though justly mine,
With sword undrawn I purpose to resign.
On aught beside, I once for all command,
Lay not, I charge thee, thy presumptuous hand.
Come not within my reach, nor dare advance,
Or thy heart's blood shall reek upon my lance."
Thus both in foul debate prolong'd the day.
The council broke, each takes his separate way.

Achilles seeks his tent with restless mind;
Patroclus and his train move slow behind.
  Meantime, a bark was haul'd along the sand,
Twice ten selected Greeks, a brawny band,
Tug the tough oars, at the great king's command.
The gifts, the hecatomb, the captive fair,
Are all intrusted to Ulysses' care.
They mount the deck. The vessel takes its [flight,
Bounds o'er the surge, and lessens to the sight.
  Next he ordains along the winding coast
By hallow'd rites to purify the host.
A herd of chosen victims they provide,
And cast their offals on the briny tide.
Fat bulls and goats to great Apollo die.
In clouds the savory steam ascends the sky.
  The Greeks to Heaven their solemn vows addrest;
But dire revenge roll'd in the monarch's breast.
Obsequious at his call two heralds stand:
To them in frowns he gives this harsh command.
"Ye heralds, to Achilles' tent repair;
Then swift the female slave Briseïs bear.
With arms, if disobey'd, myself will come.
Bid him resign her, or he tempts his doom."
  The heralds, though unwillingly, obey.
Along the sea-beat shore they speed their way:
And, now the Myrmidonian quarter past,
At his tent-door they find the hero plac'd.
Disturb'd the solemn messengers he saw;
They too stood silent, with respectful awe,

Before the royal youth, they neither spoke.
He guess'd their message, and the silence broke:
"Ye ministers of gods and men, draw near,
Not you, but him whose heralds ye appear,
Robb'd of my right I blame. Patroclus, bring
The damsel forth for this disdainful king.
But ye, my wrongs, O heralds, bear in mind,
And clear me to the gods and all mankind,
Ev'n to your thoughtless king; if ever more
My aid be wanted on the hostile shore.
Thoughtless he is, nor knows his certain doom,
Blind to the past, nor sees the woes to come,
His best defence thus rashly to forego,
And leave a naked army to the foe."
He ceas'd. Patroclus his dear friend obey'd,
And usher'd in the lovely weeping maid.
Sore sigh'd she, as the heralds took her hand,
And oft look'd back, slow-moving o'er the strand.
The widow'd hero, when the fair was gone,
Far from his friends sat bath'd in tears alone.
On the cold beach he sat, and fix'd his eyes
Where black with storms the curling billows rise,
And as the sea wide-rolling he survey'd,
With outstretch'd arms to his fond mother pray'd:
"Since to short life thy hapless son was born,
Great Jove stands bound by promise to adorn
His stinted course with an immortal name.
Is this the great amends? the promis'd fame?
The son of Atreus, proud of lawless sway,
Demands, possesses, and enjoys my prey."

Near her old sire enthron'd, she heard him weep
From the low silent caverns of the deep :
Then in a morning mist her head she rears,
Sits by her son, and mingles tears with tears ;
Close grasps her darling's hand. "My son," she cries,
"Why heaves thy heart? and why o'erflow thy eyes?
O tell me, tell thy mother all thy care,
That both may know it, and that both may share."
"Oh! goddess!" cry'd he, with an inward groan,
"Thou know'st it all: to thee are all things known.
Eëtian Thebes we sack'd, their ransack'd towers,
The plunder of a people, all was ours.
We stood agreed the booty to divide.
Chryseïs, rosy-cheek'd and glossy-ey'd,
Fell to the king; but holy Chryses bore
Vast gifts of ransom, to the tented shore:
His sceptre stretching forth (the golden rod
Hung round with hallow'd garlands of his god)
Of all the host, of every princely chief,
But first of Atreus' sons, he begg'd relief.
Throughout the host consenting murmurs ran,
To yield her to the venerable man ;
But the harsh king deny'd to do him right,
And drove the trembling prophet from his sight.
Apollo heard his injur'd suppliant's cry,
And dealt his arrows through th' infected sky ;

The swift contagion, sent by his commands,
Swept thro' the camp, and thinn'd the Grecian
bands.
The guilty cause a sacred augur show'd,
And I first mov'd to mitigate the god.
At this the tyrant storm'd, and vengeance vow'd;
And now too soon hath made his threatnings good.
Chryseïs first with gifts to Chrysa sent,
His heralds came this moment to my tent,
And bore Briseïs thence, my beauteous slave,
Th' alloted prize, which the leagu'd Grecians gave.
Thou goddess, then, and thou, I know, hast power,
For thine own son the might of Jove implore.
Oft in my father's house I've heard thee tell,
When sudden fears on Heaven's great monarch
fell,
Thy aid the rebel deities o'ercame,
And sav'd the mighty Thunderer from shame.
Pallas, and Neptune, and great Juno, bound
The sire in chains, and hemm'd their sovereign
round.
Thy voice, O goddess, broke their idle bands,
And call'd the giant of the hundred hands,
The prodigy, whom Heaven and Earth revere,
Briareus nam'd above, Ægeon here.
His father Neptune he in strength surpass'd;
At Jove's right hand his hideous form he plac'd,
Proud of his might. The gods with secret
dread,
Beheld the huge enormous shape and fled.

Remind him then: for well thou know'st the art:
Go, clasp his knees, and melt his mighty heart.
Let the driven Argians, hunted o'er the plain,
Seek the last verge of this tempestuous main:
There let them perish, void of all relief,
My wrongs remember, and enjoy their chief.
Too late with anguish shall his heart be torn,
That the first Greek was made the public scorn."
  Then she (with tears her azure eyes ran o'er:)
"Why bore I thee! or nourish'd, when I bore!
Blest, if within thy tent, and free from strife,
Thou might'st possess thy poor remains of life.
Thy death approaching now the Fates foreshow;
Short is thy destin'd term, and full of woe.
Ill-fated thou! and oh unhappy I!
But hence to the celestial courts I fly,
Where, hid in snow, to Heaven Olympus swells,
And Jove, rejoicing in his thunder, dwells.
Meantime, my son, indulge thy just disdain:
Vent all thy rage, and shun the hostile plain,
Till Jove returns. Last night my waves he cross'd,
And sought the distant Ethiopian coast:
Along the skies his radiant course he steer'd,
Behind him all the train of gods appear'd,
A bright procession. To the holy feast
Of blameless men he goes a grateful guest.
To heaven he comes, when twice six days are o'er!
Then shall his voice the sire of gods implore,

Then to my lofty mansion will I pass,
Founded on rocks of ever-during brass:
There will I clasp his knees with wonted art,
Nor doubt, my son, but I shall melt his heart."
  She ceas'd: and left him lost in doubtful care,
And bent on vengeance for the ravish'd fair.
  But, safe arriv'd near Chrysa's sacred strand,
The sage Ulysses now advanc'd to land.
Along the coast he shoots with swelling gales,
Then lowers the lofty mast, and furls the sails;
Next plies to port with many a well-tim'd oar,
And drops his anchors near the faithful shore.
The bark now fix'd amidst the rolling tide,
Chryseïs follows her experienc'd guide:
The gifts to Phœbus from the Grecian host,
A herd of bulls went bellowing o'er the coast.
To the god's fane, high looking o'er the land,
He led, and near the altar took his stand,
Then gave her to the joyful father's hand.
"All hail! Atrides sets thy daughter free,
Sends offerings to thy god, and gifts to thee.
But thou entreat the power, whose dreadful sway
Afflicts his camp, and sweeps his host away."
  He said, and gave her. The fond father smil'd
With secret rapture, and embrac'd his child.
  The victims now they range in chosen bands,
And offer gifts with unpolluted hands:
When with loud voice, and arms uprear'd in air,
The hoary priest preferr'd this powerful prayer:

" Dread warrior with the silver bow, give ear,
Patron of Chrysa and of Cilla, hear.
About this dome thou walk'st thy constant round
Still have my vows thy power propitious found.
Rous'd by my prayers ev'n now thy vengeance burns,
And smit by thee, the Grecian army mourns.
Hear me once more; and let the suppliant foe
Avert thy wrath, and slack thy dreadful bow."
He pray'd; and great Apollo heard his prayer.
The suppliants now their votive rites prepare:
Amidst the flames they cast the hallow'd bread,
And heavenward turn each victim's destin'd head:
Next slay the fatted bulls, their skins divide,
And from each carcase rend the smoking hide;
On every limb large rolls of fat bestow,
And chosen morsels round the offerings strow:
Mysterious rites. Then on the fire divine
The great high priest pours forth the ruddy wine;
Himself the offering burns. On either hand
A troop of youths, in decent order, stand.
On sharpen'd forks, obedient to the sire,
They turn the tasteful fragments in the fire,
Adorn the feast, see every dish well-stor'd,
And serve the plenteous messes to the board.
When now the various feasts had cheer'd their souls,
With sparkling wines they crown the generous bowls,
The first libations to Apollo pay,
And solemnize with sacred hymns the day:

His praise in Iö Pæans loud they sing,
And soothe the rage of the far-shooting king.
At evening, through the shore dispers'd, they sleep,
Hush'd by the distant roarings of the deep.
When now, ascending from the shades of night,
Aurora glow'd in all her rosy light,
The daughter of the dawn: th' awaken'd crew
Back to the Greeks encamp'd their course renew,
The breezes freshen: for with friendly gales
Apollo swell'd their wide, distended, sails:
Cleft by the rapid prow, the waves divide,
And in hoarse murmurs break on either side,
In safety to the destined port they pass'd,
And fix their bark with grappling haulsers fast;
Then dragg'd her farther, on the dry-land coast,
Regain'd their tents, and mingled in the host.
But fierce Achilles, still on vengeance bent,
Cherish'd his wrath, and madden'd in his tent.
Th' assembled chiefs he shunn'd with high disdain,
A band of kings: nor sought the hostile plain;
But long'd to hear the distant troops engage,
The strife grow doubtful, and the battle rage.
Twelve days were past; and now th' ethereal train,
Jove at their head, to Heaven return'd again:
When Thetis, from the deep prepar'd to rise,
Shot through a big-swoln wave, and pierc'd the skies.
At early morn she reach'd the realms above,
The court of gods, the residence of Jove.

On the top-point of high Olympus, crown'd
With hills on hills, him far apart she found,
Above the rest. The Earth beneath display'd
(A boundless prospect) his broad eye survey'd.
Her left hand grasp'd his knees, her right she
    rear'd,
And touch'd with blandishment his awful beard;
Then, suppliant, with submissive voice implor'd
Old Saturn's son, the god by gods ador'd:
  "If e'er, by rebel deities opprest,
My aid reliev'd thee, grant this one request.
Since to short life my hapless son was born,
Do thou with fame the scanty space adorn.
Punish the king of men, whose lawless sway
Hath sham'd the youth, and seiz'd his destin'd prey.
Awhile let Troy prevail, that Greece may grieve,
And doubled honours to my offspring give."
  She said. The god vouchsaf'd not to reply
(A deep suspense sat in his thoughtful eye):
Once more around his knees the goddess clung,
And to soft accents form'd her artful tongue:
  "Oh speak. O grant me, or deny my prayer.
Fear not to speak, what I am doom'd to bear;
That I may know, if thou my prayer deny,
The most despis'd of all the gods am I."
  With a deep sigh the Thundering Power
    replies:
"To what a height will Juno's anger rise!
Still doth her voice before the gods upbraid
My partial hand, that gives the Trojans aid.

I grant thy suit. But, hence! depart unseen,
And shun the sight of Heaven's suspicious queen.
Believe my nod, the great, the certain sign,
When Jove propitious hears the powers divine;
The sign that ratifies my high command,
That thus I will: and what I will shall stand."
This said, his kingly brow the sire inclin'd;
The large black curls fell awful from behind,
Thick shadowing the stern forehead of the god:
Olympus trembled at th' almighty nod.
The goddess smil'd: and, with a sudden leap,
From the mountain plung'd into the deep.
But Jove repair'd to his celestial towers:
And, as he rose, uprose the immortal powers.
In ranks, on either side, th' assembly cast,
Bow'd down, and did obeisance as he pass'd.
To him enthron'd (for whispering she had seen
Close at his knees the silver-footed queen,
Daughter of him, who, low beneath the tides,
Aged and hoary in the deep resides)
Big with invectives, Juno silence broke,
And thus opprobrious her resentments spoke:
"False Jove! what goddess whispering did I see?
O fond of counsels, still conceal'd from me!
To me neglected, thou wilt ne'er impart
One single thought of thy close-cover'd heart."
To whom the sire of gods and men reply'd;
"Strive not to find, what I decree to hide.
Laborious were the search, and vain the strife,
Vain ev'n for thee, my sister and my wife.

The thoughts and counsels proper to declare,
Nor god nor mortal shall before thee share:
But, what my secret wisdom shall ordain,
Think not to reach, for know the thought were vain."
"Dread Saturn's son, why so severe?" replies
The goddess of the large majestic eyes.
"Thy own dark thoughts at pleasure hide, or show;
Ne'er have I ask'd, nor now aspire to know.
Nor yet my fears are vain, nor came unseen
To thy high throne, the silver-footed queen,
Daughter of him, who low beneath the tides
Aged and hoary in the deep resides.
Thy nod assures me she was not deny'd:
And Greece must perish for a madman's pride."
To whom the god, whose hand the tempest forms,
Drives clouds on clouds, and blackens Heaven with storms,
Thus wrathful answer'd: "Dost thou still complain?
Perplex'd for ever, and perplex'd in vain!
Should'st thou disclose the dark event to come!
How wilt thou stop the irrevocable doom!
This serves the more to sharpen my disdain;
And woes foreseen but lengthen out thy pain.
Be silent then. Dispute not my command;
Nor tempt the force of this superior hand:
Lest all the gods, around thee leagu'd, engage
In vain to shield thee from my kindled rage."

Mute and abash'd she sat without reply,
And downward turn'd her large majestic eye,
Nor further durst the offended sire provoke:
The gods around him trembled, as he spoke.
When Vulcan, for his mother sore distress'd,
Turn'd orator, and thus his speech addrest;
"Hard is our fate, if men of mortal line
Stir up debate among the powers divine,
If things on Earth disturb the blest abodes,
And mar th' ambrosial banquet of the gods!
Then let my mother once be rul'd by me,
Though much more wise than I pretend to be:
Let me advise her silent to obey,
And due submission to our father pay.
Nor force again his gloomy rage to rise,
Ill-tim'd, and damp the revels of the skies.
For should he toss her from th' Olympian hill,
Who could resist the mighty monarch's will?
Then thou to love the Thunderer reconcile,
And tempt him kindly on us all to smile,"
He said: and in his tottering hands upbore
A double goblet, fill'd, and foaming o'er.
"Sit down, dear mother, with a heart content,
Nor urge a more disgraceful punishment,
Which if great Jove inflict, poor I, dismay'd,
Must stand aloof, nor dare to give thee aid.
Great Jove shall reign for ever, uncontroll'd:
Remember, when I took thy part of old,
Caught by the heel he swung me round on high,
And headlong hurl'd me from th' ethereal sky:

From morn to noon I fell, from noon to night;
Till pitch'd on Lemnos, a most piteous sight,
The Sintians hardly could my breath recall,
Giddy and gasping with the dreadful fall."
She smil'd: and, smiling, her white arm display'd
To reach the bowl her awkward son convey'd.
From right to left the generous bowl he crown'd,
And dealt the rosy nectar fairly round.
The gods laugh'd out, unweary'd, as they spy'd
The busy skinker hop from side to side.
Thus, feasting to the full, they pass'd away,
In blissful banquets, all the livelong day.
Nor wanted melody. With heavenly art
The Muses sung; each Muse perform'd her part,
Alternate warbling; while the golden lyre,
Touch'd by Apollo, led the vocal choir.
The Sun at length declin'd, when every guest
Sought his bright palace, and withdrew to rest;
Each had his palace on th' Olympian hill,
A masterpiece of Vulcan's matchless skill.
Ev'n he, the god, who Heaven's great sceptre sways,
And frowns amid the lightning's dreadful blaze,
His bed of state ascending, lay compos'd;
His eyes a sweet refreshing slumber clos'd;
And at his side, all glorious to behold,
Was Juno lodg'd in her alcove of gold.

TO

THE EARL OF WARWICK,

ON THE DEATH OF MR. ADDISON.

If, dumb too long, the drooping Muse hath stay'd,
And left her debt to Addison unpaid,
Blame not her silence, Warwick, but bemoan,
And judge, Oh judge, my bosom by your own.
What mourner ever felt poetic fires!
Slow comes the verse that real woe inspires:
Grief unaffected suits but ill with art,
Or flowing numbers with a bleeding heart.
Can I forget the dismal night that gave
My soul's best part for ever to the grave!
How silent did his old companions tread,
By midnight lamps, the mansions of the dead,
Through breathing statues, then unheeded things,
Through rows of warriors, and through walks of kings!
What awe did the slow solemn knell inspire;
The pealing organ, and the pausing choir;
The duties by the lawn-rob'd prelate pay'd;
And the last words that dust to dust convey'd!
While speechless o'er thy closing grave we bend,
Accept these tears, thou dear departed friend.

Oh, gone for ever; take this long adieu;
And sleep in peace, next thy lov'd Montague.
To strew fresh laurels, let the task be mine,
A frequent pilgrim, at thy sacred shrine;
Mine with true sighs thy absence to bemoan,
And grave with faithful epitaphs thy stone.
If e'er from me thy lov'd memorial part,
May shame afflict this alienated heart;
Of thee forgetful if I form a song,
My lyre be broken, and untun'd my tongue,
My grief be doubled from thy image free,
And mirth a torment, unchastis'd by thee.
  Oft let me range the gloomy aisles alone,
Sad luxury! to vulgar minds unknown,
Along the walls where speaking marbles show
What worthies form the hallow'd mould below;
Proud names, who once the reins of empire held;
In arms who triumph'd; or in arts excell'd;
Chiefs, grac'd with scars, and prodigal of blood;
Stern patriots, who for sacred freedom stood;
Just men, by whom impartial laws were given;
And saints who taught, and led the way to Heaven;
Ne'er to these chambers, where the mighty rest,
Since their foundation, came a nobler guest;
Nor e'er was to the bowers of bliss convey'd
A fairer spirit or more welcome shade.
  In what new region, to the just assign'd,
What new employments please th' unbody'd
A winged *Virtue*, through th' ethereal sky, [mind?
From world to world unweary'd does he fly?

Or curious trace the long laborious maze
Of Heaven's decrees, where wondering angels gaze?)
Does he delight to hear bold seraphs tell
How Michael battled, and the dragon fell;
Or, mix'd with milder cherubim, to glow
In hymns of love, not ill essay'd below?
Or dost thou warn poor mortals left behind,
A task well suited to thy gentle mind?
Oh! if sometimes thy spotless form descend:
To me, thy aid, thou guardian genius, lend!
When rage misguides me, or when fear alarms,
When pain distresses, or when pleasure charms,
In silent whisperings purer thoughts impart,
And turn from ill, a frail and feeble heart;
Lead through the paths thy virtue trod before,
Till bliss shall join, nor death can part us more.

That awful form, which, so the Heavens decree,
Must still be lov'd and still deplor'd by me;
In nightly visions seldom fails to rise,
Or, rous'd by Fancy, meets my waking eyes.
If business calls, or crowded courts invite,
Th' unblemish'd statesman seems to strike my sight;
If in the stage I seek to soothe my care,
I meet his soul which breathes in Cato there;
If pensive to the rural shades I rove,
His shape o'ertakes me in the lonely grove;
'Twas there of just and good he reason'd strong,
Clear'd some great truth, or rais'd some serious song:

There patient show'd us the wise course to steer,
A candid censor, and a friend severe;
There taught us how to live; and (oh! too high
The price for knowledge) taught us how to die.
Thou Hill, whose brow the antique structures grace,
Rear'd by bold chiefs of Warwick's noble race,
Why, once so lov'd, whene'er thy bower appears,
O'er my dim eyeballs glance the sudden tears!
How sweet were once thy prospects fresh and fair,
Thy sloping walks, and unpolluted air!
How sweet the glooms beneath thy aged trees,
Thy noontide shadow, and thy evening breeze!
His image thy forsaken bowers restore;
Thy walks and airy prospects charm no more;
No more the summer in thy glooms allay'd,
Thy evening breezes, and thy noonday shade.
From other hills, however Fortune frown'd;
Some refuge in the Muse's art I found;
Reluctant now I touch the trembling string,
Bereft of him, who taught me how to sing;
And these sad accents, murmur'd o'er his urn,
Betray that absence, they attempt to mourn.
O! must I then (now fresh my bosom bleeds,
And Craggs in death to Addison succeeds)
The verse, begun to one lost friend, prolong,
And weep a second in th' unfinish'd song!
These works divine, which, on his death-bed laid
To thee, O Craggs, th' expiring sage convey'd,

Great, but ill-omen'd, monument of fame,
Nor he surviv'd to give, nor thou to claim.
Swift after him thy social spirit flies,
And close to his, how soon! thy coffin lies.
Blest pair! whose union future bards shall tell
In future tongues: each other's boast! farewell,
Farewell! whom join'd in fame, in friendship try'd,
No chance could sever, nor the grave divide.

COLIN AND LUCY.

A BALLAD.

Of Leinster, fam'd for maidens fair,
  Bright Lucy was the grace;
Nor e'er did Liffy's limpid stream
  Reflect so sweet a face:
Till luckless love, and pining care,
  Impair'd her rosy hue,
Her coral lips, and damask cheeks,
  And eyes of glossy blue.

Oh! have you seen a lily pale,
  When beating rains descend?
So droop'd the slow-consuming maid,
  Her life now near its end.

By Lucy warn'd, of flattering swains
 Take heed, ye easy fair:
Of vengeance due to broken vows,
 Ye perjur'd swains, beware.

Three times, all in the dead of night,
 A bell was heard to ring;
And shrieking at her window thrice,
 The raven flapp'd his wing.
Too well the love-lorn maiden knew
 The solemn boding sound:
And thus, in dying words, bespoke
 The virgins weeping round:

"I hear a voice, you cannot hear,
 Which says, I must not stay;
I see a hand, you cannot see,
 Which beckons me away.
By a false heart, and broken vows,
 In early youth I die:
Was I to blame, because his bride
 Was thrice as rich as I?

"Ah, Colin! give not her thy vows,
 Vows due to me alone:
Nor thou, fond maid, receive his kiss,
 Nor think him all thy own.
To-morrow, in the church to wed,
 Impatient, both prepare!
But know, fond maid; and know, false man,
 That Lucy will be there!

"Then bear my corse, my comrades, bear,
This bridegroom blithe to meet,
He in his wedding-trim so gay,
I in my winding-sheet."
She spoke, she dy'd, her corse was borne,
The bridegroom blithe to meet,
He in his wedding trim so gay,
She in her winding-sheet.

Then what were perjur'd Colin's thoughts?
How were these nuptials kept?
The bridesmen flock'd round Lucy dead,
And all the village wept.
Confusion, shame, remorse, despair,
At once his bosom swell:
The damps of death bedew'd his brow,
He shook, he groan'd, he fell.

From the vain bride, ah, bride no more!
The varying crimson fled,
When, stretch'd before her rival's corse,
She saw her husband dead.
Then to his Lucy's new-made grave,
Convey'd by trembling swains,
One mould with her, beneath one sod,
For ever he remains.

Oft at this grave, the constant hind
And plighted maid are seen;
With garlands gay, and true-love knots.
They deck the sacred green;

But swain forsworn, whoe'er thou art,
  This hallow'd spot forbear;
Remember Colin's dreadful fate,
  And fear to meet him there.

TO SIR GODFREY KNELLER,

AT HIS COUNTRY SEAT.

To Whitton's shades, and Hounslow's airy plain,
Thou, Kneller, tak'st thy summer flights in vain,
In vain thy wish gives all thy rural hours
To the fair villa, and well-order'd bowers;
To court thy pencil early at thy gates,
Ambition knocks, and fleeting Beauty waits;
The boastful Muse, of others' fame so sure,
Implores thy aid to make her own secure;
The great, the fair, and, if aught nobler be,
Aught more belov'd, the Arts solicit thee.
  How canst thou hope to fly the world, in vain
From Europe sever'd by the circling main;
Sought by the kings of every distant land,
And every hero worthy of thy hand?
Hast thou forgot that mighty Bourbon fear'd
He still was mortal, till thy draught appear'd?

That Cosmo chose thy glowing form to place,
Amidst her masters of the Lombard race?
See, on her Titian's and her Guido's urns,
Her falling arts forlorn Hesperia mourns;
While Britain wins each garland from her brow,
Her wit and freedom first, her painting now.
  Let the faint copier, on old Tiber's shore,
Nor mean the task, each breathing bust explore,
Line after line, with painful patience trace,
This Roman grandeur, that Athenian grace:
Vain care of parts; if, impotent of soul,
Th' industrious workman fails to warm the whole,
Each theft betrays the marble whence it came,
And a cold statue stiffens in the frame.
Thee Nature taught, nor Art her aid deny'd,
The kindest mistress, and the surest guide,
To catch a likeness at one piercing sight,
And place the fairest in the fairest light;
Ere yet thy pencil tries her nicer toils
Or on thy palette lie the blended oils,
Thy careless chalk has half achiev'd thy art,
And her just image makes Cleora start.
  A mind that grasps the whole is rarely found,
Half learn'd, half painters, and half wits abound;
Few, like thy genius, at proportion aim,
All great, all graceful, and throughout the same.
  Such be thy life, O since the glorious rage
That fir'd thy youth, flames unsubdued by age!
Though wealth, nor fame, now touch thy sated mind,
Still tinge the canvas, bounteous to mankind;

Since after thee may rise an impious line,
Coarse manglers of the human face divine,
Paint on, till Fate dissolve thy mortal part,
And live and die the monarch of thy art.

ON THE DEATH OF THE EARL OF CADOGAN.

Of Marlborough's captains, and Eugenio's friends,
The last, Cadogan, to the grave descends:
Low lies each hand, whence Blenheim's glory sprung,
The chiefs who conquer'd, and the bards who sung,
From his cold corse though every friend be fled,
Lo! Envy waits, that lover of the dead:
Thus did she feign o'er Nassau's hearse to mourn;
Thus wept insidious, Churchill, o'er thy urn;
To blast the living, gave the dead their due,
And wreaths, herself had tainted, trimm'd anew,
Thou, yet unnam'd to fill his empty place,
And lead to war thy country's growing race,
Take every wish a British heart can frame,
Add palm to palm, and rise from fame to fame.
An hour must come, when thou shalt hear with rage
Thyself traduc'd, and curse a thankless age:

Nor yet for this decline the generous strife,
These ills, brave man, shall quit thee with thy life,
Alive though stain'd by every abject slave,
Secure of fame and justice in the grave.
Ah! no——when once the mortal yields to Fate,
The blast of Fame's sweet trumpet sounds too late,
Too late to stay the spirit on its flight,
Or soothe the new inhabitant of light;
Who hears regardless, while fond man, distress'd,
Hangs on the absent, and laments the blest.
Farewell then Fame, ill sought thro' fields and blood,
Farewell unfaithful promiser of good:
Thou music, warbling to the deafen'd ear!
Thou incense wasted on the funeral bier!
Through life pursued in vain, by death obtain'd,
When ask'd deny'd us, and when given disdain'd.

AN ODE

INSCRIBED TO THE EARL OF SUNDERLAND AT WINDSOR.

Thou Dome, where Edward first enroll'd
His red-cross knights and barons bold,
Whose vacant seats, by Virtue bought,
Ambitious emperors have sought:

Where Britain's foremost names are found,
In peace belov'd, in war renown'd,
Who made the hostile nations moan,
Or brought a blessing on their own:

Once more a son of Spencer waits,
A name familiar to thy gates;
Sprung from the chief whose prowess gain'd
The Garter while thy founder reign'd,
He offer'd here his dinted shield,
The dread of Gauls in Cressi's field,
Which, in thy high-arch'd temple rais'd,
For four long centuries hath blaz'd.

These seats our sires, a hardy kind,
To the fierce sons of war confin'd,
The flower of chivalry, who drew
With sinew'd arm the stubborn yew:
Or with heav'd pole-axe clear'd the field;
Or who, in justs and tourneys skill'd,
Before their ladies' eyes renown'd,
Threw horse and horseman to the ground.

In after-times, as courts refin'd,
Our patriots in the list were join'd.
Not only Warwick stain'd with blood,
Or Marlborough near the Danube's flood,
Have in their crimson crosses glow'd;
But, on just lawgivers bestow'd,

These emblems Cecil did invest,
And gleam'd on wise Godolphin's breast.

So Greece, ere arts began to rise,
Fix'd huge Orion in the skies,
And stern Alcides, fam'd in wars,
Bespangled with a thousand stars;
Till letter'd Athens round the pole
Made gentler constellations roll;
In the blue heavens the lyre she strung,
And near the Maid the Balance [1] hung.

Then, Spencer, mount amid the band,
Where knights and kings promiscuous stand.
What though the hero's flame repress'd
Burns calmly in thy generous breast!
Yet who more dauntless to oppose
In doubtful days our home-bred foes!
Who rais'd his country's wealth so high,
Or view'd with less desiring eye!

The sage, who, large of soul, surveys
The globe, and all its empires weighs,
Watchful the various climes to guide,
Which seas, and tongues, and faiths, divide,
A nobler name in Windsor's shrine
Shall leave, if right the Muse divine,

[1] Names of constellations.

Than sprung of old, abhorr'd and vain,
From ravag'd realms and myriads slain.
Why praise we, prodigal of fame,
The rage that sets the world on flame?
My guiltless Muse his brow shall bind
Whose godlike bounty spares mankind.
For those, whom bloody garlands crown,
The brass may breathe, the marble frown,
To him through every rescued land,
Ten thousand living trophies stand.

KENSINGTON GARDEN.

....Campos, ubi Troja fuit. VIRG.

WHERE Kensington, high o'er the neighbouring lands
Midst greens and sweets, a regal fabric, stands,
And sees each spring, luxuriant in her bowers,
A snow of blossoms, and a wild of flowers,
The dames of Britain oft in crowds repair
To gravel walks, and unpolluted air.
Here, while the town in damps and darkness lies,
They breathe in sunshine, and see azure skies;
Each walk, with robes of various dyes bespread,
Seems from afar a moving tulip-bed,
Where rich brocades and glossy damasks glow,
And chints, the rival of the showery bow.

Here England's daughter, darling of the land,
Sometimes, surrounded with her virgin band,
Gleams through the shades. She, towering o'er the rest,
Stands fairest of the fairer kind confest,
Form'd to gain hearts, that Brunswick's cause deny'd,
And charm a people to her father's side.
Long have these groves to royal guests been known,
Nor Nassau first preferr'd them to a throne.
Ere Norman banners wav'd in British air;
Ere lordly Hubba with the golden hair
Pour'd in his Danes; ere elder Julius came;
Or Dardan Brutus gave our isle a name;
A prince of Albion's lineage grac'd the wood,
The scene of wars, and stain'd with lovers' blood.
You, who through gazing crowds your captive throng,
Throw pangs and passions, as you move along,
Turn on the left, ye fair, your radiant eyes,
Where all unlevell'd the gay garden lies:
If generous anguish for another's pains
Ere heav'd your hearts, or shiver'd through your veins,
Look down attentive on the pleasing dale,
And listen to my melancholy tale.
That hollow space, were now in living rows
Line above line the yew's sad verdure grows,
Was, ere the planter's hand its beauty gave,
A common pit, a rude unfashion'd cave.

The landscape now so sweet we well may praise:
But far, far sweeter in its ancient days,
Far sweeter was it, when its peopled ground
With fairy domes and dazzling towers was crown'd.
Where in the midst those verdant pillars spring,
Rose the proud palace of the Elfin king;
For every edge of vegetable green,
In happier years a crowded street was seen;
Nor all those leaves that now the prospect grace,
Could match the numbers of its pygmy race,
What urg'd this mighty empire to its fate,
A tale of woe and wonder, I relate.
 When Albion rul'd the land, whose lineage came
From Neptune mingling with a mortal dame,
Their midnight pranks the sprightly fairies play'd
On every hill, and danc'd in every shade.
But, foes to sunshine, most they took delight
In dells and dales conceal'd from human sight:
There hew'd their houses in the arching rock;
Or scoop'd the bosom of the blasted oak;
Or heard, o'ershadow'd by some shelving hill,
The distant murmurs of the falling rill.
They, rich in pilfer'd spoils, indulg'd their mirth,
And pity'd the huge wretched sons of Earth.
Ev'n now, 'tis said, the hinds o'erhear their strain,
And strive to view their airy forms in vain:
They to their cells at man's approach repair,
Like the shy leveret, or the mother-hare,
The whilst poor mortals startle at the sound
Of unseen footsteps on the haunted ground.

Amid this garden, then with woods o'ergrown,
Stood the lov'd seat of royal Oberon.
From every region to his palace-gate
Came peers and princes of the fairy state,
Who, rank'd in council round the sacred shade,
Their monarch's will and great behests obey'd.
From Thames' fair banks, by lofty towers adorn'd,
With loads of plunder oft his chiefs return'd:
Hence in proud robes, and colours bright and gay,
Shone every knight and every lovely fay.
Whoe'er on Powell's dazzling stage display'd,
Hath fam'd king Pepin and his court survey'd,
May guess, if old by modern things we trace,
The pomp and splendour of the fairy-race.

By magic fenc'd, by spells encompass'd round,
No mortal touch'd this interdicted ground;
No mortal enter'd, those alone who came
Stol'n from the couch of some terrestrial dame:
For oft of babes they robb'd the matron's bed,
And left some sickly changeling in their stead.

It chanc'd a youth of Albion's royal blood
Was foster'd here, the wonder of the wood.
Milkah for wiles above her peers renown'd,
Deep-skill'd in charms and many a mystic sound,
As through the regal dome she sought for prey,
Observ'd the infant Albion where he lay
In mantles broider'd o'er with georgeous pride,
And stole him from the sleeping mother's side.

Who now but Milkah triumphs in her mind!
Ah, wretched nymph, to future evils blind?

The time shall come when thou shall dearly pay
The theft, hard-hearted! of that guilty day:
Thou in thy turn shalt like the queen repine,
And all her sorrows doubled shall be thine:
He who adorns thy house, the lovely boy
Who now adorns it, shall at length destroy.
Two hundred moons in their pale course had seen
The gay-rob'd fairies glimmer on the green,
And Albion now had reach'd in youthful prime
To nineteen years, as mortals measure time.
Flush'd with resistless charms he fir'd to love
Each nymph and little Dryad of the grove;
For skilful Milkah spar'd not to employ
Her utmost art to rear the princely boy;
Each supple limb she swath'd, and tender bone,
And to the Elfin standard kept him down;
She robb'd dwarf-elders of their fragrant fruit,
And fed him early with the daisy's root,
Whence through his veins the powerful juices ran,
And form'd in beauteous miniature the man.
Yet still, two inches taller than the rest,
His lofty port his human birth confest;
A foot in height, how stately did he show!
How look superior on the crowd below!
What knight like him could toss the rushy lance!
Who move so graceful in the mazy dance!
A shape so nice, or features half so fair,
What elf could boast! or such a flow of hair!

Bright Kenna saw, a princess born to reign,
And felt the charmer burn in every vein.
She, heiress to this empire's potent lord,
Prais'd like the stars, and next the Moon ador'd.
She, whom at distance thrones and princedoms view'd,
To whom proud Oriel and Azuriel sued,
In her high palace languish'd, void of joy,
And pin'd in secret for a mortal boy.
He too was smitten, and discreetly strove
By courtly deeds to gain the virgin's love.
For her he cull'd the fairest flower that grew,
Ere morning suns had drain'd their fragrant dew;
He chas'd the hornet in his mid-day flight,
And brought her glowworms in the noon of night;
When on ripe fruits she cast a wishing eye,
Did ever Albion think the tree too high!
He show'd her where the pregnant goldfinch hung,
And the wren-mother brooding o'er her young;
To her th' inscription on their eggs he read,
(Admire, ye clerks, the youth whom Milkah bred)
To her he show'd each herb of virtuous juice,
Their powers distinguish'd, and describ'd their use:
All vain their powers, alas! to Kenna prove,
And well sung Ovid, "There's no herb for love."
As when a ghost, enlarg'd from realms below,
Seeks its old friend to tell some secret woe,
The poor shade shivering stands, and must not break
His painful silence, till the mortal speak:

So far'd it with the little love-sick maid,
Forbid to utter, what her eyes betray'd.
He saw her anguish, and reveal'd his flame,
And spar'd the blushes of the tongue-ty'd dame.
The day would fail me, should I reckon o'er
The sighs they lavish'd, and the oaths they swore
In words so melting, that compar'd with those
The nicest courtship of terrestrial beaux
Would sound like compliments, from country
clowns [gowns.
To red cheek'd sweethearts in their home-spun
All in a lawn of many a various hue
A bed of flowers (a fairy forest) grew;
'Twas here one noon, the gaudiest of the May,
The still, the secret, silent, hour of day,
Beneath a lofty tulip's ample shade
Sat the young lover and th' immortal maid.
They thought all fairies slept, ah, luckless pair!
Hid, but in vain, in the Sun's noon-tide glare!
When Albion, leaning on his Kenna's breast,
Thus all the softness of his soul exprest:
"All things are hush'd. The Sun's meridian
rays
Veil the horizon in one mighty blaze:
Nor moon nor star in Heaven's blue arch is seen
With kindly rays to silver o'er the green,
Grateful to fairy eyes; they secret take
Their rest, and only wretched mortals wake.
This dead of day I fly to thee alone,
A world to me, a multitude in one.

Oh, sweet as dew-drops on these flowery lawns,
When the sky opens, and the evening dawns!
Straight as the pink, that towers so high in air,
Soft as the blow-bell! as the daisy, fair!
Blest be the hour, when first I was convey'd
An infant captive to this blissful shade!
And blest the hand that did my form refine,
And shrunk my stature to a match with thine!
Glad I for thee renounce my royal birth,
And all the giant-daughters of the Earth.
Thou, if thy breast with equal ardour burn,
Renounce thy kind, and love for love return.
So from us two, combin'd by nuptial ties,
A race unknown of demi-gods shall rise.
O speak, my love! my vows with vows repay,
And sweetly swear my rising fears away."

To whom (the shining azure of her eyes
More brighten'd) thus th' enamour'd maid replies:

"By all the stars, and first the glorious moon,
I swear, and by the head of Oberon,
A dreadful oath! no prince of fairy line
Shall e'er in wedlock plight his vows with mine.
Wheree'er my footsteps in the dance are seen,
May toadstools rise, and mildews blast the green,
May the keen east-wind blight my favourite flowers,
And snakes and spotted adders haunt my bowers.
Confin'd whole ages in an hemlock shade
There rather pine I a neglected maid,
Or worse, exil'd from Cynthia's gentle rays,
Parch in the sun a thousand summer-days,

Than any prince, a prince of fairy line,
In sacred wedlock plight his vows with mine."
  She ended: and with lips of rosy hue
Dipp'd five times over in ambrosial dew,
Stifled his words. When, from his covert rear'd,
The frowning brow of Oberon appear'd.
A sunflower's trunk was near, whence (killing
      sight!)
The monarch issued, half an ell in height:
Full on the pair a furious look he cast,
Nor spoke; but gave his bugle-horn a blast,
That through the woodland echoed far and wide,
And drew a swarm of subjects to his side.
A hundred chosen knights, in war renown'd,
Drive Albion banish'd from the sacred ground;
And twice ten myriads guard the bright abodes,
Where the proud king, amidst his demi-gods,
For Kenna's sudden bridal bids prepare,
And to Azuriel gives the weeping fair.
  If fame in arms, with ancient birth combin'd,
A faultless beauty, and a spotless mind,
To love and praise can generous souls incline,
That love, Azuriel, and that praise, was thine.
Blood only less than royal fill'd thy veins,
Proud was thy roof, and large thy fair domains.
Where now the skies high Holland-House in-
      vades,
And short-liv'd Warwick sadden'd all the shades,
Thy dwelling stood: nor did in him afford
A nobler owner, or a lovelier lord.

For thee a hundred fields produc'd their store,
And by thy name ten thousand vassals swore;
So lov'd thy name, that, at their monarch's choice,
All fairy shouted with a general voice.
Oriel alone a secret rage suppress,
That from his bosom heav'd the golden vest.
Along the banks of Thame his empire ran,
Wide was his range, and populous his clan.
When cleanly servants, if we trust old tales,
Beside their wages had good fairy vails,
Whole heaps of silver tokens, nightly paid,
The careful wife, or the neat dairy-maid,
Sunk not his stores. With smiles and powerful bribes
He gain'd the leaders of his neighbour tribes,
And ere the night the face of Heaven had chang'd,
Beneath his banners half the fairies rang'd.
Meanwhile, driven back to Earth, a lonely way
The cheerless Albion wander'd half the day,
A long, long journey, chok'd with brakes and thorns
Ill-measur'd by ten thousand barley-corns.
Tir'd out at length a spreading stream he spied
Fed by old Thame, a daughter of the tide:
'Twas then a spreading stream, though now its fame
Obscur'd, it bears the Greek's inglorious name,
And creeps, as through contracted bounds it strays,
A leap for boys in these degenerate days.

On the clear crystal's verdant bank he stood,
And thrice look'd backward on the fatal wood,
And thrice he groan'd, and thrice he beat his
breast,
And thus in tears his kindred gods addrest:
"If true, ye watery powers, my lineage came
From Neptune mingling with a mortal dame;
Down to his court, with coral garlands crown'd,
Through all your grottos waft my plaintive sound,
And urge the god, whose trident shakes the Earth,
To grace his offspring, and assert my birth."
He said. A gentle Naiad heard his prayer,
And, touch'd with pity for a lover's care,
Shoots to the sea, where low beneath the tides
Old Neptune in th' unfathom'd deep resides.
Rous'd at the news, the sea's stern sultan swore
Revenge, and scarce from present arms forbòre;
But first the nymph his harbinger he sends,
And to her care the favourite boy commends.
As thro' the Thames her backward course she
guides,
Driv'n up his current by the refluent tides,
Along his banks the pygmy legions spread
She spies, and haughty Oriel at their head.
Soon with wrong'd Albion's name the host she fires,
And counts the ocean's god, among his sires;
"The ocean's god, by whom shall be o'erthrown,
(Styx heard his oath) the tyrant Oberon.
See here beneath a toadstool's deadly gloom
Lies Albion; him the Fates your leader doom.

Hear, and obey; 'tis Neptune's powerful call,
By him Azuriel and his king shall fall."
  She said. They bow'd: and on their shields upbore
With shouts their new-saluted emperor.
E'en Oriel smil'd: at least to smile he strove,
And hopes of vengeance triumph'd over love.
  See now the mourner of the lonely shade
By gods protected, and by hosts obey'd,
A slave, a chief, by fickle Fortune's play,
In the short course of one revolving day.
What wonder if the youth, so strangely blest,
Felt his heart flutter in his little breast!
His thick embattled troops, with secret pride,
He views extended half an acre wide;
More light he treads, more tall he seems to rise,
And struts a straw-breadth nearer to the skies.
  O for thy Muse, great Bard,[1] whose lofty strains
In battle join'd the Pygmies and the Cranes;
Each gaudy knight, had I that warmth divine,
Each colour'd legion in my verse should shine.
But simple I, and innocent of art,
The tale, that sooth'd my infant years, impart,
The tale I heard whole winter-eves, untir'd,
And sing the battles, that my nurse inspir'd.
  Now the shrill corn-pipes, echoing loud to arms,
To rank and file reduce the straggling swarms,

[1] Mr. Addison.

Thick rows of spears at once, with sudden glare,
A grove of needles, glitter in the air;
Loose in the winds small ribbon-streamers flow,
Dipt in all colours of the heavenly bow,
And the gay host, that now its march pursues,
Gleams o'er the meadows in a thousand hues.
On Buda's plains thus formidably bright,
Shone Asia's sons, a pleasing, dreadful sight.
In various robes their silken troops were seen,
The blue, the red, and Prophet's sacred green:
When blooming Brunswick, near the Danube's flood,
First stain'd his maiden sword in Turkish blood.
Unseen and silent march the slow brigades
Through pathless wilds, and unfrequented shades.
In hope already vanquish'd by surprise,
In Albion's power the fairy empire lies;
Already has he seiz'd on Kenna's charms,
And the glad beauty trembles in his arms.
The march concludes: and now in prospect near,
But fenc'd with arms, the hostile towers appear.
For Oberon, or Druids falsely sing,
Wore his prime vizier in a magic ring,
A subtle spright, that opening plots foretold
By sudden dimness on the beamy gold.
Hence, in a crescent form'd, his legions bright
With beating bosoms waited for the fight;
To charge their foes they march, a glittering band,
And in their van doth bold Azuriel stand.

What rage that hour did Albion's soul possess,
Let chiefs imagine, and let lovers guess!
Forth issuing from his ranks, that strove in vain
To check his course, athwart the dreadful plain
He strides indignant, and with haughty cries
To single fight the fairy prince defies.
Forbear! rash youth, th' unequal war to try;
Nor, sprung from mortals, with immortals vie.
No god stands ready to avert thy doom,
Nor yet thy grandsire of the waves is come.
My words are vain—no words the wretch can move,
By Beauty dazzled, and bewitch'd by Love:
He longs, he burns, to win the glorious prize,
And sees no danger, while he sees her eyes.
Now from each host the eager warriors start,
And furious Albion flings his hasty dart,
'Twas feather'd from the bee's transparent wing,
And its shaft ended in a hornet's sting;
But, tost in rage, it flew without a wound,
High o'er the foe, and guiltless pierc'd the ground.
Not so Azuriel's: with unerring aim
Too near the needle-pointed javelin came,
Drove through the seven-fold shield, and silken vest,
And lightly ras'd the lover's ivory breast.
Rous'd at the smart, and rising to the blow,
With his keen sword he cleaves his fairy foe,
Sheer from the shoulder to the waste he cleaves,
And of one arm the tottering trunk bereaves.

His useless steel brave Albion wields no more,
But sternly smiles, and thinks the combat o'er:
So had it been, had aught of mortal strain,
Or less than fairy, felt the deadly pain.
But empyreal forms, howe'er in fight
Gash'd and dismember'd, easily unite.
As some frail cup of China's purest mould,
With azure varnish'd, and bedropt with gold,
Though broke, if cur'd by some nice virgin's hands,
In its old strength and pristine beauty stands;
The tumults of the boiling Bohea braves,
And holds secure the coffee's sable waves:
So did Azuriel's arm, if Fame say true,
Rejoin the vital trunk whence first it grew;
And whilst in wonder fix'd poor Albion stood,
Plung'd the curs'd sabre in his heart's warm blood.
The golden broidery, tender Milkah wove,
The breast, to Kenna sacred and to Love,
Lie rent and mangled, and the gaping wound
Pours out a flood of purple on the ground.
The jetty lustre sickens in his eyes,
On his cold cheeks the bloomy freshness dies;
"Oh Kenna, Kenna, "thrice he tried to say,
"Kenna, farewell!" and sigh'd his soul away.
His fall the Dryads with loud shrieks deplore,
By sister Naiads echo'd from the shore,

Thence down to Neptune's secret realms convey'd,
Through grots, and glooms, and many a coral shade.
The sea's great sire, with looks denouncing war,
The trident shakes, and mounts the pearly car;
With one stern frown the wide-spread deep deforms,
And works the madding ocean into storms.
O'er foaming mountains, and through bursting tides,
Now high, now low, the bounding chariot rides,
Till through the Thames in a loud whirlwind's roar
It shoots, and lands him on the destin'd shore.
Now fix'd on earth his towering stature stood,
Hung o'er the mountains, and o'erlook'd the wood.
To Brumpton's Grove one ample stride he took,
(The valleys trembled, and the forests shook,)
The next huge step reach'd the devoted shade,
Where chok'd in blood was wretched Albion laid:
Where now the vanquish'd, with the victors join'd,
Beneath the regal banners stood combin'd.
Th' embattled dwarfs with rage and scorn he past,
And on their town his eye vindictive cast.
In deep foundations his strong trident cleaves,
And high in air th' uprooted empire heaves;
On his broad engine the vast ruin hung,
Which on the foe with force divine he flung:
Aghast the legions in th' approaching shade,
Th' inverted spires and rocking domes survey'd,

That, downward tumbling on the host below,
Crush'd the whole nation at one dreadful blow.
Towers, arms, nymphs, warriors, are together lost,
And a whole empire falls to soothe said Albion's ghost.
Such was the period, long restrain'd by Fate,
And such the downfall of the fairy state.
This dale, a pleasing region, not unblest,
This dale possest they ; and had still possest ;
Had not their monarch, with a father's pride,
Rent from her lord th' inviolable bride,
Rash to dissolve the contract seal'd above,
The solemn vows and sacred bonds of love.
Now, where his elves so sprightly danc'd the round,
No violet breathes, nor daisy paints the ground,
His towers and people fill one common grave,
A shapeless ruin, and a barren cave.
Beneath huge hills of smoking piles he lay
Stunn'd and confounded a whole summer's day,
At length awak'd (for what can long restrain
Unbody'd spirits !) but awak'd in pain :
And as he saw the desolated wood,
And the dark den where once his empire stood,
Grief chill'd his heart : to his half-open'd eyes
In every oak a Neptune seem'd to rise :
He fled : and left, with all his trembling peers,
The long possession of a thousand years.

Through bush, through brake, through groves, and gloomy dales [vales,
Through dank and dry, o'er streams and flowery
Direct they fled; but often look'd behind,
And stopt and started at each rustling wind.
Wing'd with like fear, his abdicated bands
Disperse and wander into different lands.
Part hid beneath the Peak's deep caverns lie,
In silent glooms, impervious to the sky;
Part on fair Avon's margin seek repose,
Whose stream o'er Britain's midmost region flows,
Where formidable Neptune never came,
And seas and oceans are but known by fame:
Some to dark woods and secret shade retreat:
And some on mountains choose their airy seat.
There haply by the ruddy damsel seen,
Or shepherd-boy, they featly foot the green,
While from their steps a circling verdure springs;
But fly from towns, and dread the courts of kings.
Meanwhile said Kenna, loth to quit the grove,
Hung o'er the body of her breathless love,
Try'd every art, (vain arts!) to change his doom,
And vow'd (vain vows!) to join him in the tomb.
What could she do? the Fates alike deny
The dead to live, or fairy forms to die.
An herb there grows (the same old Homer[1] tells
Ulysses bore to rival Circe's spells)

[1] Odyss. Lib. x.

Its root is ebon-black, but sends to light
A stem that bends with flow'rets milky white,
Moly the plant, which gods and fairies know,
But secret kept from mortal men below.
On his pale limbs its virtuous juice she shed,
And murmur'd mystic numbers o'er the dead,
When lo! the little shape by magic power
Grew less and less, contracted to a flower;
A flower, that first in this sweet garden smil'd,
To virgins sacred, and the Snowdrop styl'd.
The new-born plant with sweet regret she view'd,
Warm'd with her sighs, and with her tears bedew'd,
Its ripen'd seeds from bank to bank convey'd,
And with her lover whiten'd half the shade.
Thus won from death each spring she sees him grow,
And glorious in the vegetable snow,
Which now increas'd through wide Britannia's plains,
Its parent's warmth and spotless name retains,
First leader of the flowery race aspires,
And foremost catches the Sun's genial fires,
'Mid frosts and snows triumphant dares appear,
Mingles the seasons, and leads on the year.
Deserted now of all the pygmy race,
Nor man nor fairy touch'd this guilty place.
In heaps on heaps, for many a rolling age,
It lay accurs'd, the mark of Neptune's rage,
Till great Nassau recloth'd the desert shade,
Thence sacred to Britannia's monarchs made.

'Twas then the green-rob'd nymph, fair Kenna, came,
(Kenna that gave the neighbouring town its name.)
Proud when she saw th' ennobled garden shine
With nymphs and heroes of her lover's line,
She vow'd to grace the mansions once her own,
And picture out in plants the fairy town.
To far-fam'd Wise her flight unseen she sped,
And with gay prospects fill'd the craftsman's head,
Soft in his fancy drew a pleasing scheme,
And plann'd that landscape in a morning dream.
With the sweet view the sire of Gardens fir'd,
Attempts the labour by the nymph inspir'd,
The walls and streets in rows of yew designs,
And forms the town in all its ancient lines;
The corner trees he lifts more high in air,
And girds the palace with a verdant square;
Nor knows, while round he views the rising scenes,
He builds a city as he plants his greens.
With a sad pleasure the aërial maid
This image of her ancient realms survey'd,
How chang'd, how fall'n from its primeval pride!
Yet here each moon, the hour her lover died,
Each moon his solemn obsequies she pays,
And leads the dance beneath pale Cynthia's rays;
Pleas'd in these shades to head her fairy train,
And grace the groves where Albion's kinsmen reign.

TO A LADY BEFORE MARRIAGE.

Oh! form'd by Nature, and refin'd by Art,
With charms to win, and sense to fix the heart!
By thousands sought, Clotilda, canst thou free
Thy croud of captives and descend to me?
Content in shades obscure to waste thy life,
A hidden beauty and a country wife?
O! listen while thy summers are my theme,
Ah! soothe thy partner in his waking dream!
In some small hamlet on the lonely plain, [train;
Where Thames, through meadows, rolls his mazy
Or where high Windsor, thick with greens array'd
Waves his old oaks, and spreads his ample shade,
Fancy has figur'd out our calm retreat;
Already round the visionary seat
Our limes begin to shoot, our flowers to spring,
The brooks to murmur, and the birds to sing.
Where dost thou lie, thou thinly-peopled green,
Thou nameless lawn, and village yet unseen,
Where sons, contented with their native ground,
Ne'er travell'd further than ten furlongs round,
And the tann'd peasant, and his ruddy bride,
Were born together, and together died;

Where early larks best tell the morning light,
And only Philomel disturbs the night?
'Midst gardens here my humble pile shall rise,
With sweets surrounded of ten thousand dies;
All savage where th' embroider'd gardens end,
The haunt of echoes, shall my woods ascend;
And oh! if Heaven th' ambitious thought approve,
A rill shall warble cross the gloomy grove,
A little rill, o'er pebbly beds convey'd,
Gush down the steep, and glitter through the glade.
What cheering scents these bordering banks exhale!
How loud that heifer lows from yonder vale!
That thrush how shrill! his note so clear, so high,
He drowns each feather'd minstrel of the sky.
Here let me trace beneath the purpled morn,
The deep-mouth'd beagle, and the sprightly horn;
Or lure the trout with well dissembled flies,
Or fetch the fluttering partridge from the skies.
Nor shall thy hand disdain to crop the vine,
The downy peach, or flavour'd nectarine;
Or rob the bee-hive of its golden hoard,
And bear th' unbought luxuriance to thy board.
Sometimes my books by day shall kill the hours,
While from thy needle rise the silken flowers,
And thou, by turns, to ease my feeble sight,
Resume the volume, and deceive the night.
Oh! when I mark thy twinkling eyes opprest,
Soft whispering, let me warn my love to rest;

Then watch thee, charm'd, while sleep locks every sense,
And to sweet Heaven commend thy innocence.
Thus reign'd our fathers o'er the rural fold,
Wise, hale, and honest, in the days of old;
Till courts arose, where substance pays for show,
And specious joys are bought with real woe.
See Flavia's pendants large, well spread and right;
The ear that wears them hears a fool each night.
Mark how th' embroider'd col'nel sneaks away,
To shun the withering dame that made him gay;
That knave, to gain a title, lost his fame;
That rais'd his credit by a daughter's shame;
This coxcomb's ribband cost him half his land,
And oaks, unnumber'd, bought that fool a wand.
Fond man, as all his sorrows were too few,
Acquires strange wants that nature never knew,
By midnight lamps he emulates the day,
And sleeps, perverse, the cheerful suns away;
From goblets high-embost, his wine must glide,
Round his clos'd sight the gorgeous curtain slide;
Fruits ere their time to grace his pomp must rise,
And three untasted courses glut his eyes.
For this are nature's gentle calls withstood,
The voice of conscience, and the bonds of blood;
This wisdom thy reward for every pain,
And this gay glory all thy mighty gain.
Fair phantoms woo'd and scorn'd from age to age,
Since bards began to laugh, and priests to rage.

And yet, just curse on man's aspiring kind!
Prone to ambition, to example blind,
Our children's children shall our steps pursue,
And the same errors be for ever new.
Meanwhile in hope a guiltless country swain,
My reed with warblings cheers the imagin'd plain.
Hail humble shades, where truth and silence dwell!
The noisy town and faithless court farewell!
Farewell ambition, once my darling flame!
The thirst of lucre, and the charm of fame!
In life's by-road, that winds through paths unknown,
My days, though number'd, shall be all my own.
Here shall they end, (O! might they twice begin)
And all be white the Fates intend to spin.

A POEM

IN PRAISE OF THE HORNBOOK.

WRITTEN UNDER A FIT OF THE GOUT.

Magni magna patrant, nos non nisi ludicra........
....................Podagra hæc otia fecit.

Hail! ancient Book, most venerable code!
Learning's first cradle, and its last abode!
The huge unnumber'd volumes which we see,
By lazy plagiaries are stol'n from thee.
Yet future times, to thy sufficient store,
Shall ne'er presume to add one letter more.
  Thee will I sing, in comely wainscot bound,
And golden verge enclosing thee around;
The faithful horn before, from age to age,
Preserving thy invaluable page;
Behind, thy patron saint in armour shines,
With sword and lance, to guard thy sacred lines:
Beneath his courser's feet the dragon lies
Transfix'd; his blood thy scarlet cover dies;
Th' instructive handle 's at the bottom fix'd,
Lest wrangling critics should pervert the text.

Or if to gingerbread thou shalt descend,
And liquorish learning to thy babes extend;
Or sugar'd plane, o'erspread with beaten gold,
Does the sweet treasure of thy letters hold;
Thou still shalt be my song——Apollo's choir
I scorn t' invoke; Cadmus my verse inspire:
'Twas Cadmus who the first materials brought
Of all the learning which has since been taught,
Soon made complete! for mortals ne'er shall know
More than contain'd of old the Christ-cross row;
What masters dictate, or what doctors preach,
Wise matrons hence, e'en to our children teach:
But as the name of every plant and flower
(So common that each peasant knows its power)
Physicians in mysterious cant express,
T' amuse the patient, and enhance their fees;
So from the letters of our native tongue,
Put in Greek scrawls, a mystery too is sprung,
Schools are erected, puzzling grammars made,
And artful men strike out a gainful trade;
Strange characters adorn the learned gate,
And heedless youth catch at the shining bait;
The pregnant boys the noisy charms declare,
And Tau's, and Delta's,[1] make their mothers stare;
Th' uncommon sounds amaze the vulgar ear,
And what's uncommon never costs too dear.
Yet in all tongues the Hornbook is the same,
Taught by the Grecian master, or the English dame.

1 The Greek letters T, Δ.

But how shall I thy endless virtues tell,
In which thou dost all other books excel?
No greasy thumbs thy spotless leaf can soil,
Nor crooked dogsears thy smooth corners spoil;
In idle pages no errata stand,
To tell the blunders of the printer's hand:
No fulsome dedication here is writ,
Nor flattering verse, to praise the author's wit:
The margin with no tedious notes is vex'd,
Nor various reading to confound the text:
All parties in thy literal sense agree,
Thou perfect centre of concordancy!
Search we the records of an ancient date,
Or read what modern histories relate,
They all proclaim what wonders have been done
By the plain letters taken as they run:
"Too high the floods of passion us'd to roll,
And rend the Roman youth's impatient soul;
His hasty anger furnish'd scenes of blood,
And frequent deaths of worthy men ensued:
In vain were all the weaker methods tried,
None could suffice to stem the furious tide,
Thy sacred line he did but once repeat,
And laid the storm, and cool'd the raging heat." [1]
Thy heavenly notes, like angels' music, cheer
Departing souls, and soothe the dying ear.
An aged peasant, on his latest bed,
Wish'd for a friend some godly book to read;

[1] The advice given to Augustus, by Athenodorus the stoic philosopher.

The pious grandson thy known handle takes,
And (eyes lift up) this savory lecture makes:
"Great A," he gravely read; the important sound
The empty walls and hollow roof rebound:
Th' expiring ancient rear'd his drooping head,
And thank'd his stars that Hodge had learn'd to read.
"Great B," the younker bawls: O heavenly breath!
What ghostly comforts in the hour of death!
What hopes I feel! "Great C," pronounc'd the boy;
The grandsire dies with ecstasy of joy.
  Yet in some lands such ignorance abounds,
Whole parishes scarce know thy useful sounds.
Of Essex-Hundreds Fame gives this report,
But Fame, I ween, says many things in sport.
Scarce lives the man to whom thou'rt quite unknown,
Though few th' extent of thy vast empire own.
Whatever wonders magic spells can do
On earth, in air, in sea, in shades below;
What words profound and dark wise Mahomet spoke,
When his old cow an angel's figure took;
What strong enchantments sage Canidia knew,
Or Horace sung, fierce monsters to subdue,
O mighty Book, are all contain'd in you!
All human arts, and every science meet,
Within the limits of thy single sheet:

From thy vast root all learning's branches grow,
And all her streams from thy deep fountain flow.
And, lo! while thus thy wonders I indite,
Inspir'd I feel the power of which I write;
The gentler gout his former rage forgets,
Less frequent now, and less severe the fits:
Loose grew the chains which bound my useless
feet;
Stiffness and pain from every joint retreat;
Surprising strength comes every moment on,
I stand, I step, I walk, and now I run.
Here let me cease, my hobbling numbers stop.
And at thy handle[1] hand my crutches up.

THERISTES, OR THE LORDLING,

THE GRANDSON OF A BRICKLAYER, GREAT-GRANDSON OF A BUTCHER.

THERISTES of amphibious breed,
Motley fruit of mongrel seed:
By the dam from lordlings sprung,
By the sire exhal'd from dung:

[1] Votiva Tabula. HOR.

Think on every vice in both,
Look on him, and see their growth.
View him on the mother's side,
Fill'd with falsehood, spleen, and pride,
Positive and overbearing,
Changing still, and still adhering,
Spiteful, peevish, rude, untoward,
Fierce in tongue, in heart a coward;
When his friends he most is hard on,
Cringing comes to beg their pardon;
Reputation ever tearing,
Ever dearest friendship swearing;
Judgment weak, and passion strong;
Always various, always wrong;
Provocation never waits,
Where he loves, or where he hates;
Talks whate'er comes in his head,
Wishes it were all unsaid.
Let me now the vices trace,
From his father's scoundrel race,
Who could give the looby such airs?
Were they masons? Were they butchers?
Herald lend the Muse an answer,
From his atavus and grandsire!
This was dexterous at his trowel,
That was bred to kill a cow well:
Hence the greasy clumsy mien,
In his dress and figure seen:
Hence that mean and sordid soul,
Like his body, rank and foul:

Hence that wild suspicious peep,
Like a rogue that steals a sheep:
Hence he learn'd the butcher's guile,
How to cut a throat and smile:
Like a butcher doom'd for life,
In his mouth to wear his knife:
Hence he draws his daily food,
From his tenant's vital blood.
  Lastly, let his gifts be tried,
Borrow'd from the mason-side.
Some, perhaps, may think him able
In the state to build a Babel;
Could we place him in a station
To destroy the old foundation.
True, indeed, I should be gladder
Could he learn to mount a ladder.
May he at his latter end
Mount alive, and dead descend.
In him tell me, which prevail,
Female vices most, or male?
What produc'd them, can you tell?
Human race, or imp of Hell?

OXFORD, A POEM,[1]

INSCRIBED TO LORD LONSDALE,[2] 1707.

Unum opus est intactæ Palladis urbem
Carmine perpetuo celebrare—

HOR. I. Od. 7.

WHILST you, my lord, adorn that stately seat,
Where shining Beauty makes her soft retreat,
Enjoying all those graces, uncontroll'd,
Which noblest youths would die but to behold;
Whilst you inhabit Lowther's awful pile,
A structure worthy of the founder's toil,

[1] Added by the express direction of Dr. Johnson; by whom (together with another piece) it was originally appended to his Life of Tickell, with this introduction: "The two poems which follow would have been inserted in the collection, if the compilers could have obtained copies of them. To complete the poetical works of Tickell, they are here copied from the Select Collection of Miscellaneous Poems, 1780." *N.*

[2] Richard, second Lord Viscount Lonsdale. He died of the smallpox, December 1, 1713. *N.*

Amaz'd we see the former Lonsdale[3] shine
In each descendant of his noble line:
But most transported and surpris'd we view
His ancient glories all reviv'd in you,
Where charms and virtues join their equal grace,
Your father's godlike soul, your mother's lovely
face.
Me fortune and kind Heaven's indulgent care
To famous Oxford and the Muses bear,
Where, of all ranks, the blooming youths combine
To pay due homage to the mighty Nine,
And snatch, with smiling joy, the laurel crown,
Due to the learned honours of the gown.
Here I, the meanest of the tuneful throng,
Delude the time with an unhallow'd song,
Which thus my thanks to much-lov'd Oxford pays,
In no ungrateful, though unartful lays.
Where shall I first the beauteous scene disclose,
And all the gay variety expose?
For wheresoe'er I turn my wondering eyes,
Aspiring towers and verdant groves arise,
Immortal greens the smiling plains array,
And mazy rivers murmur all the way.
O! might your eyes behold each sparkling dome,
And freely o'er the beauteous prospect roam,

[3] Sir John Lowther, one of the early promoters of the Revolution, was constituted vice-chamberlain to King William and Queen Mary on their advancement to the throne; created Baron Lowther and Viscount Lonsdale, May 28, 1696; and appointed lord privy-seal in 1699. He died July 10, 1700. *N.*

Less ravish'd your own Lowther you'd survey,
Though pomp and state the costly seat display,
Where Art so nicely has adorn'd the place,
That Nature's aid might seem an useless grace;
Yet Nature's smiles such various charms impart,
That vain and needless are the strokes of Art.
In equal state our rising structures shine,
Fram'd by such rules, and form'd by such design,
That here, at once surpris'd and pleas'd, we view
Old Athens lost and conquer'd in the new;
More sweet our shades, more fit our bright abodes
For warbling Muses and inspiring Gods.
  Great Vanbrook's[4] self might own each artful draught
Equal to models in his curious thought,
Nor scorn a fabric by our plans to frame,
Or in immortal labours sing their fame;
Both ways he saves them from destroying Fate,
If he but praise them, or but imitate.
  See, where the sacred Sheldon's[5] haughty dome
Rivals the stately pomp of ancient Rome,
Whose form, so great and noble, seems design'd
T' express the grandeur of its founder's mind.
Here, in one lofty building, we behold
Whate'er the Latian pride could boast of old.
True, no dire combats feed the savage eye,
And strew the sand with sportive cruelty;
But, more adorn'd with what the Muse inspires,
It far outshines their bloody theatres.

[4] Sir John Vanbrugh. *N.*

[5] The Theatre. *T.*

Delightful scene! when here, in equal verse,
The youthful bards their godlike queen rehearse,
To Churchill's wreaths Apollo's laurel join,
And sing the plains of Hockstet and Judoign.
Next let the Muse record our Bodley's seat [6],
Nor aim at numbers, like the subject, great:
All hail, thou fabric, sacred to the Nine,
Thy fame immortal, and thy form divine!
Who to thy praise attempts the dangerous flight,
Should in thy various tongues be taught to write;
His verse, like thee, a lofty dress should wear,
And breathe the genius which inhabits there;
Thy proper lays alone can make thee live,
And pay that fame, which first thyself didst give.
So fountains, which through secret channels flow,
And pour above the floods they take below,
Back to their father Ocean urge their way,
And to the sea, the streams it gave, repay.
No more we fear the military rage,
Nurs'd up in some obscure barbarian age;
Nor dread the ruin of our arts divine,
From thick-skull'd heroes of the Gothic line,
Though pale the Romans saw those arms advance,
And wept their learning lost in ignorance.
Let brutal rage around its terrour spread,
The living murder, and consume the dead,
In impious fires let noblest writings burn,
And with their authors share a common urn;

[6] The Bodleian Library. *T.*

Only, ye Fates, our lov'd Bodleian spare,
Be IT, and Learning's self shall be your care,
Here every art and every grace shall join,
Collected Phœbus here alone shall shine,
Each other seat be dark, and this be all divine.
Thus when the Greeks imperial Troy defac'd,
And to the ground its fatal walls debas'd,
In vain they burn the work of hands divine,
And vow destruction to the Dardan line,
Whilst good Æneas flies th' unequal wars,
And, with his guardian gods, Iülus bears,
Old Troy for ever stands in him alone,
And all the Phrygian kings survive in one.
Here still presides each sage's reverend shade,
In soft repose and easy grandeur laid;
Their deathless works forbid their fame to die,
Nor Time itself their persons shall destroy,
Preserv'd within the living gallery.[7]
What greater gift could bounteous Heaven bestow,
Than to be seen above, and read below?
With deep respect I bend my duteous head,
To see the faithful likeness of the dead;
But O! what Muse can equal warmth impart?
The painter's skill transcends the poet's art.
When round the pictur'd founders I descry,
With goodness soft, and great with majesty,
So much of life the artful colours give,
Scarce more within their colleges they live;

[7] The Picture Gallery. *T.*

My blood begins in wilder rounds to roll,
And pleasing tumults combat in my soul;
An humble awe my downcast eyes betray,
And only less than adoration pay.
Such were the Roman Fathers, when, o'ercome,
They saw the Gauls insult o'er conquer'd Rome;
Each captive seem'd the haughty victor's lord,
And prostrate chiefs their awful slaves ador'd.
Such art as this adorns your Lowther's hall,
Where feasting gods carouse upon the wall;
The nectar, which creating paint supplies,
Intoxicates each pleas'd spectator's eyes;
Who view, amaz'd, the figures heavenly fair,
And think they breathe the true Elysian air.
With strokes so bold, great Verrio's hand has drawn
The gods in dwellings brighter than their own.
Fir'd with a thousand raptures, I behold.
What lively features grac'd each bard of old;
Such lips, I think, did guide his charming tongue,
In such an air as this the poet sung;
Such eyes as these glow'd with the sacred fire,
And hands like these employ'd the vocal lyre.
Quite ravish'd, I pursue each image o'er,
And scarce admire their deathless labours more.
See where the gloomy Scaliger appears,
Each shade is critic, and each feature sneers;
The artful Ben so smartly strikes the eye,
I more than see a fancy'd comedy;

The muddy Scotus crowns the motley show,
And metaphysics cloud his wrinkled brow.
But distant awe invades my beating breast,
To see great Ormond in the paint expreſt;
With fear I view the figure from afar,
Which burns with noble ardour for the war;
But near approaches free my doubting mind,
To view such sweetness with such grandeur join'd.
 Here studious heads the graver tablet shows,
And there with martial warmth the picture glows;
The blooming youth here boasts a brighter hue,
And painted virgins far outshine the true.
 Hail, Colours, which with Nature bear a strife,
And only want a voice to perfect life!
The wondering stranger makes a sudden stand,
And pays low homage to the lovely band;
Within each frame a real fair believes,
And vainly thinks the mimic canvas lives;
Till, undeceiv'd, he quits th' enchanting shew,
Pleas'd with the art, though he laments it too.
 So when his Juno bold Ixion woo'd,
And aim'd at pleasures worthy of a god,
A beauteous cloud was form'd by angry Jove,
Fit to invite, though not indulge his love;
The mortal thought he saw his goddess shine,
And all the lying graces look'd divine;
But when with heat he clasp'd her fancied charms,
The empty vapour baulk'd his eager arms.
 Loth to depart, I leave th' inviting scene,
Yet scarce forbear to view it o'er again;

But still new objects give a new delight,
And various prospects bless the wandering sight.
Aloft in state the airy towers arise,
And with new lustre deck the wondering skies!
Lo! to what height the schools ascending reach,
Built with that art which they alone can teach;
The lofty dome expands her spacious gate,
Where all the decent graces jointly wait;
In every shape the god of art resorts,
And crowds of sages fill th' extended courts.
With wonders fraught the bright Museum see,
Itself the greatest curiosity!
Where Nature's choicest treasure, all combin'd,
Delight at once, and quite confound the mind;
Ten thousand splendours strike the dazzled eye,
And form on Earth another galaxy.
Here colleges in sweet confusion rise,
There temples seem to reach their native skies;
Spires, towers, and groves, compose the various shew,
And mingled prospects charm the doubting view;
Who can deny their characters divine,
Without resplendent, and inspir'd within?
But, since above my weak and artless lays,
Let their own poets sing their equal praise.
One labour more my grateful verse renews,
And rears aloft the low-descending Muse;
The building,[8] parent of my young essays,

[8] Queen's College Library. See the Poem on Queen Caro

Asks in return a tributary praise.
Pillars sublime bear up the learned weight,
And antique sages tread the pompous height;
Whilst guardian Muses shade the happy piles,
And all around diffuse propitious smiles.
Here Lancaster, adorn'd with every grace,
Stands chief in merit, as the chief in place:
To his lov'd name our earliest lays belong,
The theme at once, and patron of our song.
Long may he o'er his much-lov'd Queen's preside,
Our arts encourage, and our counsels guide;
Till after-ages, fill'd with glad surprise,
Behold his image all majestic rise,
Where now in pomp a venerable band,
Princes and queens and holy fathers, stand.
Good Egglesfield[9] claims homage from the eye,
And the hard stone seems soft with piety;
The mighty monarchs still the same appear,
And every marble frown provokes the war;
Whilst rugged rocks, mark'd with Philippa's face,
Soften to charms, and glow with new-born grace.
A sightless noble did the warriors yield,
Transform'd to statues by the Gorgon shield;
Distorting fear the coward's form confest,
And fury seem'd to heave the hero's breast;
The lifeless rocks each various thought betray'd,
And all the soul was in the stone display'd.

line's rebuilding the Lodgings of the Black Prince and Henry V. p. 101, the other of the "two poems" alluded to in p. 130. *N.*

[9] Robert Egglesfield, B. D. the founder, 1340. *N.*

Too high, my verse! has been thy daring flight,
Thy softer numbers now the groves invite,
Where silent shades provoke the speaking lyre,
And cheerful objects happy songs inspire,
At once bestow rewards, and thoughts infuse,
Compose a garland, and supply a Muse.
Behold around, and see the living green
In native colours paints a blooming scene;
The eternal buds no deadly Winter fear,
But scorn the coldest season of the year;
Apollo sure will bless the happy place,
Which his own Daphne condescends to grace;
For here the everlasting laurels grow,
In every grotto, and on every brow.
Prospects so gay demand a Congreve's strains,
To call the gods and nymphs upon the plains;
Pan yields his empire o'er the sylvan throng,
Pleas'd to submit to his superior song;
Great Denham's genius looks with rapture down,
And Spenser's shade resigns the rural crown.
Fill'd with great thoughts, a thousand sages rove
Through every field and solitary grove;
Whose souls, ascending an exalted height,
Out-soar the drooping Muse's vulgar flight,
That longs to see her darling votaries laid
Beneath the covert of some gentle shade,
Where purling streams and warbling birds conspire
To aid th' enchantments of the trembling lyre.
Bear me, some god, to Christ-Church, royal seat,
And lay me softly in the green retreat,

Where Aldrich holds o'er Wit the sovereign power,
And crowns the poets which he taught before.
To Aldrich Britain owes her tuneful Boyle,
The noblest trophy of the conquer'd isle;
Who adds new warmth to our poetic fire,
And gives to England the Hibernian lyre.
Philips, by Phœbus and his Aldrich taught,
Sings with that heat wherewith his Churchill fought,
Unfetter'd, in great Milton's strain he writes,
Like Milton's angels whilst his hero fights;
Pursues the bard, whilst he with honour can,
Equals the poet, and excels the man.
O'er all the plains, the streams, and woods around,
The pleasing lays of sweetest bards resound;
A faithful echo every note returns,
And listening river-gods neglect their urns.
When Codrington [1] and Steele their verse unrein,
And form an easy, unaffected strain,
A double wreath of laurel binds their brow,
As they are poets and are warriors too.
Trapp's lofty scenes in gentle numbers flow,
Like Dryden great, as soft as moving Rowe.
When youthful Harrison,[2] with tuneful skill
Makes Woodstock Park scarce yield to Cooper's Hill;
Old Chaucer from th' Elysian Fields looks down,

[1] The great benefactor to All-souls College. *N.*

[2] Of whom, see Select Collection, vol iv. p. 180. *N.*

And sees at length a genius like his own;
Charm'd with his lays, which reach the shades below,
Fair Rosamonda intermits her woe,
Forgets the anguish of an injur'd soul,
The fatal poignard, and envenom'd bowl.
Apollo smiles on Magd'len's peaceful bowers,
Perfumes the air, and paints the grot with flowers,
Where Yalden learn'd to gain the myrtle crown,
And every Muse was fond of Addison.
Applauded man! for weightier trusts design'd,
For once disdain not to unbend thy mind;
Thy mother Isis and her groves rehearse,
A subject not unworthy of thy verse;
So Latian fields will cease to boast thy praise,
And yield to Oxford, painted in thy lays:
And when the age to come, from envy free,
What thou to Virgil giv'st shall give to thee,
Isis, immortal by the poet's skill,
"Shall, in the smooth description, murmur still[3];"
New beauties shall adorn our sylvan scene,
And in thy numbers grow for ever green.
Danby's fam'd gift[4] such verse as thine requires,
Exalted raptures, and celestial fires;
Apollo here should plenteously impart,
As well his singing, as his curing art;

[3] Letter from Italy, by Mr. Addison. *T.*

[4] The Physic-garden at Oxford. This hint was happily taken up in 1713, by Dr. Evans. See Select Collection, 1780, vol. iii. p. 145. *N.*

Nature herself the healing garden loves,
Which kindly her declining strength improves,
Baffles the strokes of unrelenting Death,
Can break his arrows, and can blunt his teeth.
How sweet the landscape! where, in living trees,
Here frowns a vegetable Hercules!
There fam'd Achilles learns to live again;
And looks yet angry in the mimic scene;
Here artful birds, which blooming arbours show
Seem to fly higher, whilst they upwards grow,
From the same leaves both arms and warriors
rise,
And every bough a different charm supplies.
So when our world the great Creator made,
And, unadorn'd, the sluggish chaos laid,
Horrour and Beauty own'd their sire the same,
And Form itself from Parent Matter came,
That lumpish mass alone was source of all,
And Bards and Themes had one original.
In vain the groves demand my longer stay,
The gentle Isis wafts the Muse away;
With ease the river guides her wandering stream,
And hastes to mingle with uxorious Thame,
Attempting poets on her banks lie down,
And quaff, inspir'd, the better Helicon,
Harmonious strains adorn their various themes,
Sweet as the banks, and flowing as the streams.
Bless'd we, whom bounteous Fortune here has
thrown.
And made the various blessings all our own!

Nor crowns, nor globes, the pageantry of state,
Upon our humble, easy slumbers wait;
Nor aught that is Ambition's lofty theme
Disturbs our sleep, and gilds the gaudy dream.
Touch'd by no ills which vex th' unhappy great,
We only read the changes in the state,
Triumphant Marlborough's arms at distance hear,
And learn from Fame the rough events of war;
With pointed rhymes the Gallic tyrant pierce,
And make the cannon thunder in our verse.
See how the matchless youth their hours improve,
And in the glorious way to knowledge move!
Eager for fame, prevent the rising Sun,
And watch the midnight labours of the Moon.
Not tender years their bold attempts restrain,
Who leave dull Time, and hasten into man,
Pure to the soul, and pleasing to the eyes,
Like angels youthful, and like angels wise.
Some learn the mighty deeds of ages gone,
And, by the lives of heroes, form their own;
Now view the Granique chok'd with heaps of slain,
And warring worlds on the Pharsalian plain;
Now hear the trumpets clangour from afar,
And all the dreadful harmony of war;
Now trace those secret tricks that lost a state,
And search the fine-spun arts that made it great,
Correct those errours that its ruin bred,
And bid some long-lost empire rear its ancient head.

Others, to whom persuasive arts belong,
(Words in their looks, and music on their tongue)
Instructed by the wit of Greece and Rome,
Learn richly to adorn their native home;
Whilst listening crowds confess the sweet surprise,
With pleasure in their breasts, and wonder in their
eyes.
Here curious minds the latent seeds disclose,
And Nature's darkest labyrinths expose;
Whilst greater souls the distant worlds descry,
Pierce to the out-stretch'd borders of the sky,
Enlarge the searching mind, and broad expand the
eye.
O you, whose rising years so great began,
In whose bright youth I read the shining man,
O Lonsdale, know what noblest minds approve,
The thoughts they cherish, and the hearts they
love:
Let these examples your young bosom fire,
And bid your soul to boundless height aspire.
Methinks I see you in our shades retir'd,
Alike admiring, and by all admir'd:
Your eloquence now charms my ravish'd ear,
Which future senates shall transported hear,
Now mournful verse inspires a pleasing woe,
And now your cheeks with warlike fury glow,
Whilst on the paper fancy'd fields appear,
And prospects of imaginary war;
Your martial soul sees Hockstet's fatal plain,
Or fights the fam'd Ramilia o'er again.

But I in vain these lofty names rehearse,
Above the faint attempts of humble verse,
Which Garth should in immortal strains design,
Or Addison exalt with warmth divine;
A meaner song my tender voice requires,
And fainter lays confess the fainter fires,
By Nature fitted for an humble theme
A painted prospect, or a murmuring stream,
To tune a vulgar note in Echo's praise,
Whilst Echo's self resounds the flattering lays;
Or, whilst I tell how Myra's charms surprise,
Paint roses on her cheeks, and suns within her eyes.
O, did proportion'd height to me belong,
Great Anna's name should grace th' ambitious song;
Illustrious dames should round their queen resort,
And Lonsdale's mother crown the splendid court;
Her noble son should boast no vulgar place,
But share the ancient honours of his race;
Whilst each fair daughter's face and conquering eyes
To Venus only should submit the prize.
O matchless beauties! more than heavenly fair,
Your looks resistless, and divine your air,
Let your bright eyes their bounteous beams diffuse,
And no fond Bard shall ask an useless Muse;
Their kindling rays excite a noble fire,
Give beauty to the song, and music to the lyre.

This charming theme I ever could pursue,
And think the inspiration ever new,
Did not the god my wandering pen restrain;
And bring me to his Oxford back again.
Oxford, the goddess Muse's native home,
Inspir'd like Athens, and adorn'd like Rome!
Hadst thou of old been Learning's fam'd retreat,
And pagan Muses chose thy lovely seat,
O, how unbounded had their fiction been!
What fancy'd visions had adorn'd the scene!
Upon each hill a sylvan Pan had stood,
And every thicket boasted of a god;
Satyrs had frisk'd in each poetic grove,
And not a stream without its nymphs could move;
Each summit had the train of Muses show'd,
And Hippocrene in every fountain flow'd;
The tales, adorn'd with each poetic grace,
Had look'd almost as charming as the place.
Ev'n now we hear the world with transports own
Those fictions by more wondrous truths outdone;
Here pure Eusebia keeps her holy seat,
And Themis smiles from Heaven on this retreat;
Our chaster Graces own refin'd desires,
And all our Muses burn with vestal fires;
Whilst guardian-angels our Apollos stand,
Scattering rich favours with a bounteous hand,
To bless the happy air and sanctify the land.
O pleasing shades! O ever-green retreats!
Ye learned grottoes! and ye sacred seats!

Never may you politer arts refuse,
But entertain in peace the bashful Muse!
So may you be kind Heaven's distinguish'd care,
And may your fame be lasting, as 'tis fair!
Let greater Bards on fam'd Parnassus dream,
Or taste th' inspir'd Heliconian stream;
Yet, whilst our Oxford is the bless'd abode
Of every Muse, and every tuneful god,
Parnassus owns its honours far outdone,
And Isis boasts more Bards than Helicon.
A thousand blessings I to Oxford owe,
But you, my Lord, th' inspiring Muse bestow;
Grac'd with your name th' unpolish'd poem shines,
You guard its faults, and consecrate the lines,
O might you here meet my desiring eyes,
My drooping song to nobler heights would rise:
Or might I come to breathe your northern air,
Yet should I find an equal pleasure there;
Your presence would the harsher climate soothe,
Hush every wind, and every mountain smooth;
Would bid the groves in springing pomp arise,
And open charming vistas to the eyes;
Would make my trifling verse be heard around,
And sportive Echo play the empty sound:
With you I should a better Phœbus find,
And own in you alone the charms of Oxford join'd.

THE END.

www.ingramcontent.com/pod-product-compliance
Lightning Source LLC
LaVergne TN
LVHW010155110826
845151LV00002B/528